IEPs for ELs

AND OTHER DIVERSE LEARNERS

John J. Hoover

James R. Patton

CORWIN

A SAGE Publishing Company

FOR INFORMATION

Corwin

A SAGE Company

2455 Teller Road

Thousand Oaks, California 91320

(800) 233-9936

www.corwin.com

SAGE Publications Ltd.

1 Oliver's Yard

55 City Road

London, EC1Y 1SP

United Kingdom

SAGE Publications India Pvt. Ltd.

B 1/I 1 Mohan Cooperative Industrial Area

Mathura Road, New Delhi 110 044

India

SAGE Publications Asia-Pacific Pte. Ltd.

3 Church Street

#10-04 Samsung Hub

Singapore 049483

Program Director: Jessica Allan

Senior Associate Editor: Kimberly Greenberg

Editorial Assistant: Katie Crilley

Production Editor: Veronica Stapleton Hooper

Copy Editor: Patrice Sutton

Typesetter: Hurix Systems Pvt. Ltd.

Proofreader: Sarah J. Duffy

Indexer: J. Naomi Linzer Indexing Services

Cover Designer: Anthony Paular

Marketing Manager: Charline Maher

ISBN: 978-1-5063-2818-8

This book is printed on acid-free paper.

17 18 19 20 21 10 9 8 7 6 5 4 3 2 1

IEPs for ELs

Contents

Acknowledgments

We wish to acknowledge that this book is written for all the K–12 culturally and linguistically diverse learners, and their families and educators, with whom we have had the privilege of instructing and collaborating with over the past several decades. English language and other diverse learners and their families bring diverse values, qualities, and strengths to the Individualized Education Program (IEP) development and implementation process providing the foundation for the development of this book.

This book is the result of efforts of several contributing authors whose research, experience, and professional insight provide invaluable expertise to the topic of IEPs for diverse learners. Specifically, we wish to acknowledge Donna Sacco for providing expertise in academic language development in Chapter 3, Le Tran for her contributions to Chapters 4 and 7, Molly Betty for her contribution detailing SMART goals and IEPs in Chapter 5, Leah Teeters for developing Chapter 10 on the topic of IEP team meeting specifics, and Le Tran for assisting with the development of the authentic samples of elementary and secondary grade–level culturally and linguistically responsive IEPs. Collectively, these contributors are sharing expertise acquired from many years of work with English language and other diverse learners with and without disabilities, providing guidance to readers of this book for the proper development and implementation of culturally and linguistically responsive IEPs.

PUBLISHER'S ACKNOWLEDGMENTS

Corwin gratefully acknowledges the contributions of the following reviewers.

Renee Bernhardt
Supervisor, Special Education
Cherokee County School District
Canton, Georgia

Stephanie M. Corbett, MA
Special Education Teacher Grades K–3
Oak Creek Franklin Joint School
    District—Cedar Hills Elementary
Oak Creek, Wisconsin

Sonya Erickson
ESOL Teacher (1.5 years),
    ESE Coordinator (1 year),
    ESE Teacher (14 years)
Indian Pines Elementary School
Lake Worth, Florida

About the Authors

John J. Hoover is associate research professor at the University of Colorado Boulder and a former K–12 special educator, teaching diverse students representing multiple languages and cultures in western, southwestern, and midwestern states. He earned a BA in elementary and special education (intellectual disabilities), an MA in learning disabilities and emotional disorders with an emphasis in reading, and a PhD in curriculum specializing in special education. His research agenda for the past two decades has focused on the topic of culturally and linguistically responsive special education referral and assessment of English language and other diverse learners. He is currently principal investigator (PI) on a multiyear-grant-funded project addressing English learners and multi-tiered supports, special education referral and assessment of culturally and linguistically diverse learners, and graduate-level teacher preparation for teaching English language and other diverse learners with and without disabilities. Select, recently coauthored/coedited books include *Why Do English Learners Struggle With Reading? Distinguishing Language Acquisition From Learning Disabilities* (Corwin); *Linking Assessment to Instruction in Multi-Tiered Models: A Teacher's Guide to Selecting Reading, Writing and Mathematics Interventions* (Pearson); *Differentiating Learning Differences From Learning and Behavioral Disabilities: Teaching Diverse Learners Through Multi-Tiered Response to Intervention* (Allyn & Bacon); and *Methods for Teaching Culturally and Linguistically Diverse Exceptional Learners* (Pearson Merrill). He also is coauthor of a nationally normed reading test, *Early Reading Assessment* (Pro-Ed), and of a research-based educator self-assessment and professional development tool, *Core ESL Instructional Practices (CEIP) Guide.* Recent refereed journal publications include "Increasing Usage of ESL Instructional Practices in a Rural County Elementary School," *Rural Educator* (2015); "Culturally Responsive Special Education Referrals of English Learners in One Rural County School District: Pilot Project," *Rural Special Education Quarterly* (2015); and "Reducing Unnecessary Referrals: Guidelines for Teachers of Diverse Learners," *Teaching Exceptional Children* (2012).

Dr. James R. Patton is an adjunct associate professor in the Department of Special Education at the University of Texas at Austin and independent consultant. He formerly was a special education teacher, having taught students with special needs at the elementary, secondary, and postsecondary levels of schooling. He has written books, chapters, articles, and tests in the area of special education. Dr. Patton's current areas of professional interest are the assessment of the transition strengths and needs of students, differentiating instruction for diverse students with special needs in general education settings, and the ways that disability is portrayed in the media. He also works as an intellectual disability forensic specialist in death penalty cases throughout the country. Dr. Patton received his BS from the University of Notre Dame and obtained his MEd and EdD from the University of Virginia.

About the Contributors

Dr. Leah Teeters is a research fellow in clinical and translational research in the Department of Pediatrics at Vanderbilt University Medical Center. Her professional career is dedicated to promoting equity. Her experience as a K–12 educator led her to expand her research to look at equity both in the classroom and in community settings, where she considers how to design more equitable learning environments and opportunities for advancement. She aims to develop community-engaged research methodologies that recognize and leverage diverse epistemologies and generate new opportunities for participation.

Donna Sacco is a doctoral candidate and adjunct professor at George Mason University. She received her master of education degree in bilingual special education from George Washington University, where she also worked as an adjunct professor. Holding dual certification in special education and ESL, she taught elementary school in Arlington, Virginia, for twelve years. While in Arlington, she worked across the continuum of services in multiple school settings and across all disability areas. She is a former member of the Council for Exceptional Children Board of Directors and continues to serve on its committees. In addition, she is actively involved in the Council for Learning Disabilities and is a member of the Leadership Academy's Sixth Cohort.

Molly Betty is a special education teacher in Denver, Colorado. She received her master of science in education degree from Bank Street College of Education, where she studied special education and elementary education. She taught elementary school in New York City before moving to Colorado. She has worked in a variety of educational settings and across many disability areas. In 2015, Ms. Betty co-presented a session on IEP development at the annual Council for Exceptional Children Convention. She is deeply committed to promoting equity and access for all special education students.

Le M. Tran is a doctoral student in the Department of Special Education at the University of Texas at Austin. She received her BEd in unified early childhood and her MEd in special education from the University of Kansas. She has taught students with special needs at the early childhood, elementary, and secondary levels of schooling. Her current professional interests are instructional practices for culturally and/or linguistically diverse exceptional students, designing instructional strategies in math for diverse learners, and supervising preservice special education teachers in their internships.

Introduction

Blueprint of IEPs for ELs and Other Diverse Learners

IEPs for ELs and Other Diverse Learners provides practitioners contemporary information and skill sets necessary to develop and implement culturally and linguistically responsive Individualized Education Programs (IEPs). This book is purposefully titled to reflect the unique features and needs that students in the process of acquiring English as a second language bring to the IEP process, in addition to the features and needs of other diverse learners who are English proficient. "Approximately half of all culturally and linguistically diverse PreK–12 students have limited English language proficiency and are classified as English language learners" (Navarrete & Watson, 2013, p. 1). Specifically, IEPs for English language learners must address the English language development aspects of teaching and learning, in addition to attending to academic, social, and cultural features that diverse non-English learners bring to the special education instructional environment. Therefore, readers will acquire knowledge and skills to meet the IEP expectations of both English learners (ELs) as well as other diverse students with disabilities who are English proficient.

The Individualized Education Program has been in existence since PL 94–142 was signed into law during the mid-1970s. Throughout the past several decades, an IEP has been used as a mandated educational blueprint framing the instruction for all learners found eligible for special education services. Though its use in educational settings to inform families, educators, and students about necessary services is well intended, over the years, the IEP has become more of a legal mandate rather than an instructional tool to meet academic and social-emotional needs of students with disabilities. However, if developed properly, an IEP is a highly valuable instructional tool containing clearly articulated goals, objectives, services, accommodations, and supplemental supports necessary to deliver effective teaching and learning to a student with a disability in the least restrictive environment along with age and grade-level peers.

Our purpose for writing this book is to provide guidance to practitioners in the development of an Individualized Education Program for English language and other diverse students properly placed into special education with an identified disability. Though much of the material in this highly practical book is appropriate for any learner's IEP, specific attention focuses on ways to make the IEP culturally and linguistically responsive. Therefore, the central focus of this book is to guide educators in the development and implementation of an Individualized Education Program for all diverse learners who are properly identified as having a disability and placed for special education services.

UNDERLYING ASSUMPTIONS OF THE IEP DEVELOPMENT STAGE

In developing the contents of this book, several assumptions are made relative to the referral, assessment, eligibility decision making, and placement of English language and other diverse learners for special education services:

1. Learner was properly referred and assessed within the special education comprehensive evaluation process consistent with mandated procedures identified in the 2004 reauthorization of the Individual with Disabilities Education Improvement Act (IDEIA).

2. English language proficiency level was properly identified using a nationally accepted assessment instrument (e.g., WIDA ACCESS) with results incorporated into the special education assessment process to reduce bias.

3. Multiple forms of assessment were used in the evaluation of the placed English language or other diverse learner to make certain that a culturally and linguistically responsive process framed the eligibility and placement decision.

4. Eligibility decision-making team included members with expertise in the education of English language and other diverse learners.

The extent that one or more of the above four assumptions is not met limits practitioners' abilities to generate an informed IEP for English language and other diverse learners. Therefore, framed within the above referral, assessment, and placement assumptions, the task of generating a culturally and linguistically responsive IEP ensues. As stated, although the chapters of this book include discussion and presentation of items required of any IEP, the primary emphasis is on ways to make the IEP appropriate for and responsive to all diverse learners and their families.

TOPICAL AREAS AND TERMINOLOGY

Key features of a culturally and linguistically responsive IEP examined in this book include these items:

- Documentation of present performance levels that incorporate culturally and linguistically diverse qualities and strengths

- Incorporation of language development in the annual goals and short-term objectives
- Emphasis on continued development of English academic language proficiency
- Determination of involvement in general class curriculum in culturally responsive ways
- Use of responsive monitoring practices to measure achievement and affective progress of English language and other diverse learners
- Interrelated significance of the role and function of English language development in IEP goal attainment is evident

Throughout the book, the development and implementation of an IEP for English language and other diverse learners within a multi-tiered system of supports (MTSS) is examined, detailing its potential for framing effective education for all students with disabilities. Below is a listing of the chapter structure of the book's material:

- Understanding a Culturally and Linguistically Diverse Multi-Tiered System of Supports (Chapter 1)
- Essential Components of IEPs for English Language and Other Diverse Learners (Chapter 2)
- Role and Function of Academic Language in IEPs (Chapter 3)
- Culturally and Linguistically Responsive Present Levels of Academic Achievement and Functional Performance (Chapter 4)
- IEPs and the Development of Measurable Annual Goals Using SMART Principles (Chapter 5)
- Delivering Appropriate IEP Services (Chapter 6)
- Special Considerations and Diversity (Chapter 7)
- IEP Progress Monitoring and Diverse Needs (Chapter 8)
- Culturally and Linguistically Responsive Transition Planning and Services (Chapter 9)
- Guidelines for Successful IEP Meetings for Diverse Learners (Chapter 10)
- Putting the IEP Pieces Together (Chapter 11)

Given the various perspectives and definitions associated with terminology and features connected to IEPs, we define a few select terms as used throughout the book:

Term	Description
Accommodation	Learner completes the exact same task, addressing same standard as others while being provided changes to time, format, setting, schedule, and/or presentation without altering what the test measure or assignment requires.
Benchmark	An IEP learning target specifying knowledge and skills students acquire relative to a broader standard.
Content Objective	IEP statement that describes the content knowledge/skills to be acquired by the students through completion of lessons and units of study.

(Continued)

(Continued)

Term	Description
Culturally and Linguistically Diverse (CLD) Learner	A student who brings diverse ethnic, cultural, and/or linguistic qualities to the teaching and learning environment possessing English language proficiency that may range from emerging to full proficiency levels.
Culturally and Linguistically Responsive	Incorporating and valuing learners' diverse characteristics, backgrounds, languages, experiences, and home teachings into the planning and delivery of an IEP and associated instruction.
Diverse Learner	Term used interchangeably with the term *CLD learner.*
English Learner (EL)	A student who has a home language other than English and who is in the process of acquiring English as a second or other language.
Language Objective	Objective that specifically addresses the functions of language (e.g., compare, contrast, evaluate), vocabulary relevant to the lesson, and form (e.g., adjective, sentence structure) in the four domains (listening, speaking, reading, writing).
Modification	Adjustment to assignments or tasks that may alter a standard or expectations of what is completed or measured (e.g., an alternate task in which the learner addresses only part of a standard or achievement expectation).
Other Diverse Learner	Culturally and linguistically diverse student who is bilingual and/or English proficient.

NOTE: Several different features and strengths characterize diverse learners, and as such three types of terminologies are used throughout this book when referring to diverse students, depending on the particular topic of discussion or area of emphasis:

Culturally and Linguistically Diverse (CLD) is used when the topic of discussion pertains to any diverse learner irrespective of first or second language proficiency levels.

English Learner (EL) is used when the topic of discussion pertains specifically to an individual in the process of acquiring English as a second language.

English Language and Other Diverse Learners is used when the topic of discussion pertains to both individuals in the process of acquiring English as a second language as well as other diverse learners who are either bilingual or fluent English speakers.

Additional terminology is defined when introduced throughout the chapters. Though specific content, components, and visual layout of an IEP varies across school districts, several features are mandated by law (IDEA, 2004; Shinn & Shinn, 2000). We begin our discussions by examining a culturally and linguistically responsive MTSS in Chapter 1, followed by required IEP elements presented in Chapter 2.

Understanding a Culturally and Linguistically Diverse Multi-Tiered System of Supports

1

Practitioner's Perspective . . .

What are the key features of a Multi-Tiered System of Supports (MTSS)? How does an MTSS framework best serve culturally and linguistically diverse learners? How is an IEP best delivered within an MTSS model for English language and other diverse learners?

In order to develop an Individualized Education Program (IEP) that reflects the cultural and linguistic diversity of English language and other diverse learners, educators must possess a working knowledge of culturally and linguistically responsive principles and practices. Specifically, abilities associated with culturally and linguistically responsive teaching are critical to informed IEPs for diverse students. This chapter provides an overview of the unique qualities and strengths that English language and other diverse learners bring to the teaching and learning environment. The following topics are addressed: (a) MTSS in today's schools, (b) MTSS and cultural and linguistic diversity, (c) key features of culturally and linguistically responsive teaching and stages to becoming a culturally proficient educator, and (d) suggestions for applying MTSS knowledge and skills in the development of culturally and linguistically responsive IEPs for English language and other diverse learners with disabilities. We begin with an overview of an MTSS framework for meeting needs of struggling learners, including diverse students with disabilities.

OVERVIEW OF MTSS

The eventual placement of a student into special education is framed within a multi-tiered model that includes documentation of lack of progress leading to referral. Once placed, the development, delivery, and refinement of an Individualized Education Program for English language and other diverse learners occur within the school-wide instructional framework designed to educate all students. Over the past several decades, we have educated students with and without disabilities through a variety of structures that included self-contained, resource, mainstreaming, inclusion, full inclusion, response to treatment, response to instruction, and response to intervention models (Hoover, 2013). No matter how the instruction is framed in a school, it serves as a backdrop and perspective, requiring a working level of understanding to best inform effective instruction provided through delivery of an IEP.

The contemporary framework for educating all learners in today's schools is through delivery of a multi-tiered system of supports (MTSS). What is an MTSS model and how does it differ from previous models? Though specific definitions vary in how an MTSS is characterized, a recent American Association of Colleges for Teacher Education report captures the key aspects typically found in most MTSS definitions:

> *A comprehensive system of differentiated supports that includes evidence-based instruction, universal screening, progress monitoring, formative assessments, research-based interventions matched to student needs, and educational decision making using student outcome data.* (Blanton, Pugach, & Florian, 2011, p. 15)

An MTSS model of instruction serves as the foundation of IEP development by incorporating key features associated with response to intervention (RTI) and positive behavioral interventions and supports (PBIS), thereby emphasizing the interrelated features of academic and affective learner development. Similar to IEPs, the structure of an MTSS model varies across schools and school districts; however, the Colorado state MTSS model contains several common components found in most models as illustrated in Table 1.1. The model components are first presented in the table as essential for addressing educational needs of all learners, which is followed by specific examples of how cultural and linguistic features should be incorporated to generate an MTSS model most relevant to English language and other diverse learners.

Specifics concerning the application and implementation of an MTSS framework vary based on school district size, population, geographic location, available resources, and other related factors. However, each of the six features listed in Table 1.1 is important to include in a school- or district-wide MTSS model. Our purpose for presenting the core features of an MTSS model is to remind practitioners of the most important aspects that frame effective instruction for all learners, especially English language and other diverse learners, instruction that eventually may be drawn upon for informed IEP development and implementation. For additional and more detailed information about different MTSS models, the reader is referred to Center on Response to Intervention (n.d.), Hoover (2013), Vanderwood and Nam (2007).

Table 1.1   MTSS Framework for All Learners

MTSS Feature	*Implementation Description*
Shared Leadership	Shared input, supports, and decision making to include representatives from the district, home-community, school, and classroom settings.
Data-Based Problem Solving and Decision Making	Achievement and affective rate of progress, proficiency, and gap analysis data form the foundation for making instructional, eligibility, and placement decisions.
Multi-Tiered Continuum of Supports	Instruction layered along a dynamic continuum of supports often includes three tiers: Universal (Tier 1: All learners); Targeted (Tier 2: Learners struggling with Tier 1); and Intensive (Tier 3: Learners who struggle with Tiers 1 and 2). Level of support provided is based on learner progress in the tiers, with increased instructional intensity and duration at each higher layer of instruction.
Evidence-Based Instruction, Intervention, Assessment	An efficient MTSS model is grounded in evidence-based practice in which effectiveness of methods is demonstrated for an intended (a) purpose (e.g., reading fluency) and (b) learner (e.g., EL). Multi-level models require use of high-quality instruction and intervention procedures and methods, along with assessment devices and practices matched to the needs of students based on standards (e.g., culturally responsive).
Universal Screening and Progress Monitoring	General assessment of all students to screen for at-risk and struggling learners occurs 2–3 times per year in most districts (i.e., universal screening), and the monitoring of student growth and progress for learners who are struggling occurs more frequently (e.g., weekly, daily, every other week; i.e., progress monitoring).
Family, School, Community Partnerships	An effectively implemented MTSS values the learners' families, guardians, and community members who assume key roles in the overall process, including decision making, while tapping into funds of knowledge and interactive home-school supports.

MTSS AND CULTURAL AND LINGUISTIC DIVERSITY

A properly developed and implemented MTSS should by its very nature meet the diverse needs of all learners. However, as seen in many of our previous models of instruction (e.g., mainstreaming, response to intervention) without specific attention to cultural and linguistic diversity, the models may be appropriate in general for diverse learners yet lack specificity required to bring them to a more culturally responsive level (Ortiz et al., 2011). Therefore, attention to some of the key instructional qualities and strengths brought to the instructional environment by CLD learners is necessary. Each of the six MTSS features summarized above contains embedded opportunities for making certain that the model is appropriate for English language and other diverse learners, leading to informed IEPs.

Shared Leadership. Educators with expertise (i.e., training, experience) in the education of culturally and linguistically diverse learners bring much needed knowledge, skills, and perspective to the MTSS leadership. Too often we operate from the perspective of a one size fits all model, which serves only to undermine the concept and practice of *diversity.* Educational leadership in the development and implementation of an MTSS model requires representation from experts in curriculum, content, and management as well as from those most knowledgeable about the influences of cultural and linguistic diversity on the implementation of that curriculum, content, and management. Effective leadership throughout instructional delivery within a school-wide MTSS framework is necessary to ensure proper development of an IEP for diverse learners with a disability.

> *A key question to ponder:* Does the team leadership in your school or district include educators with expertise in the education of culturally and linguistically diverse learners?

Data-Based Problem Solving and Decision Making. A cornerstone of MTSS is the gathering, charting, and analyzing of data reflecting learners' academic and affective growth, followed by decisions based on those data. Procedures in the data process need to be standardized, so comparisons across time may be made using tools or assessment measures designed to assess the specific area (e.g., self-management behaviors, reading fluency rate, mathematics reasoning). However, a critical area of caution when implementing this feature of an MTSS model is making certain that the data collection procedures are appropriate for English language and other diverse learners by taking into account cultural and linguistic qualities (Hoover & Klingner, 2011). Oftentimes, we use in good faith an instrument to gather data that has not been validated for use with English learners, or it fails to address in its development the various stages of second language acquisition. Of most significance in the implementation of this MTSS feature is the possibility that if decision making and problem solving for an English language or other diverse learner are based on data that are not culturally responsive, thereby inaccurately demonstrating a learner's actual progress, then subsequent instructional adjustments, multi-tiered placements, possible referral for special education, or the contents of an IEP may also be inaccurate.

> *A key question to ponder:* To what extent is the data-based decision making for English language and other diverse learners in your MTSS based on data collected using culturally and linguistically responsive methods and devices?

Multi-Tiered Continuum of Supports. The concept of layered instruction, increasing in duration and intensity, provides the framework for delivering education in our schools. Though easy to comprehend in theory, actual practice of tiered instruction often represents unique challenges to educators of English language and other diverse learners (Hoover & Klingner, 2011). Of most concern is the delivery of tiered instruction in a way that meets the needs of all

learners in a classroom or grade, differentiated sufficiently to be cultⁿ
linguistically responsive. Multi-tiered supports are only effective if th
diverse learners sufficient opportunities to learn, particularly in Tⁱ
Though the MTSS structure in a school is the same for all lear
making concerning high-quality differentiated instruction for Er
and other diverse learners requires emphasis on language skill ac.
typically necessary for non-English learners. Incorporating academic la.
development (see Chapter 3) in the education of English learners is fundamentꜜ
to providing sufficient opportunities to learn (Gottlieb & Ernst-Slavit, 2014), and
it is essential to consider when addressing IEP needs in MTSS models.

> *A key question to ponder:* What features within your school's MTSS provide evidence that the model reflects cultural and linguistic diversity in the education of all learners to ensure accurate special education referral, placement, and subsequent IEP development?

Evidence-Based Instruction, Intervention, Assessment. A most critical aspect in the education of diverse learners pertains to the extent that education incorporates methods, materials, classroom management, cooperative groupings, curriculum-based measurement, or access to content reflective of cultural and linguistic backgrounds of the students. Most curricula, assessment devices, and expectations for achieving benchmarks are almost always reflective of a mainstream, Anglo, middle-class perspective—a perspective that may vary significantly from values, teachings and expectations of many English language and other diverse learners educated in today's schools and classrooms (Hoover, 2013; Orosco, de Schonewise, de Onis, Klingner, & Hoover, 2016). Similar to use of data discussed above, we often in good faith implement instruction and interventions including methods, materials, or management that were not designed or are inappropriate for use with English learners, students from diverse cultural backgrounds, or those with limited experiences due to lack of appropriate learning opportunities. Yet as we assess progress to determine growth, we fail to recognize that delivery of instruction, interventions, or assessments that are not culturally and linguistically responsive has little chance of facilitating growth expectations for diverse students as compared to non-English learners and other mainstream students. The influence and direction of *shared leadership* is critical when implementing this evidence-based feature within an MTSS model to make certain that instruction, intervention, and assessment are culturally and linguistically responsive. Development of proper IEPs can be achieved only if this MTSS feature is properly delivered to all learners prior to and subsequent to special education referral and placement, especially English language and other diverse learners.

> *A key question to ponder:* What evidence exists to confirm that the instruction provided in Tier 1, intervention in Tier 2, and associated assessments used are culturally and linguistically responsive to properly educate English language and other diverse learners prior to referral?

Universal Screening and Progress Monitoring. The practice of screening learners for evidence of struggle two to three times per school year is standard in today's districts. Similarly, more frequent monitoring to maintain current data on a struggling student's progress is also standard practice. In regard to English language and other diverse learners, the practice of universal screening or progress monitoring represents a challenge to educators due to lack of valid and reliable devices (Basterra, Trumbull, & Solano-Flores, 2011; Hoover & Klingner, 2011). Though most nationally developed, normed, and standardized screening and monitoring devices are appropriate for non-English learners and mainstream students, when used with diverse students, they often yield invalid or inaccurate results, due to English language proficiency levels or cultural expectations that some English language or other diverse learners do not possess (Hoover, Baca, & Klingner, 2016). This, in turn, leads to instructional, referral, and/or placement decisions that may also be inaccurate. The significance of using curriculum-based measurement (CBM) to screen and monitor English language and other diverse learners' progress via many of the current devices becomes highly important, since educators are able to develop or modify CBMs that meet cultural and linguistic needs that many existing devices lack (see Chapter 8 for discussion about CBMs). Therefore, universal screening and progress monitoring when used with diverse students require educators to view existing practices through a cultural and linguistic lens, making proper adjustments as necessary particularly when incorporating findings into IEP development.

> *A key question to ponder:* What evidence exists to support use of the universal screening and progress-monitoring devices and practices in your school, demonstrating that each is culturally and linguistically responsive for diverse learners?

Family, School, Community Partnerships. An MTSS model is most effective when grounded in a well-established partnership that values collaboration among home, community, and school (Hoover, Barletta, & Klingner, 2016). Valuing contributions of family and community as partners in the education of students serves the best interests of all involved with education. Depending on cultural expectations, parents/guardians and community members may vary in their expectations for collaboration, which educators should respect by accommodating differences to best support learners' education. Additionally, the importance of community and family support in the education of English language and other diverse learners cannot be overstated. As partnerships are strengthened through collaboration, educators become more informed of student strengths, qualities, learning preferences, and needs. Comprehensive education provided through an MTSS framework requires involvement and commitment from a variety of people in students' lives given the diversity seen in today's classrooms. Additionally, parental or guardian involvement is required in IEP development, further highlighting the importance of collaboration and effective communication.

> *A key question to ponder:* How are family and community involved in the education of English language and other diverse learners at your school?

CULTURALLY AND LINGUISTICALLY RESPONSIVE TEACHING QUALITIES

The education of students in today's classrooms requires teachers to have a working knowledge and understanding of key features that define diversity in schools. Culturally and linguistically diverse learners have a significant stake in the success of multi-tiered support systems (Hoover & Klingner, 2011; Vanderwood & Nam, 2007). Knowledge of CLD instructional qualities leading to culturally and linguistically responsive (CLR) teaching is essential to providing high-quality instruction, while also avoiding erroneously thinking that a learning disability exists when in fact the student is exhibiting differences in learning preferences (Hoover, Baca, & Klingner, 2016). Adhering to the following, derived from material found in Hoover (2011), assists educators to apply CLR teaching principles in the development and delivery of an IEP for English language and other diverse learners:

- Incorporating culturally and linguistically diverse values and practices is required to provide diverse students sufficient opportunities to learn.
- Interventions need to be validated with English learners and other diverse populations to achieve satisfactory IEP progress.
- IEPs need to reflect English language proficiency levels in instruction and assessment.
- Students' English language proficiency and cultural values/norms inform necessary accommodations to best meet IEP goals.
- Culturally responsive educators (see Table 1.2) need to be involved in the development and implementation of IEPs for diverse learners.

Consideration of these items facilitates the successful development and implementation of the IEP within an MTSS framework, while reducing the tendency to perceive lack of opportunity as lack of progress. "Teachers who utilize CRT [culturally responsive teaching] practices value students' cultural and linguistic resources and view this knowledge as capital to build upon rather than as a barrier to learning" (Aceves & Orosco, 2014, p. 7).

In addition, cultural proficiency is achieved through a long-term process as educators integrate experience with and knowledge about different cultures (Gay, 2000; Mason, 1993). This experience and knowledge, in turn, informs the development of responsive IEPs for diverse learners. Literature searches yield a variety of definitions describing culturally responsive teaching and instruction (Gay, 2002; Hoover, 2012; Ladson-Billings, 1995; Richards, Brown, & Forde, 2007; Villegas & Lucas, 2007; Wlodkowski & Ginsburg, 1995). One definition frequently cited and applied was put forth by a leading researcher in the field

Table 1.2   Stages of Cultural Proficiency

Development Stage	Relevance to IEP Development and Implementation
1. Cultural Destructiveness	Cultural diversity is viewed as a highly negative aspect and is excluded totally from MTSS and IEPs.
2. Cultural Incapacity	Cultural diversity is viewed indifferently, ignored, and given little if any credibility in the implementation of MTSS and IEPs.
3. Cultural Blindness	Existence of cultural diversity is acknowledged yet is viewed as having little significance in the implementation of MTSS or IEP development and implementation.
4. Cultural Precompetence	Cultural diversity is valued as evidenced through greater personal awareness and sensitivity with some, although limited, applications within MTSS and IEP development and implementation.
5. Cultural Competence	Perceptions about cultural diversity move from awareness and sensitivity to application and incorporation within MTSS and IEP development and implementation.
6. Cultural Proficiency	Cultural diversity is significantly embedded into MTSS and IEP development and implementation including both general and special education at the school/district levels.

who defined culturally responsive teaching as "using the cultural characteristics, experiences, and perspectives of ethnically diverse students as conduits for teaching them more effectively" (Gay, 2002, p. 106). In regard to cultural proficiency in teaching, Table 1.2 summarizes stages associated with educator development (Cross, Bazron, Dennis, & Isaacs, 1989; Gay, 2000; Hoover, Klingner, Baca, & Patton, 2008; Mason, 1993) as applied to MTSS and IEP implementation.

The initial stages (i.e., Stages 1–3) are very incompatible with culturally responsive teaching, while Stages 4–6 reflect preferred and necessary MTSS practices, attitudes, and values along with appropriate IEPs for English language and other diverse learners.

WHAT MAKES AN IEP CULTURALLY AND LINGUISTICALLY RESPONSIVE?

Though it is essential to *exclude* culture and language as primary causes leading to a struggling learner's lack of academic or affective progress, diverse learners who are appropriately placed into special education continue to bring

> Cultural and linguistic diversity does not cease to be integral to diverse students' teaching and learning once they are placed in special education.

their cultural and linguistic diversity to the teaching and learning environment. That is, cultural and linguistic qualities that diverse students bring to the special education environment continue to be relevant and, therefore, require continued incorporation into instruction similar to the teaching provided in the general classroom prior and subsequent to referral and placement.

Thus, an IEP for a culturally and linguistically diverse learner must incorporate cultural and linguistic features into its development and implementation to be responsive to the learner's needs. Stated differently, if a CLD learner's

IEP addresses only factors typically addressed for non-CLD students with little or no attention to culture and language, then it lacks the cultural and linguistic responsiveness needed to properly provide a diverse learner special education. As will be discussed and illustrated throughout this book, in order for an IEP to be responsive, it must include documented practical considerations and instructional suggestions for meeting diverse culture and language needs within several IEP component areas:

(a) present level of performance statement(s)

(b) measurable annual goals and short-term objectives

(c) instructional and assessment accommodations

(d) progress monitoring devices and procedures

(e) special considerations, related services, and supplemental aids

The significance of incorporating cultural and linguistic content and considerations in these, and the other mandated IEP components, is a central focus of the material in this book, providing practitioners contemporary perspectives about diversity and disability education embedded into IEP development and implementation.

EDUCATIONAL FRAMEWORK FOR DIVERSE LEARNERS WITH DISABILITIES

Successful education of English language and other diverse learners who have a disability requires educators to become knowledgeable about the content and skills described above. However, when diverse learners possess a disability, another dimension in teaching and learning emerges requiring consideration of the interaction between diversity and disability. Figure 1.1 illustrates one way of thinking about or conceptualizing skill sets required to provide sufficient

Figure 1.1   Conceptualizing the Education of Diverse Learners With Disabilities

opportunities to learn for diverse learners with disabilities. The figure, developed from material found in numerous sources (e.g., Aceves & Orosco, 2014; Gay, 2002; Hoover, Baca, & Klingner, 2016; Hoover & Klingner, 2011; IRIS Center, 2015; Ortiz et al., 2011), illustrates three skill sets that shape effective instruction for English language and other diverse learners with disabilities.

Skill Set 1: Role of cultural diversity. As illustrated in Table 1.2, cultural competence and proficiency become evident when diverse cultural values, teachings, and heritages are integral to the curriculum being used in overall teaching and learning. That is, in order for educators to become culturally proficient (i.e., Stage 6), the ways of learning must reflect best practices that demonstrate educator understanding of the role that culture assumes in teaching and learning, such as diverse (a) ways of thinking about history, (b) views about the same set of events shaping society, (c) home and community teachings in the curricula, or (d) perceptions about a disability in society, to name a few. Therefore, this first key skill set necessary to develop and implement a culturally and linguistically responsive IEP is for all educators to understand the significant role and positive contributions that cultural diversity assumes in the classroom.

Skill Set 2: Significance of native language use. It is well documented that English learners' success with English development and with learning in English is strengthened by strategic use of native, or first, language in the instruction, especially when more complex issues, vocabulary, concepts, and comprehension are involved (August, Shanahan, & Shanahan, 2006; Goldenberg, 2008; Hoover, Baca, & Klingner, 2016). Successful education of English language and other diverse learners requires opportunities in the teaching and learning environment for students to use their first language skills, even if the classroom teacher is not proficient in that language. Therefore, this second skill set emphasizes the importance of educators knowing the value of first language usage by second language learners, which should be evident in various aspects within the IEP.

Skill Set 3: Diversity and disability intersection. One of the more frequently discussed topics in the teaching of diverse learners is educators' abilities to distinguish second language acquisition and learning differences from a language or learning disability. Critical to the successful development and implementation of an IEP is the understanding that culturally and linguistically diverse learner qualities and strengths are not indicators of a disability. This third essential skill set requires educators to become proficient in recognizing similarities and differences between expected second language acquisition behaviors, culturally taught behaviors, and disability characteristics—sufficient to a level where acquisition behaviors and cultural teachings are not misinterpreted as disability characteristics.

Overall, the conceptual framework for educating English language and other diverse learners must be shaped by educators' (a) positive perceptions about the role of diverse cultures in teaching and learning; (b) recognition and application of first language use in acquiring English and in learning and comprehending skills, concepts, and academic vocabulary in English; and (c) abilities to distinguish second language acquisition and culturally diverse values from language or learning disabilities. These core essential skill sets are examined further in various chapters of this book. For more in-depth consideration of this conceptual framework and its three features, the reader is referred to the sources cited above and those found in the previous two sections. In summary, knowledge of the role of cultural diversity, native language usage, and interaction between diversity and disability is foundational to the development and implementation of an IEP for diverse learners, especially those in the process of acquiring English as a second language.

IEP DEVELOPMENT PRINCIPLES FOR ENGLISH LANGUAGE AND OTHER DIVERSE LEARNERS

English language proficiency is used relative to an individual whose challenges in speaking, reading, writing, or understanding the English language may deny them the ability to meet expected proficiency levels of achievement. Students acquiring English as a second language progress through several stages, each of which reflects specific behaviors; these stages are necessary for educators to understand to best provide sufficient opportunities for diverse learners (see Chapter 4 for additional discussion). Overall, the composition of culturally responsive teaching includes adhering to several core principles reflecting important classroom structures, supports, and practices. Below are nine principles to guide IEP development and delivery to meet diverse student needs based on material found in several sources (see Baca & Cervantes, 2004; Grossman, 1995; Hoover, 2009; Hoover, Baca, & Klingner, 2016; Orosco & Klingner, 2010):

> *Principle 1*—Language development, content knowledge, and academic vocabulary should be reinforced across different subjects to properly contextualize the IEP goals and objectives.
>
> *Principle 2*—IEPs should contain both English language development and content goals to be culturally responsive for diverse learners.
>
> *Principle 3*—IEPs for English language and other diverse learners should document challenging goals and objectives, rather than low-level outcomes, to ensure sufficient opportunities to learn.
>
> *Principle 4*—IEPs' present level of performance statement(s) should include reference to instructional types found to be successful with the learner, such as cooperative, active, or inquiry-based learning tasks.
>
> *Principle 5*—IEP content and suggested accommodations should reflect students' cultural, linguistic, experiential, and family backgrounds.
>
> *Principle 6*—Opportunities should be provided to allow learners to utilize their cultural and linguistic experiences, languages, and strengths in their learning.
>
> *Principle 7*—IEPs should document needed supports for using various learning strategies consistent with language proficiency and cultural and family teachings.

Principle 8—IEP objectives should incorporate co-teaching within collaboratively structured learning environments to make certain culturally and linguistically diverse methods and assessments are employed.

Principle 9—Diverse learners should be provided ongoing reciprocal dialogue in their instruction to be successful in meeting IEP goals and objectives through English language development.

CONCLUSION

The education of English language and other diverse learners requires educators to possess training and experience working within culturally diverse environments to best provide sufficient opportunities. Understanding the MTSS model of education contributes to informed IEP development, especially since one mandated IEP element requires documentation of the extent to which student will participate in and access general education along with nondisabled peers. Culturally and linguistically responsive teaching practices facilitate needed language and cultural supports to assist with academic learning and English language development of diverse learners who have a disability. Developing and maintaining knowledge and expertise in cultural and linguistic responsiveness that shape the conceptual framework for educating diverse learners with disabilities provide a solid foundation from which culturally and linguistically responsive IEPs are best developed.

The contents of this chapter only introduce the reader to the complex task of educating English language and other diverse learners with IEPs. Additional study and experience are required to become fully proficient in the special education referral, assessment, and instruction of diverse learners, and readers are referred to the various sources cited in this chapter and throughout the remainder of this book for additional study in these areas. Best practices specific to the development and implementation of IEPs for diverse students in today's schools and classrooms introduced in this chapter are discussed in subsequent chapters of this book.

Essential Components of IEPs for English Language and Other Diverse Learners

2

Practitioner's Perspective . . .

What components of an IEP are mandated by IDEA? Why are present levels of both academic achievement and functional performance important to include in an IEP? How does knowledge of cultural and linguistic features inform development of the various mandated IEP components, such as present levels, annual goals, accommodations, and assessment for English language and other diverse learners?

An Individualized Education Program (IEP) is a document required by law that outlines a student's instructional goals, objectives, accommodations, general class participation, and necessary related services, to meet needs connected to the disability identified as the basis for special education eligibility and placement. The IEP provides educators and parents a document to guide the teaching and learning of a student with a disability who has been properly placed for services consistent with state and federal laws.

REQUIRED COMPONENTS OF IEPs PER IDEA

IEP structures and components vary in design, presentation, content, and online formatting. However, all IEPs must include several items mandated by the Individuals with Disabilities Education Act (IDEA; 2004). These are presented in Table 2.1, developed from material found in several sources including Bateman and Herr (2006), Gibb and Dyches (2016), IDEA (2004), Martin and Hauth (2015), and Siegel (2014).

In addition to the table items, frequency, duration, and location of services are also required items to be documented on the IEP. School districts include various formats for documenting material on an IEP to meet the mandated components highlighted in the table. The challenge is to document meaningful and relevant material.

Table 2.1 Key IEP Components With Culturally/Linguistically Responsive (CLR) Implications

Mandated IEP Component	Description	CLR Perspective
Present Level of Academic Achievement and Functional Performance	Brief, detailed summary of student's academic and functional performance at time IEP is generated	Include present level of English language proficiency at home and school.
Measureable Annual Goals	Structured statements (i.e., SMART) stating progress expectations by end of current academic school year, including short-term objectives	Incorporate academic language development into statements. Include academic, functional, *and* language annual goals and short-term objectives.
Special Education/ Related Services/ Supplemental Aids and Services	Description of specially designed instruction to meet annual and short-term goals and objectives, and location/duration of services, includes accommodations	Use evidence-based intervention processes with English learners, which may differ from those used with non-English learners; location of services should be with "true peers" as much as possible.
General-Education Curriculum Participation	Description of conditions under which learner will/will not participate in general education curricula or in settings with general class peers	It is essential that English learners receive continued development in English while receiving special education and that instruction include attention to academic language development.
Progress Monitoring	Procedures for gathering data and other evidence to monitor progress toward goals and objectives, method for informing parents of child's progress required in monitoring procedures	Reduce bias and increase validity by using multiple sources/devices designed for use with diverse learners, matching the language used in the monitoring to English proficiency level of English learners.
Participation Considerations in State and District Assessments	Summary of required test accommodations or modifications in high stakes assessment/alternative options	Accommodations based on English language proficiency are essential to document for meaningful participation in mandated assessments.
Transition Services	Assist learners for post-secondary success	Cultural values influence postsecondary expectations.

Present Performance Levels

Once a student has been properly referred, followed by the comprehensive evaluation leading to an appropriate eligibility placement decision, an IEP is developed to describe the instruction the student will receive. The foundation for framing the documented instruction is based on the descriptions about present level of academic and functional performance. Present levels of academic achievement and functional performance (PLAAFP) specify current strengths and needs, while also reflecting cultural and linguistic considerations that support diverse students' effective learning. The present level of performance component contains two related elements succinctly describing the learner's existing skill sets and performance levels at the time the IEP is generated (Gibb & Dyches, 2016), thereby serving as the baseline from which instruction begins.

Academic Performance—Refers to the core academic skills and abilities relevant to the disability area of need reflective of reading, writing, and/or mathematics since these are foundational to success with other academic areas (e.g., social studies, science). Academic achievement performance describes the student's current academic strengths and needs in both quantitative and qualitative terms (e.g., reading grade level of 3.2; proficient with 60 of the top 100 high-frequency vocabulary words; uses finger to point when reading; interacts well in small math groups; prefers to read aloud in pairs rather than whole-class settings).

It is essential to document both quantitative achievement level and clarifying qualitative statements, in order to generate annual goals and relevant short-term objectives necessary for measuring annual progress and for linking assessment with instruction. It is also important to note that for English language and other diverse learners, the academic performance statements should reflect cultural and linguistic qualities (e.g., learner is proficient with WIDA Can Do skills at Stage 3 of English language development; based on input from parents student prefers to interact and work in cooperative groups over independent, competitive task completion; student requires more "wait time" prior to responding to a question to best use English language skills). Therefore, the current academic performance levels include documentation of the specific defined levels (e.g., third-grade reading comprehension level) while also clarifying under which conditions student best learns or prefers to learn (e.g., small groups, sufficient time to think through a question). Simply providing a reading or math grade level in the present performance level limits the value of this foundational aspect of an IEP, as it says little about *how* a student best learns, which is essential to identifying and selecting effective instruction and related services to meet annual goals.

Functional Performance—In addition to skills and needs related to present levels of academics, an IEP must also include relevant functional performance skills and abilities. Functional skills are those abilities that reflect necessary daily living and classroom performance expectations essential to success regardless of academic area. When developing an IEP, functional skills that directly affect learner performance in school should be documented, such as hygiene, interpersonal interactions, organization/time management, healthy life style, and so on. These and similar abilities should be documented on an IEP if they represent sufficient need areas for effective "functional" performance in school and society. Similar to academic achievement performance, culturally and linguistically diverse values and norms affect functional performance. For example, lack of eye contact or extended periods of silence may be taught as a sign of respect and therefore should not be misinterpreted as a functional performance deficit. Family input and cultural knowledge are essential to making certain that culturally and linguistically diverse values and norms are incorporated in functional skill performance statements as well as academic achievement statements. The topic of cultural and linguistic diversity and IEPs was discussed in Chapter 1, and performance levels are examined in greater detail in Chapter 4.

Measurable Annual Goals/Short-Term Instructional Objectives

Once performance levels are properly identified and recorded, the task of generating annual goals begins. Annual goals are statements defining progress expectations by the end of the academic year (e.g., student applies three self-management strategies during whole-group instruction; learner increases reading comprehension to fourth-grade reading level), which by IDEA mandate must be stated in measurable terms (Twachtman-Cullen & Twachtman-Bassett, 2011). It is essential to understand that annual goals are only as good as the associated performance level statements. That is, weak present level of performance statements lead to weak or ineffective annual goals, which is why IEP team members must exhibit the highest level of attention to properly written present levels of academic and functional performance described in both quantitative and qualitative terms. Annual goals then become a natural, logical, and measurable extension of the present performance abilities. Though no longer mandated by law, an IEP may contain short-term objectives to provide intermediate steps that connect to the annual goal. A short-term objective provides a breakdown of the annual goal into manageable and measurable targets that provide educators, parents, and students with evidence of ongoing progress as illustrated in the example below:

"An annual goal is written to show learner mastery of reading comprehension at grade level over an eight-month time frame. Select short-term objectives could provide a breakdown into four two-month segments with emphasis on mastery of different comprehension skill sets (e.g., compare-contrast, evaluation, synthesis). Process includes (a) providing a properly written present performance statement about existing comprehension skills, (b) generating associated annual reading comprehension goal and short-term objectives, and (c) monitoring progress to demonstrate reading comprehension mastery."

In reference to IEPs for English language and other diverse learners, writing the annual goal and associated short-term objectives provides an opportunity for educators to incorporate cultural and linguistic features and qualities into the delivery of responsive instruction (e.g., include the need for additional wait time when responding to verbal questions to reflect learner's level of second language acquisition). Selected examples of culturally and linguistically responsive items to include in the annual goals and short-term objectives are provided in Table 2.2.

Illustrated are different learner behaviors summarized from various WIDA Can Do Descriptors, which are skill sets based on English language acquisition proficiency levels and stages of development. Connecting descriptors and language proficiency, such as the examples provided in Table 2.2, in IEP development and implementation is essential for delivering appropriate specially

Table 2.2   Incorporating Cultural and Linguistic Features in IEPs

Representative WIDA Can Do Descriptors	Sample Expected Second Language Acquisition (SLA) Stage Behaviors
WIDA Level 1: Entering	**SLA Stage: Preproduction**
Listening: Learner is able to point to pictures, words, or phrases; follow one-step directions given orally; and match objects to oral statements. *Speaking:* Learner is able to name objects, people, and pictures and respond to who, what, when, where, which questions. *Reading:* Learner is able to match symbols to words or phrases and identify print concepts and text features. *Writing:* Learner is able to label objects and pictures, draw an illustration in response to a prompt, or produce symbols and words to convey messages.	Silent Period • Very little English spoken by learner: may respond nonverbally by nodding yes or no, drawing, and pointing • May not respond when spoken to • May have difficulty following directions • May have difficulty understanding questions • May have difficulty expressing needs • May experience confusion with locus of control • May be withdrawn/show low self-esteem • May seem to exhibit poor attention and concentration
WIDA Level 2: Beginning	**SLA Stage: Early Production**
Listening: Learner is able to sort pictures and objects based on oral instructions, follow two-step oral directions, and match information from oral descriptions to objects. *Speaking:* Learner is able to ask Wh-questions, orally describe pictures or events, and restate facts. *Reading:* Learner is able to find and classify information, identify facts, and determine language patterns connected to facts.	• Limited English spoken by learner: usually speaks in one- or two-word phrases • Uses present-tense verbs • May respond to who, what, where, and either/or questions with one-word answers • May complete sentences when given sentence starters • May participate using key words and familiar phrases • May memorize short language chunks (with or without errors)
WIDA Level 3: Developing	**SLA Stage: Production**
Listening: Learner is able to locate and select information from oral discourse, complete several steps of instructions, and categorize/sequence orally presented material. *Speaking:* Learner is able to predict, hypothesize, describe procedures, and retell stories. *Reading:* Learner is able to sequence, identify main ideas, and use context clues appropriately in reading. *Writing:* Learner is able to generate basic text, use compare and contrast statements, and describe in writing events, people, and procedures.	Speech Emergence • Increasing proficiency: speaks in short phrases and simple sentences • Writing may contain grammatical errors • Speech may contain grammatical and pronunciation errors • Developing sight word vocabulary • May be able to describe, compare, and make predictions • Can answer how/why questions • May be withdrawn/show signs of frustration • May seem to have trouble concentrating • Limited participation in group discussions

(Continued)

Table 2.2   (Continued)

Representative WIDA Can Do Descriptors	Sample Expected Second Language Acquisition (SLA) Stage Behaviors
WIDA Level 4: Expanding	**SLA Stage: Intermediate**
Listening: Learner is able to compare/contrast functions and relationships from oral material, conduct analyses of oral information, and engage in cause and effect discussions. *Speaking:* Learner is able to discuss issues and concepts, deliver a speech, present orally, and engage in creative problem solving and solutions generation. *Reading:* Learner interprets material and data, locates details, supports main ideas, and identifies word families. *Writing:* Learner is able to summarize, edit, revise, and create original ideas.	• English is approaching age-appropriate levels, but learner still makes grammatical errors in writing, grammatical and pronunciation errors in speech • May engage in dialogue • Receptive and expressive language mismatch: may understand more than she/he is able to demonstrate, or may seem more proficient than she/he is • May seem slow processing challenging language • May be confused by idioms/slang conveyed in English • May seem to have poor auditory memory
WIDA Level 5: Bridging	
Listening: Learner is able to draw conclusions from oral material, develop models reflecting oral discussions, and make connections to orally presented material and ideas. *Speaking:* Learner debates, provides detailed examples and justifications for reasoning, and is able to defend viewpoint. *Reading:* Learner conducts research using multiple sources and draws conclusions from different forms of text. *Writing:* Learner is able to apply material in a new context and author multiple forms of writing. *Writing:* Learner is able to compile a list of items, develop drawings, generate short phrases, and provide responses to requested information.	
WIDA Level 6: Reaching	**SLA Stage: Advanced**
	• Language usage, meaning, and fluency are age-appropriate; learner has very good comprehension • Academic, behavioral, cultural, and social skills are second language age-appropriate

Source: Hoover (2016b). Reprinted by permission.

designed instruction to English language and other diverse learners with disabilities. For additional Can Do Descriptors and detailed examination of English language proficiency levels from which Table 2.2 was developed, readers are referred to the WIDA.us website.

IEP annual goals and short-term objectives should incorporate use and development of skills commensurate with present levels of English language acquisition to meet academic and functional needs, thereby providing English language and other diverse learners with disabilities sufficient opportunities to learn and progress. Detailed discussion of development of SMART IEP annual goals and short-term objectives is provided in Chapter 5.

Assessment Procedures

Assessment procedures to measure progress toward annual goals and/ or instructional objectives, including participation in state assessments or need for an alternate assessment, are documented on a learner's IEP. In today's schools and classrooms, three types of assessments are used to measure achievement and social-emotional growth: (a) universal screening, (b) progress monitoring, and (c) diagnostic. Each type has its unique place in the function of an IEP.

Universal Screening and IEPs. Universal screening is the process of measuring learner progress toward annual core instructional benchmarks most typically associated with grade-level expectations in the content areas of reading, writing, and mathematics along with English language development for second language learners (Hoover, 2009). Students in most school systems are screened three times per year (e.g., September, January, April). Screening results alert educators of learners at risk and those who are beginning to fall behind grade- or age-level peers. Annual screening is foundational to determining instructional adjustment needs for becoming more intensive based on progress. Though students with IEPs are provided more specific and targeted assessment toward annual goals, they are still included in the annual universal screenings, thereby providing an important piece of evidence, connecting IEP instruction to continued general education core instruction as well as specialized instruction resulting from a disability.

Progress Monitoring and IEPs. The regular monitoring of progress toward IEP goals and associated instructional objectives is framed within progress monitoring procedures that are documented on the learner's IEP. Monitoring often takes the form of curriculum-based measurement (CBM), given CBM's process, to monitor progress based on shorter segments of instruction, and its direct connection to curriculum used during the instructional delivery of an IEP. It is essential to ensure that the IEP includes documentation of the procedures to be used to measure learner progress toward IEP goals and objectives. This includes the (a) device to be used (e.g., Dynamic Indicator of Basic Early Literacy Skills [DIBELS], Development Reading Assessment [DRA2]), (b) timing (e.g., every two weeks for ten weeks), (c) process (e.g., reading a 200-word passage aloud for fluency), and (d) charting (e.g., graph monitoring results to visually illustrate learner progress). Additionally, the progress monitoring procedures should clearly connect to the curricular goals and instructional methods to be most valid, thereby ensuring use of devices or practices that link the assessment to instruction.

Diagnostic.   Selective and strategic use of individual diagnostic assessment measures to determine IEP annual progress provides highly useful and relevant information to educators, families, and students. Though most monitoring of IEP progress should include use of CBMs as discussed above, the addition of an individual diagnostic assessment (e.g., Early Reading Assessment, Test of Written Language, Test of Mathematic Ability) supports the documentation of learner progress particularly when comparison with grade- and age-level peers is desired. In some instances, using an individual diagnostic assessment to provide pre-post IEP implementation progress assists educators to document present level of performance at the beginning and subsequent levels at the end of the academic school year. However, similar to the other two types of assessments, diagnostic measures must be valid and reliable for intended purposes and uses with English language and other diverse learners to ensure accurate results, followed by appropriate instructional decision making.

Assessment of English Learners and IEPs. In regard to English language and other diverse learners, each of the three types of assessments requires the same level of validity and reliability to be of value in IEP development, implementation, and evaluation. Of particular concern is the use of assessment devices designed to measure a content area (e.g., reading, math) with learners with whom the device was not researched or validated. As emphasized in the previous chapter and throughout the remaining chapters of this book, if learners lack sufficient English skills to successfully understand the test material, then the test becomes an English test rather than a test of existing knowledge and skills in that content area. To best understand these concerns, Table 2.3 provides linguistic and instructional examples that influence test development and completion. Educators should consider these features in the IEP screening and progress monitoring process during test selection, use, and interpretation of results for students in the process of acquiring English as a second language.

As shown, the more frequent linguistic features used on most English tests may present unique problems for students who are in the process of acquiring English. Attention to these linguistic features prior to assessment selection assists to reduce use of inappropriate devices. This is of particular concern for learners who fall within the developing or emerging stages of development (e.g., WIDA English proficiency stages 3 and 4), as summarized in Table 2.2. These learners may appear to possess sufficient English skills through oral interactions, yet they lack the more in-depth academic language necessary to take most tests in English. The topic of academic language is discussed in greater detail in Chapter 3, with additional discussion about appropriate assessment of IEP progress presented in Chapter 8.

State and District Assessment Participation. Each IEP is required to document the extent to which the learner will participate in the mandated state or district assessments provided to all students. Extent of participation in these assessments is based on the type and significance of the identified disability. This may include participation in alternative assessments. Additionally, participation should be strengthened by including use of any approved accommodation to

Table 2.3   Assessment Linguistic Features for English Learners

Linguistic Feature	*Instructional Example*	*Assessment Considerations for English Learners*
Word Frequency/ Familiarity	Words most frequently used in reading/spoken language	Words high on a general frequency list for English are likely to be familiar to most readers because they are encountered often. Readers who encounter familiar words are more likely to interpret them quickly and correctly, enjoying a positive impact on comprehension and test results.
Word Length	Use of single-syllable to multisyllable words	Words tend to be longer as their frequency of use decreases. In one study, language minority students performed better on math test items with shorter word lengths than items with longer word lengths.
Sentence Length	Two- to three-word sentences through lengthy multi-word sentences	The length of a sentence serves as an index for its complexity and can be used to predict comprehension difficulty.
Active/ Passive Voice	Use of active (e.g., "Juan hit the ball") vs. passive (e.g., "The ball was hit by Juan") structure	Passive constructions can be especially challenging to nonnative English speakers.
Long Noun Phrases	Sentences that contain several interconnected phrases requiring learners to comprehend more complex ideas	Noun phrases with several modifiers provide a potential source of difficulty in test items. Romance languages (e.g., Spanish, French, Italian, Portuguese) make less use of compounding than English.
Long Question Phrases	Questions that contain longer phrases and numerous words	Longer question phrases occur less frequently than short question phrases. Low-frequency expressions (long question phrases) are often harder to read/understand.
Comparative Structures	Comparing/contrasting ideas	Comparative constructions often represent potential sources of difficulty for nonnative speakers and for speakers acquiring a second language.
Prepositional Phrases	Phrases within a sentence that begin with a preposition	Students may experience difficulty with prepositions. English and Spanish may differ in their use of prepositions.
Sentence and Discourse Structure	Complexities of words/phrases used in a sentence or group of sentences	Although sentences may have a similar number of words, one may be more difficult to understand due to syntax complexities or discourse relationships among sentences.
Subordinate Clause	Clauses in sentences designed to show relationships and connect ideas that do not stand alone	For many students, subordinate clauses may increase the complexity of the sentence, generating confusion or lack of understanding.
Relative Clauses	Clauses that characterize (e.g., "The dog, who loves bones, barked for a treat.")	Relative clauses are less frequent in spoken English than in written English, and some students may have limited exposure to them and their usage in writing/reading.
Concrete vs. Abstract/ Impersonal Presentations	Use of concrete examples or statements, avoiding the use of vague abstractions	Students tend to perform better when content is presented in concrete rather than abstract terms.
Negation	Use of negatives in sentences (e.g., no, not, none, never)	Sentences that contain negations are more difficult to understand than affirmative sentences. In Spanish, double negative constructions retain a negative meaning rather than the affirmative meaning as in English.

Source: Hoover & Barletta (2016). Reprinted by permission.

provide the student sufficient opportunity to (a) participate in the assessment and (b) demonstrate valid and instructionally meaningful results. Similar to access to general curriculum, all learners with IEPs should be provided access to state and district assessments commensurate with their disability needs.

Specialized and Related Services/Supplemental Aids and Services

An individual's IEP must document any specialized services and related supports required to achieve annual goals and address needs associated with the disability. Specialized and related services include a variety of supports such as counseling, medical, occupational therapy, transportation, and social work to name a few. Professionals delivering the related services include those trained in the specific skill area, such as guidance counselor, school psychologist, social worker, school nurse, or speech and language specialist. The IEP includes documentation of the specialized/related service, the service provider, and the duration and location of the services. It is important to note that specialized and related services are those supports necessary to assist the learner to achieve the annual IEP goals and make satisfactory interim progress as addressed through short-term objectives.

In addition to the specialized and related services, many students with IEPs require what is referred to as "supplemental" services or aids. These supports are "provided in regular education classes or other education-related settings to enable students with disabilities to be educated with nondisabled peers to the maximum extent possible" (Gibb & Dyches, 2007, p. 70). These types of supports may include large-print materials to address visual impairment needs, lip-reading proximity for learners with hearing impairments, use of dictation or oral presentation for those with motor skill challenges, or seating location in the classroom to reduce direct exposure to external noises or other visual distractions. These and similar types of supports are incorporated into both general and specialized services to meet the needs of learners with disabilities.

General Education Access and Participation

The extent to which a student with an IEP continues to receive instruction through the general-education curriculum with general education peers is also documented. Building on the present levels of performance, the delivery of instruction to meet annual IEP goals and associated short-term objectives should facilitate access to the general-education curriculum delivered with general classroom peers as much as possible. Though pull-out situations are often necessary and appropriate, education in the least restrictive environment (LRE), which is primarily in general education, is central to IDEA (2004) and related special education legislation. As discussed above for English learners, continued English language development (ELD; e.g., daily ELD for forty-five minutes) and/or incorporating research-based ESL instructional practices in general class core instruction is essential and necessary to provide diverse students sufficient opportunities to participate with peers and make adequate annual IEP progress.

> Diminished emphasis on ELD once delivery of an IEP begins may situate the learner to fail—lack of English development directly influences lack of academic progress expected from delivery of the IEP.

Table 2.4   Assessment and Instructional Accommodations

Accommodation	*Use accommodation if . . .*
Setting	changing the location for learning in the classroom or school provides the student with increased motivation and confidence in abilities to attend to and complete the assessment and instructional tasks.
Presentation	a modified presentation of assessment or instructional material provides the learner with increased opportunities to acquire and/or demonstrate knowledge and skills.
Response	allowing the learner to respond in an alternate or different manner (e.g., oral vs. written, using computer vs. paper-pencil, portfolio) results in increased attention in learning and accuracy in demonstrating knowledge and skills.
Scheduling	adjusting the schedule for task completion (e.g., breaking task into three segments) or conducting assessment (e.g., delivering assessment in morning rather than after lunch) provides the learner a fairer opportunity to demonstrate true abilities and skills.
Time	providing additional time facilitates increased task completion or greater accuracy in demonstrating knowledge and skills.

Accommodations

Instructional and assessment accommodations reflecting both disability needs and cultural and linguistic diversity are considered and documented on the IEP to best improve learning. Specifically, five accommodations are typically considered in the delivery of assessment and instruction for learners on an IEP, illustrated in Table 2.4, developed from material in several sources (see Hoover, Baca, & Klingner, 2016; Orosco, 2005).

Strategic use of the above accommodations to meet disability needs provides all learners, especially English language and other diverse learners, with much needed supports to make certain that instruction is appropriate and assessment is valid.

Transition Services

For secondary learners, the IEP must delineate procedures for helping them transition from secondary education to postsecondary areas, such as employment, higher education, trade school skills development, or independent/semi-independent living, to name a few. As will be discussed in detail in Chapter 9, educators and parents collaborate to document appropriate supports to help learners achieve smooth and equitable transition to adult living. Cultural preferences and teachings are essential to developing meaningful transition planning, which can be achieved only through valued parental/family and community input.

OTHER MANDATED IEP CONSIDERATIONS PER IDEA

Several additional areas associated with the documentation of learner strengths and needs require consideration to properly develop an IEP, as illustrated in Table 2.5. Select items presented in the table are addressed in greater detail

Table 2.5 Other Mandated IEP Instructional Factors

Factor	*Description*	*Diversity Considerations*
Parental/Guardian Input and Written Permission	Make certain that all procedures mandated by law are followed including securing meaningful and relevant parental input, support, and approval during the IEP development, implementation, and assessment phases.	Cultural teachings, values, and heritage shape a student's perspectives toward learning, which in turn shape the value of the IEP for diverse families. Second language acquisition development frames success with meeting IEP annual goals and must be integral to implementation for an English learner. Parental input and support are essential to generating and delivering a culturally and linguistically responsive IEP.
Team Consideration of Learner's Strengths, Parental Concerns, Evaluation Results, and Academic, Developmental, and Functional Needs	It is essential to make certain that learner strengths and the conditions under which learning best occurs are documented along with any concerns expressed by the parents.	Specific educational strengths may be manifested in ways that reflect culturally and linguistically diverse values that may vary from what is typically expected of non–culturally and linguistically diverse (CLD) learners.
English Language Development	English language development needs must be incorporated into the IEP for English learners.	It is essential to make certain that delivery of the learner's IEP occurs along with the delivery of English language development (i.e., English development is not replaced or reduced once the delivery of an IEP begins).
Consideration of Special Factors	Depending on learner needs, one or more special factors must be included on the IEP, such as positive behavioral interventions, braille, communication needs (i.e., deaf/hard of hearing), and assistive technology, devices, and services.	CLD learners require special consideration of their English language development needs, or ways of managing behavior.
IEP Review/ Modifications	Law requires an annual review of each learner's IEP with needed adjustments or modifications made with parental approval.	For many CLD learners, IEP modifications may require increased use of ESL/bilingual best practices in both general and special education settings, including additional English language development.

following the table, with the other items examined in greater detail in subsequent chapters in this book.

Parental/Guardian Input and Written Permission*

IEP procedural safeguards delineated in IDEA (2004) ensure that school personnel include in meaningful ways the input and support of families. Specifically for English language and other diverse learners, parental or guardian input, concerns, and related information reflecting cultural and linguistic

* **NOTE**: *Parental/Guardian* section includes contributions from Donna Sacco.

diversity and teachings should be incorporated into the development of the IEP. In regard to ensuring meaningful input associated with the IEP and its development, the following parental supports and activities are provided or completed (Gibb & Dyches, 2016).

Parents . . .

are active participants in the development of the IEP,

may present external evaluation information conducted by an independent evaluator,

must receive written notice, in the home or primary language, about an IEP meeting,

provide written consent to the IEP and its implementation,

provide cultural insight into the child's needs reflecting cultural and linguistic diversity,

are allowed to raise questions and issues of concern about the child's IEP, and

are informed of and may initiate due process procedures should this be desired.

Other mandated IDEA procedures provide parents/guardians with necessary IEP safeguards. In reference to English language and other diverse learners, several practices should be incorporated into procedural safeguards to reflect cultural/linguistic diversity supporting mandated procedures:

- Provide an interpreter in the most proficient language during the IEP process
- Demonstrate how English language development is continued for English learners with an IEP
- Respond to issues or questions raised about the IEP process and its implementation
- Incorporate both language development and content objectives into IEPs
- Document supplemental supports and accommodations (e.g., culturally responsive materials, research-based ESL instructional practices, instructional settings with peers) necessary to ensure that the IEP and its delivery are responsive to culturally and linguistically diverse qualities, second language acquisition, and valid instructional methods and assessment

Blending these and similar diversity practices with the mandated IEP procedural safeguards ensures that (a) parental input of all learners, including diverse students, is valued; (b) English language development continues to be central in the education of English learners along with IEP implementation; (c) selected devices, methods, and materials are appropriate for both the content area and English language proficiency levels to ensure validity in assessment and instruction; (d) present levels of performance statements reflect cultural values and teachings; and (e) specialized and general class instruction settings reflect the least restrictive environment.

Language Acquisition Considerations

For English learners, a variety of ESL instructional practices should be included in the IEP to provide sufficient opportunities to learn in general education and with grade-level peers. Hoover, Sarris, and Hill (2015) conducted a research project that prepared educators to incorporate several essential ESL themes into daily core instruction to improve learning for English language and other diverse learners. The seven themes are summarized in Table 2.6 (developed from material found in Hoover, Hopewell, & Sarris, 2014; Hoover et al., 2015) and should be incorporated in various components of the IEP (e.g., present levels, annual goals, short-term objectives, supplemental supports, accommodations) to ensure development of a culturally and linguistically responsive IEP, including general education instruction with peers.

> The task of continuing English language development is not replaced by the task of delivering an IEP; rather, both are implemented, monitored, and adjusted simultaneously to best meet the disability and English language needs of English learners placed for special education services.

Second language acquisition needs of English learners do not disappear once a diverse learner is placed for special education services. And in order to ensure appropriate delivery of specialized, related, and supplemental supports and services, the development of English must continue. All educators teaching English learners with an IEP (e.g., general educators, special educators, specialized service providers) are responsible for differentiating instruction, incorporating effective ESL practices, and delivering culturally responsive teaching.

Table 2.6   Core ESL Instructional Practices (CEIP) Themes

CEIP Theme	Description
Connections	Emphasize academic and language learning by assisting students to connect known skills and content to new material being acquired
Relevance	Ensure that diverse cultures and values are incorporated into teaching and learning, thereby building engagement and strengthening motivation
Native Language Utilization	English learners use their first languages to facilitate acquisition of English and content taught in English
English Language Development	Support use of a variety of practices in English development for second language learners including verbal interactions, visual supports, word walls, sentence stems, or appropriate wait times
Materials	Use physical and visual aids to assist English learners in a variety of instructional ways especially related to recognizing similarities/differences, building concepts and vocabulary, or connecting concrete to abstract concepts
Differentiations	Differentiated instruction is essential for providing English learners with disabilities sufficient opportunities in both general and specialized instruction and includes scaffolding, sheltering, and direct instruction
Assessment to Inform Instruction	Formative and summative classroom assessment is essential to accurately measure diverse learners' progress necessary to make informed, timely, and appropriate instructional adjustments reflecting IEP annual and interim progress

Consideration of Special Factors

In addition to the above items, IDEA mandates that an IEP contain documentation of "special factors" relevant to the learner's instructional needs. Factors requiring specific consideration by the IEP team include (a) positive behavior interventions when the student's behavior interferes with his/her own learning or that of others; (b) English language development needs of second language learners; (c) reading and writing needs of learners with visual impairments or of those who are blind, specifically instructional Braille needs; (d) communication needs of learners who are deaf or who have a hearing impairment; and (e) assistive technology needs (Center for Parent Information and Resources, 2016).

IEP TEAM: ESSENTIAL MEMBERS FOR DIVERSITY

The composition of the IEP team is crucial when considering the needs of English language and other diverse learners and often must go beyond the types of educators used in IEP meetings mandated by IDEA. However, at minimum the following are essential members of an IEP development meeting: (a) parents/guardians, (b) general education teacher, (c) special education teacher, (d) school administration representative, (e) assessment/evaluation specialist, (f) other educators with specific knowledge about the learner or disability, and (g) student (when appropriate).

Within the parameters of the above mandated types of educators, other professionals with specific skill sets and expertise specific to cultural and linguistic diversity must be included when developing the IEP for diverse learners. Though some of the individuals above may possess one or more skill sets identified below, in many situations additional IEP team members need to be included or consulted (e.g., bilingual educator, ELD teacher, ESL coordinator). In order for IEPs for English language and other diverse learners to be culturally and linguistically responsive, the following skill sets must be represented by one or more educators possessing proficiency or expertise:

- Learner's native language (e.g., bilingual educator)
- Learner's culture, heritage, and teachings
- Stages of English as a second language acquisition (e.g., ESL or ELD specialist)
- Assessment of English learners
- Culturally and linguistically responsive instruction

Educators with the above cultural and linguistic responsive skill sets provide essential input necessary to develop and implement IEPs for English language and other diverse learners. Following is an example of the essential mandated IEP components with suggestions for a diverse learner.

Culturally and Linguistically Responsive IEP Application

Many of the items discussed throughout this chapter are referenced in Table 2.7, which provides guidelines for incorporating culturally and

Table 2.7   Suggestions for Writing Culturally and Linguistically Responsive (CLR) IEPs

Overview: Suggestions for key IEP components are provided below. Within each component, representative examples illustrating CLR considerations are provided.

Meeting Information (e.g., date, time, those in attendance)

Example: 3/20/2015, 3:00 p.m., Parents, General Classroom Teacher, Special Educator, ELD Teacher, Instructional Coach, Assistant Principal

Student Information (e.g., age, home language, grade level)

Example: Age 9, Grade 4, English learner, Home language is primarily Spanish with some English

Parent/Guardian Input: Specify culturally and linguistically responsive items based on input provided by parents/guardians to incorporate into IEP.

Example:

1. Child has been taught to work with others in pairs or small groups in cooperative ways.
2. Child's second language acquisition stage requires additional time to think about a question.
3. Child likes to read material about home country.
4. Child speaks at home in native language and is "always talking and asking questions," which differs from child's responses when asked to speak in English in school.

1. Present Level of Academic Achievement and Functional Performance (PLAAFP)

IEP Mandate: One or more statements that clearly describe the student's current levels of academic achievement and functional behavioral strengths and weaknesses that pertain specifically to the disability area of need that served to make the special education eligibility and placement decision

CLR Considerations: The PLAAFP should include learner's current English language proficiency level (e.g., WIDA ACCESS Proficiency level 1–5), examples of WIDA Can Do Descriptors possessed by the student, statement(s) about cultural teachings that support student's successful learning, and ESL best practices that have been shown to be effective for the student

2. Measurable Annual Goals, Including Short-Term Objectives

IEP Mandate: Listing of each annual academic and/or functional goal and associated objectives adhering to SMART principles that clearly describe the knowledge and skills the student will achieve during the duration of the IEP. Cultural and linguistic specifics should be incorporated into annual goal(s) as necessary for diverse learners

CLR Considerations: Listed for each annual goal are short-term objectives. If student is an English learner, the short-term objectives should be classified within two headings:

1. *Academic Language:* identifying specific skills (e.g., compare, contrast) and structures (e.g., parts of speech, sentences) and the language domain most impacted (i.e., listening, speaking, reading, writing) that are necessary to successfully master the objective
2. *Academic Vocabulary:* identifying key vocabulary needed to be taught and successfully mastered to achieve the objective

3. Assessment and Progress Monitoring Toward Annual Goals/Objectives

IEP Mandate: Statement describing the periodic monitoring used to determine IEP annual progress

CLR Considerations: Describe assessment conditions most compatible with the student's English language proficiency level and appropriate WIDA ACCESS Can Do Descriptors to be considered in periodic progress monitoring, CBM, and other formative and summative assessments

4. Specialized and Related/Supplementary Services

IEP Mandate: Statement describing needed related and supplementary services, including technology or other aids to address disability needs

CLR Considerations: Incorporate ESL or bilingual instructional practices into delivery of IEP

5. General-Education Curriculum Participation

IEP Mandate: Statement, with rationale, describing the extent to which the learner's disability enables and limits the child's involvement in the general-education curriculum with nondisabled peers

CLR Considerations: Listing or description of specific ESL instructional practices found successful with the learner that should be used by the general educator to assist the student to best access the general-education classroom and curriculum

6. Participation in High Stakes Testing

IEP Mandate: Statement that identifies the extent to which learner participates in state and district high stakes testing must be included

CLR Considerations: For English learners, alignment between English language proficiency level and English proficiency required to successfully complete the high stakes assessment is documented

7. Accommodations: Assessment and Instructional

IEP Mandate: Statement that identifies instructional and testing accommodations needed to assist learner to achieve and to measure academic achievement and functional performance

CLR Considerations: For English learners, document how English language development (ELD) is continued in general education and during delivery of specialized services to support continued English language proficiency development (*i.e., role of general and special educators in ELD*)

IEP Mandate: Statement describing extent to which and the reason why the learner is permitted to use alternative assessments based on disability for annual statewide and IEP assessments

CLR Considerations: Describe assessment conditions most compatible with the student's English language proficiency level and appropriate WIDA Can Do Descriptors when considering IEP assessments

8. Transition Services and Supports (aged 14 or older)

IEP Mandate: Statement identifying measurable postsecondary goals including procedures/courses of study for transition beyond secondary education to school, employment, and/or independent living

CLR Considerations: Document culturally appropriate practices consistent with family input, desires, and teachings

linguistically responsive instruction into the various IEP components. Two representative samples of IEPs, one secondary and one elementary, are provided in the Appendix.

IEP Variations of Structure and Content

School districts are mandated through IDEA to incorporate material addressing the seven topical areas described and illustrated above. Additionally, districts may add to or elaborate on the IDEA-mandated required components leading to a variety of ways in which IEPs are structured in format and layout along with documented content. Also, technological advances make completion of IEPs electronically a more frequent occurrence in today's schools and districts. Therefore, we recognize that variation in IEP format, structure, and content exists across the hundreds of school districts nationwide.

Within this reality, however, our purpose is to maintain focus on ways to create culturally and linguistically responsive IEPs specific to the mandated IDEA components. Readers will no doubt be exposed to a variety of IEPs for diverse learners, each of which includes at minimum the core mandated IEP aspects required by law. Therefore, though we may not specifically discuss IEP items and formats that go beyond that which is required by law, we value these variations with the hope that all IEPs for English language and other diverse learners reflect cultural and linguistic responsiveness as emphasized throughout this book.

CONCLUSION

An IEP is a document mandated by law to be developed once a learner has been identified has having a disability that requires specially designed instruction to make adequate progress in school. The foundation of an IEP is the present level of academic achievement and functional performance, from which the measurable annual goals/short-term objectives are generated along with special, related, and supplemental services and aids. Additionally, processes for measuring IEP progress are documented including assessment procedures and accommodations. *An IEP is a legal document; however, if developed consistent with recommendations found in this chapter (and the others in this book), it also becomes a useful instructional tool.*

Though information required on any IEP is similar for all learners, additional material should be included for English language and other diverse learners to incorporate culturally and linguistically responsive teaching. Of most importance are two realities: (1) an IEP containing only information that is typically included for non-CLD learners falls short of being appropriate for English language and other diverse learners, and (2) the need to continue English language development remains once an English learner is placed into special education. English development should not be discontinued or replaced once the delivery of the IEP begins (i.e., the challenge is to determine how to best deliver English development and the IEP simultaneously).

Numerous examples of learner skill sets, educational practices, and suggestions for delivering sufficient opportunities to learn were provided in this chapter, guiding both general and special educators to develop and implement a culturally and linguistically responsive IEP. Readers are encouraged to periodically revisit the material in this chapter as remaining chapters of this book are studied.

3

Role and Function of
Academic Language in IEPs

By Donna Sacco

Practitioner's Perspective . . .

What is the contemporary perspective on academic language? What are four *processes* associated with academic language? How is each process important to effective development and implementation of IEPs for English language and other diverse learners?

Proficient use of academic language is foundational to unlocking success in school for students who bring cultural and linguistic diversity to the teaching and learning environment (Gottlieb & Ernst-Slavit, 2014). Yet what exactly is meant by academic language? For example, it is often referred to as the language of school, while others refer to it as standard or mainstream English. However, the term *academic language* refers to more than the language itself, capturing its subtleties, reflecting gestural, behavioral, and cognitive domains associated with language. Additionally, due to its complex nature, academic language is more than simple vocabulary, phrases, or terms used in reading, writing, or speaking (Frantz, Bailey, Starr, & Perea, 2014).

Students bring to school their language, reflective of cultural ways and teachings associated directly with levels of experience, privilege, or social justice. This chapter provides (a) an overview of what is meant by academic language, (b) the importance of academic language proficiency to the success of students in school, and (c) the significance of academic language in Individualized Education Program (IEP) development, implementation, and evaluation for English language and other diverse learners. We begin with a brief scenario that reflects the need for emphasizing academic language in IEPs for diverse learners.

Academic Language Vignette

Adrianna (second grade) and Carolina (third grade) are sisters attending a diverse elementary school in a suburban community. The sisters, the oldest of four children, came to the United States from El Salvador when they were five and six years old, respectively, and have resided in the United States for two years. At home, they are very active and engaged in playing "school," assisting with household chores, caring for their two younger brothers, or attending their place of worship. The family lives in a modest two-bedroom apartment where there are few books, papers, pencils, or crayons. Both parents speak very little English and have limited literacy skills in Spanish. The mother remains in the home during the day, caring for an infant son, and the father holds steady work in a landscaping business. Each year, during the school year, they return to El Salvador to visit family for two to three weeks.

Although they have been in the United States for such a short time, Carolina was identified as having a learning disability in reading. She was recently identified by a multilingual assessment team adhering to ecological assessment principles (Hoover, Klingner, Baca, & Patton, 2008) and was appropriately identified as having a specific learning disability. Though Carolina continues to receive English language development (ELD) in her general education classroom, a major concern was that once she began receiving special education services, she would no longer receive the additional ELD services with her peers in a pull-out setting. The special educator has some training in second language acquisition and applies this knowledge when teaching Carolina in the special education setting. With regard to Adrianna, she receives ELD services both in her large second-grade classroom as well as in a daily pull-out small-group setting. Adrianna is making steady progress—although she is very hesitant to speak English in class. She is quiet and has difficulty answering the teacher's questions unless sufficient wait time is provided. However, when she meets her sister on the playground after lunch, they have animated conversations in Spanish.

Both sisters continue to require academic language supports throughout the school day regardless of where the instruction is provided, be that in a general education setting, within an ELD small group, or in a special education resource setting. To ensure that Carolina continues to receive academic language support across all settings, the IEP can be developed in a manner that addresses her language acquisition along with academic disability needs simultaneously.

ACADEMIC LANGUAGE HISTORICAL PERSPECTIVE

Origins of research involving academic language include the seminal work of Jim Cummins (1979), who proposed that language acquisition can be looked at in two ways: basic interpersonal communication skills (BICS) and cognitive academic language proficiency (CALP). BICS was believed to be the everyday social language the students use to communicate with individuals in social settings (e.g., as they play on the playground; after school; during free time in the classroom). According to Cummins (1999), students are generally able to develop this level of language proficiency in six months to two years. CALP on the other hand was perceived to reflect specific formal academic language used in school, as it relates to the content area instruction involving speaking, listening, reading, and writing. Cummins (1999) determined that this level of language proficiency could take five to seven years to develop, although Thomas and Collier (1997) found that English learners who come to school without an academic background in their first language could take seven to ten years to acquire this level of language proficiency.

Though foundational since their initial emphasis, the concepts of BICS and CALP have evolved into a more contemporary perspective, using terminology to better reflect language usage based on updated research. Specifically, current research has shown that students acquire and use social and academic language simultaneously along a continuum. For example, Frantz et al. (2014) wrote that researchers "hypothesize that language is on a continuum whereby it is more or less academic, depending on a preponderance of traits" (p. 438). In today's school settings, social and academic languages are the preferred terms and will be used throughout this chapter and book, capturing several contexts of language use (i.e., listening, speaking, reading, writing).

Academic Language Defined.   Academic language is the language necessary for success in an academic context that facilitates frequent use of "complex grammatical structures, specialized vocabulary, and uncommon language functions" (August & Shanahan, 2010, p. 217). Contemporary emphasis on academic language in educator preparation standards and teaching is found in, at minimum, three interrelated areas (Frantz et al., 2014):

- Vocabulary—refers to word form and meaning in an academic context and includes high-frequency, general academic, specialized, and content-specific vocabulary.
- Grammatical—refers to both form and meaning based on context (e.g., science, social studies, mathematics) and includes various complexities such as those associated with sentence structure, phrases, and voice.
- Discourse—refers to various dimensions of language found in texts generated for different purposes containing variations of use connected to social, cultural, and political language; text organization patterns; structures beyond sentence levels; or other language functions specific to a particular discipline or context, to name a few.

Additional academic language examples may be included and the reader is referred to the sources cited in this chapter for more detailed coverage of the various dimensions of academic language. For our purposes, we are focused on the concept that academic language is central to teaching and learning for English language and other diverse learners, reflecting "features that are common to actual language use in academic settings" (Frantz et al., 2014, p. 442), no matter which definition is used within any academic context.

Academic Language Instructional Developments.   Framed within these earlier academic language works, educators began to research and develop instructional practices and materials regarding academic language for students who are English learners. For example, Chamot and O'Malley (1994) developed the instructional model *cognitive academic language learning approach* (CALLA), designed to improve instruction, curriculum, and staff development for English learners and their teachers. Another research-based development includes the *sheltered instruction observation protocol* (SIOP; Echevarria, Vogt, & Short, 2008) for use with lesson design and implementation, emphasizing the importance of using sheltered instruction for simultaneously meeting academic and language goals. SIOP emerged out of the work completed at the Center for Research on Education, Diversity, and Excellence (CREDE) funded by the US Department of Education between 1996 and 2003. Currently, the Center for Applied Linguistics (CAL) is continuing to research the SIOP model and its effectiveness in teaching and learning. Furthermore, WIDA has made great progress in the development of Can Do Descriptors and assessments of language proficiency. Elements of various WIDA Can Do Descriptors were introduced in Chapter 2 and will be explained in greater detail later in this chapter. Also, numerous professionals including Jeff Zwiers, Margo Gottlieb, Gisela Ernst-Slavit, and Debbie Zacarian, to name a few, have devoted themselves to developing professional resources to enhance instruction with academic language as a means of access and equity.

> To date, regardless of the model of instruction, developing academic language is considered to be one of the most critical tools for academic success in school for English learners.

Academic language development is also central to understanding the achievement gap between English learners and non-English learners in our schools. For example, Zacarian (2013) frames the achievement gap in this country as being a gap between students who are academic language *carriers* and those who are academic language *learners.* Students who carry academic language begin to have consistent exposure to a rich vocabulary from a young age. They are exposed to literacy as a cultural way of being, with dialectal skills similar to those used in school. Conversely, students who are academic language learners have consistent exposure to oral storytelling and a rich narrative of personhood and membership from a young age. However, the dialect is often distinct from school language and vernacular. During the early academic language learner stages of development, students require more explicit directions about language, often leading to limited experiences with problem solving typically seen in formal schooling. Therefore, distinguishing between academic language carriers and learners is critical when evaluating the language needs of a student during the IEP development and implementation process.

ACADEMIC LANGUAGE PROCESSES

Though various perspectives about academic language exist, we select the Four-Pronged Framework based on the work of Zacarian (2013) as the foundation for understanding and incorporating academic language into IEP development and implementation for English language and other diverse learners. In Zacarian's framework for the planning and delivery of high-quality instructional experiences, academic language learning is presented as four interrelated processes: sociocultural, developmental, academic, and cognitive. These four processes reflect various skill sets working interdependently as learners perform academic tasks at all grade levels, as illustrated in Figure 3.1.

Figure 3.1   Four-Pronged Structure Framing an Instructional Learning Environment

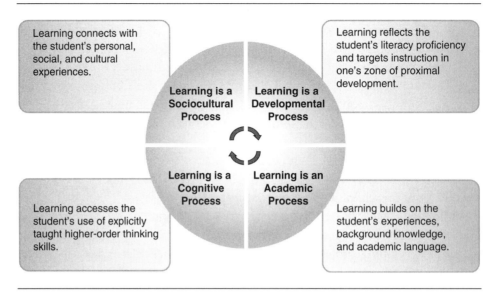

Source: Figure developed by permission from material found in Zacarian (2013), pp. 43 & 47.

As shown, the four processes reflect different, yet related, aspects of teaching and learning with specific emphasis on cultural and linguistic diversity. An overview of each of the four processes is discussed below, and the reader is referred to Zacarian (2013) for more in-depth coverage of each process.

Learning as a Sociocultural Process

Learning as a sociocultural process involves building connections with students' personal, social, cultural, and world experiences (Vygotsky, 1986; Zacarian, 2013). This process incorporates several research-based instructional practices for effectively educating English language and other diverse learners including activating prior knowledge, building background knowledge, and scaffolding by connecting to issues relevant to the students. Zacarian (2013) also includes learning as an interactive social process within this prong of the framework. Teacher creativity and planning are essential to effective use of paired and group work based on the cultural norms of the students. It is incumbent upon each classroom teacher to uncover students' interests and learning preferences based on cultural teachings and values, such as preference toward cooperative work over individual accomplishments.

To best prepare for this sociocultural academic learning component, teachers should spend the time needed to learn about students' interests, home teachings, and cultures. For example, a home visit could be conducted or an interest inventory could be developed and conducted either in writing or orally to facilitate inclusion of personal, cultural, and world knowledge of the students and families into the design and delivery of culturally relevant instruction. By using learning as an interactive process, teachers continue to acquire increased knowledge about their students, helping to build background knowledge based on students' worldviews (Zacarian, 2013). Also, by connecting to students' home cultures and teachings, educators will find that student motivation increases, which is essential for success in school for all learners, especially for those with a disability or in the process of acquiring English as a second language. In addition, research shows the effectiveness of paired and small-group work (see Haynes & Zacarian, 2010; Zacarian, 2011; Zacarian & Haynes, 2012; Zwiers & Crawford, 2011), especially when explicit instructions are provided to clarify (a) expectations in group work, (b) assigned roles, and (c) monitoring of group's activities (Klingner, Vaughn, Boardman, & Swanson, 2012). These learning as sociocultural process classroom structures provide a less intimidating setting for discussion and multiple opportunities to incorporate academic language purposefully in teaching and learning.

Learning as a Developmental Process

The developmental process prong considers the student's age, prior learning, proficiency in language, as well as exposure to literacy practices. It is rooted in the student's cultural way of being. To best understand learning as a developmental process, Zacarian (2013) stresses the importance of listening, speaking, and experience in teaching and learning. As introduced above, comparison between academic language carriers and academic language learners puts the academic literacy frame into proper context and practice. As discussed, *carriers,* from their earliest years, are surrounded by a literacy rich environment and therefore often bring rich vocabulary to the learning environment. Academic language *learners,* on the other hand, must build a rich vocabulary, requiring direct language instruction embedded within content instruction.

In discussing vocabulary within the developmental process, Zacarian refers to these four items: terms, words, idioms, and phrases (i.e., TWIPs). Additionally, the tiered levels of vocabulary discussed by Beck, McKeown, and Kucan (2002) further enhance this process:

Tier 1—Everyday words used in basic communication

Tier 2—More sophisticated vocabulary involving synonyms for Tier 1 words, along with transition and connecting words

Tier 3—Vocabulary that is academic in nature going beyond everyday communication

Explicit instruction and culturally relevant activities that engage English language and other diverse students in authentic, repeated practice are necessary for academic language learners to become familiar with TWIPs and vocabulary associated with the three tiers presented above. Incorporating multiple opportunities to practice academic language with purposeful listening and speaking activities will ultimately support reading and writing through this developmental process.

Along with vocabulary development, students require opportunities to understand the text features of content (i.e., comprehension). To best facilitate the integrated skills of vocabulary development and comprehension, students should be guided, using explicit instruction, in the before, during, and after reading task segments to support long-term use of newly acquired vocabulary and associated comprehension. Additionally, content-specific vocabulary should be reinforced using a variety of effective practices such as visual supports or anchors on word walls, table mats, sentence stems, or handouts (Baca & Cervantes, 2004; Echevarria et al., 2008; Zacarian, 2013). In summary, given the importance of listening, speaking, and experiential background in the delivery of learning as a developmental process, a most powerful tool for teaching academic language learners is academic and instructional conversations that reinforce the vocabulary and content of texts, such as the process promoted through the CREDE standards of instruction (see Tharp, 1997; Tharp et al., 2004; see also the Center for Research on Education, Diversity, and Excellence website, at end of chapter).

Learning as an Academic Process

Within the learning as an academic process prong, essential questions about required learning and key concepts are posed to best identify the necessary grade- or age-level knowledge and skills required in school. Learning as an academic process builds on students' prior learning experiences, leading to explicitly stated academic content and language goals. Using state standards as a foundation, teachers design a unit of study by determining what the students should know and be able to do at the end of the unit (i.e., annual goals). Teachers are then able to use backward chaining as a means of developing short-term instructional objectives or learning targets associated with the IEP annual content goals as well as academic language goals.

Once a teacher has determined the overarching content and language goals for the unit, each day or lesson should have its own content and language objectives. These objectives should be clearly stated in measurable, student-friendly language, defined, and displayed for all students to see. Students should also be made aware of what they will be expected to do and how they will demonstrate what they have learned during and at the end of the instructional unit. As discussed, Zacarian (2013) stresses the need to have explicit vocabulary instruction and frequent practice opportunities in challenging educational tasks. In summary, English language and other diverse learners need to be provided repeated practice, supported by teacher modeling of expected behaviors, thinking processes, and learning procedures to best master academic content and associated language outcomes through the learning as an academic process prong (Zacarian, 2013).

Learning as a Cognitive Process

Learning as a cognitive process is shaped by Bloom's taxonomy (i.e., remembering, understanding, applying, analyzing, evaluating, and creating) that intentionally teaches higher-order thinking skills. According to Zacarian (2013), properly framed cognitive skill development assists students to understand how to use language to express thinking. As students construct meaning from experience and engage in thought-provoking academic conversations, opportunities for cognitive skill development are provided. Academic language learners require continued support in this process, initially through explicit instruction to help them negotiate multiple learning tasks to use associated academic language. Visual organizers are effective in practices to support thinking when explicitly taught to students and applied in multiple learning situations. Teachers should employ various research-based instructional practices found effective for the education of English language and other diverse

Table 3.1   Sample Sentence Response Starters for Developing Academic Language

Questioning Prompt	
	What did you notice?
	Can you provide an example of _____ ?
	How might the outcome be changed?
	Why do you think _____ was important?
	What is one example of _____?
Response Frames	
	I know this because . . .
	I observed . . .
	I expected to see . . .
	I agree/disagree with you because . . .
	I understand that _____. Is that correct?

learners, including modeling expected behaviors, using think-alouds, graphic organizers, sentence frames, or sentence prompts—to name a few. Additionally, incorporating sentence response starters in unit instruction is an effective teaching practice to develop academic language such as the examples provided in Table 3.1.

An ultimate outcome of the learning as a cognitive process prong is for students to become effective problem solvers who are able to use critical thinking skills throughout their lives. However, a common misperception about instruction for English language and other diverse learners with disabilities is that they are unable to engage in higher-level cognitive tasks academically and/or in language proficiency (Hoover, Baca, & Klingner, 2016). This erroneous assumption is best addressed through effective teaching practices such as (a) strategic planning, (b) explicit instruction, (c) scaffolding and supports, and (d) multiple opportunities to practice academic language in a variety of content settings. It is through these and the other best practices identified above that learners develop and generalize cognitive skills. All English language and other diverse learners with disabilities should be provided sufficient opportunities to engage in challenging and culturally relevant tasks, documented on their IEPs, to best implement the learning as a cognitive process prong.

INCLUSION OF ACADEMIC LANGUAGE PROFICIENCY IN IEP DEVELOPMENT

How does knowledge about academic language development and use relate to writing an effective IEP? In particular, once a full profile of the student is examined, there are at minimum three areas within the IEP in which educators can ensure that language needs of the English language or other diverse student are addressed and being met:

1. The present level of academic achievement and functional performance (PLAAFP) must be used to fully describe the student's strengths and weaknesses in social, emotional, academic, *and* language proficiency.

2. Annual goals and associated short-term objectives should address those areas of academic language proficiency requiring continued support.

3. Necessary language proficiency supports and ELD instruction should be identified in one or more of the mandated components of the IEP.

IEPs and WIDA/Second Language Acquisition Skill Sets

Currently, the WIDA consortium includes over thirty states, the US Virgin Islands, and the Northern Mariana Islands. These geographic localities may use the WIDA ACCESS, which is an annual language proficiency assessment. For students who have a cognitive disability, there is the Alternate ACCESS. In addition, WIDA has developed the WIDA Measure of Developing English Language (MODEL), which is a series of English language proficiency assessments for K–12 students. The MODEL tool may be used with newly enrolled English learners in the language proficiency identification and/or placement process, or as an interim progress monitoring assessment tool (to see WIDA MODEL, visit WIDA.us). Results from these assessments allow educators to use empirical data specific to the student for planning instruction. Thus, several WIDA-developed materials provide highly useful information to educators in the development, implementation, and monitoring of an IEP. The rationale for our recommendation for WIDA usage is that it is best to use the most specific, clear, and precise measures of strengths and weaknesses in language proficiency as part of the PLAAFP in order to accurately build upon the student's skills.

One feature of a well-written IEP is the alignment of the PLAAFP (see Chapter 4) with the measurable annual goals and short-term objectives (see Chapter 5). In order to create a responsive IEP for an English language or other diverse student, the PLAAFP should include a learner's current English language proficiency level, such as that provided by the WIDA ACCESS proficiency test currently used in many states. Recall the WIDA ACCESS levels—previously presented in Table 2.2—provide a proficiency score as follows: Level 1: Entering; Level 2: Beginning; Level 3: Developing; Level 4: Expanding; Level 5: Bridging; and Level 6: Reaching. An English learner's IEP should identify the level of English proficiency to guide documentation of necessary academic language supports needed to improve progress toward mastery of the annual goals and short-term objectives.

In addition to recording the actual proficiency level, WIDA Can Do Descriptors associated with the above language proficiency levels have been generated. Can Do Descriptors identify behaviors typically possessed by the student across the four language domains of listening, speaking, reading, and writing for the one to five proficiency levels. Knowledge of the learner's English proficiency level is essential to developing a culturally and linguistically responsive IEP. Once identified, the WIDA Can Do Descriptors, or similar second language acquisition model skill sets, provide learning behaviors useful for IEP development of annual goals and short-term objectives that complement the four-pronged academic language processes discussed above (revisit Table 2.2 for representative examples of WIDA Can Do Descriptors and second language acquisition model skill sets). Reflecting on Can Do Descriptors and/or acquisition skill sets, the PLAAFP can specifically state how effectively the student is able to use and understand academic language. Completing the PLAAFP also provides opportunity for educators to describe the specific ESL/bilingual best practices that are in use with the student in general education.

For example, as we look back at the sisters in our vignette, they received an overall score as well as scores for each domain on the WIDA ACCESS assessment as they live in a state that is part of the WIDA consortium. Their English proficiency scores can be used to accurately describe their present levels of language proficiency including what they are able to do with language supports (i.e., Can Do Descriptors). The WIDA ACCESS tool will help the general education teachers as they plan instruction in an inclusive environment and also inform the development of goals and objectives for Carolina's IEP based on her WIDA scores (i.e., Beginning level 2 stage). These proficiency level scores are meaningful to the entire team including the special educator, general educator, ESL instructor, family, and student. They demonstrate what the student is able to do and from where the student will be able to best build skills.

The following examples illustrate ways to incorporate academic language proficiency, aligned from the PLAAFP, to IEP goals for Carolina. Each example provides (a) representative aspects of PLAAFP as it relates to English language proficiency and the content skills, (b) a goal, (c) several short-term objectives, and (d) suggested presentation practices. These are presented in this manner to illustrate how they are interconnected and grounded in academic language skills for an English learner in the early stages of language proficiency. The goals adhere to core SMART principles, which will be further examined in Chapter 5, which presents more refined and detailed examples of SMART goals. Each of the sample goals are written for the following student:

> Carolina is an eight-year-old third-grade student who has been in the United States for two years, who is an English learner, and whose first language is Spanish.

EXAMPLE 1—LANGUAGE PROFICIENCY AND READING

Present Level of Academic Achievement and Functional Performance

Carolina has received ESL support in the general education setting with an ESL instructor since she entered the school system. Based on the WIDA ACCESS test, she has reached an overall language proficiency Level 2 (Beginning). Her language proficiency levels in each domain are as follows:

Listening: Level 2—She can follow two-step oral directions, draw in response to oral directions, and categorize content-based pictures and objects from oral descriptions.

Speaking: Level 2—She can ask simple everyday questions, restate content-based facts, and share basic social information with peers.

Reading: Level 2—She can identify elements of a story, identify facts and an explicit message from an illustrated text, and find changes to root words.

Writing: Level 1—She can label objects or pictures with a word or phrase bank, and communicate ideas by drawing, copying words, phrases, or short sentences.

Carolina is reading at a DRA Level 6 (Lexile 150–175, Fountas & Pinnell E/F), which is at grade level 1.4. She is able to read 50 words per minute at a 90% accuracy rate. She reads word by word with little fluency. She is able to retell the story with prompting while using the book as a support. Carolina demonstrates significant confusion with letters and words, and she experiences some problems with listening comprehension in both her native language and English, further contributing to her learning disability. However, Carolina responds well to explicit instruction, repeated reading, and graphic aids in reading, as these appear to contribute to her learning of academic language skills and listening comprehension.

Reading Goal and Objectives

Goal: By May 31st of this school year, after orally reading a series of nonfiction text passages of fables and folklores from diverse cultures during each week of reading instruction, Carolina will demonstrate reading proficiency at a DRA2 level of 28.

Objective 1: Retell a story after three repeated readings to a peer with first language support, pictures from the book, and/or sentence frames to support language with correct sequencing and accurate details with 80% accuracy.

Objective 2: Answer oral questions about the repeatedly read story accurately, using the text as a reference with first language support, pictures from the book, and/or sentence frames to support language with 80% accuracy.

Objective 3: Copy words and short sentences from the text, a word bank, or sentence frames, describing a character and how the character's actions contribute to the sequence of events with 100% accuracy.

Objective 4: Orally compare and contrast two themes between two texts regarding the message, moral, topic, or culture with 90% accuracy.

Objective 5: Make text-to-self, text-to-text, and text-to-world connections verbally and in a written statement, copying words and short sentences from the text, a word bank, or sentence frames with 90% accuracy.

Presentation: Graphic aids and Venn diagrams, repeated reading strategies, paired learning

EXAMPLE 2—LANGUAGE PROFICIENCY AND MATH

Present Level of Academic Achievement and Functional Performance

Carolina is able to verbally articulate the inverse relationship between addition and subtraction with one-digit math problems. However, when asked to independently solve word problems using addition, she is unable to identify the operation to be used and cannot develop an appropriate equation 50% of the time. The academic language also presents challenges due to level of second language acquisition.

Math Goal and Objectives

Goal: By May 31st of this school year, within a thirty-minute math session, Carolina will independently solve 10 word problems requiring single-digit addition using a student-developed glossary of key terms/concepts/visual representations of the math English language vocabulary with 90% accuracy.

Objective 1: Identify math clue words for problems (e.g., addition = plus, all together, combined, sum, total of, added to; subtraction = less than, take away, minus, fewer than, less than).

Objective 2: Use think-alouds with first language support and labeling to draw an accurate representation of the math problem with two-step directions.

Objective 3: After using a student-made glossary with first language support, identify the appropriate operation to solve the word problem.

Presentation: Teacher uses think-aloud to demonstrate thought processes and mathematical thinking for problem solving; re-loop previously learned material with multiple opportunities to practice concepts and language; provide visuals of math concepts, key words, labels with first language supports for numbers, dates, money, fractions, and so on.

EXAMPLE 3—LANGUAGE PROFICIENCY AND WRITING

Present Level of Academic Achievement and Functional Performance

Carolina is able to generate and label pictures of writing topics, using two- and three-word phrases. She is able to generate ideas and develop simple sentences when dictating to another person and using language supports, such as word walls, with visual representations and sentence stems. Though Carolina is able to dictate key parts of a paragraph, she struggles with writing the same ideas in an organized manner.

Writing Goal and Objectives

Goal: By May 31st of this academic year, after verbally discussing a topic of her choice with a Spanish-speaking peer, Carolina will write a five-sentence paragraph on that topic that includes a topic sentence, three details, and a conclusion sentence with 100% accuracy.

Objective 1: Using sentence starters, complete a topic sentence for a paragraph with a verb, subject, and end punctuation.

(Continued)

(Continued)

Objective 2: Work with a peer, using brainstorming and dictation to develop a paragraph.

Objective 3: Use a visual graphic organizer with embedded sentence starters and transition words to create a three-sentence paragraph with two details following a topic sentence.

Presentation: Teacher uses think-alouds to demonstrate thought processes for writing a paragraph; provide word wall with visual supports; graphic organizers; language experience strategies.

EXAMPLE 4—LANGUAGE PROFICIENCY AND SOCIAL SCIENCE

Present Level of Academic Achievement and Functional Performance

In the content areas of science and social studies, Carolina is not able to read the texts at the Lexile level provided, nor retain information that has been primarily presented verbally. However, when the content is presented in a variety of formats including videos, visual representations, and audiotapes and at a lower Lexile level commensurate with her instructional level, Carolina is able to retain the content learned and create a timeline and sequence steps. In addition, she retains content material when the teacher or students use gesture and total physical response (TPR) to deliver key concepts and content.

Social Science Goal and Objectives

Goal: By May 31st of this academic year, Carolina will independently demonstrate knowledge of a social science topic of her choice by creating a timeline of 10 items in the proper sequence, using one or more forms of expression such as drawing, oral presentations, graphic representations, and/or total physical response with 90% accuracy.

Objective 1: Identify the key words or concepts in a lesson and create a personal glossary of important terms.

Objective 2: Answer oral questions about the content accurately, using the text as a reference with first language support, pictures from the book, and/or sentence frames to support language.

Objective 3: Copy words and short sentences from the text, a word bank, or sentence frames, describing the content learned or the activity and organize into a graphic organizer as a means of taking notes.

Objective 4: Orally compare and contrast themes between two lessons regarding the message, moral, topic, or culture (e.g., the lives of freed slaves before and after reconstruction, the life cycles of frogs compared to butterflies).

Presentation: TPR acting out key concepts or academic language; visual and graphic aids.

The above goals include aspects connected to (a) Common Core State Standards, (b) WIDA Can Do Descriptors and language domains, and/or (c) select indications for Zacarian's (2013) Four-Pronged Framework. The PLAAFP are comprehensive, conforming to our suggested guidelines for incorporating culturally and linguistically responsive material into IEP development (see Chapter 4). The goals include attention to academic language supports and are structured as SMART goals (see Chapter 5). The associated short-term objectives provide a clear description of the skills being addressed, framed within the strengths of the student documented in the PLAAFP, as well as specific criteria for measuring student progress toward the annual goal. Overall, these examples are presented here to initially illustrate the important connections between academic language and key components of the IEP, which are further examined in the remaining chapters of this book.

CONCLUSION

The foundation for school success is development, use, and mastery of academic language in the teaching and learning environment. Educators should consider the four types of processes (sociocultural, developmental, academic, cognitive) when measuring academic language proficiency and delivering associated instruction. Subsequently, consideration of academic language proficiency levels, associated skill sets, and multiple best practices lead directly to development of the IEP present level of academic achievement and functional performance for English language and other diverse learners placed into special education for a disability. This in turn leads to appropriate IEP measurable annual goals and associated short-term objectives to provide sufficient opportunities to maintain adequate IEP progress.

WEBSITES

For additional information readers are referred to the following websites and resources:

Center for Research on Education, Diversity, and Excellence (CREDE) (http://manoa.hawaii.edu/coe/crede/)

The IRIS Center for Training Enhancements (http://iris.peabody.vanderbilt.edu)

Sheltered Instruction Observation Protocol (http://www.cal.org/siop/about/)

What Works Clearinghouse (http://ies.ed.gov/ncee/wwc/)

WIDA (https://www.wida.us)

4 Culturally and Linguistically Responsive Present Levels of Academic Achievement and Functional Performance

Determining Accurate Levels and Developing Meaningful Statements

By Le M. Tran and James R. Patton

Practitioner's Perspective . . .

What are PLAAFP statements, and why are these critical to the development of an IEP? How are cultural and linguistic features best incorporated into the development of the PLAAFP statements for English language and other diverse learners? What are some examples of responsive and defensible PLAAFP statements that value the skill sets that diverse learners bring to the IEP development process?

One of the most fundamental components of the Individualized Education Program (IEP) is the documentation of what a student can and cannot do across a number of important areas at the time it is created. This information is required under the Individuals with Disabilities Education Act (IDEA) for each student who receives special education services. The identification of meaningful present levels of academic achievement and functional performance (PLAAFP) is the foundation upon which much of the IEP is based. For example, the development of useful, measurable annual goals can only occur by first establishing sound present levels of performance; present levels also inform the proper selection of relevant instructional and assessment accommodations and delivery of related services.

Additionally, as discussed in the Introduction and reflected in the title of this book, a primary purpose is to assist educators of English language and other diverse learners to develop meaningful and relevant IEPs to best value students' culturally and linguistically diverse (CLD) qualities and strengths in the delivery of special education. The development of appropriate PLAAFP statements for diverse students is therefore central to the purpose and presentation of material in this chapter, thereby meeting high instructional expectations for all learners.

This chapter introduces key concepts and illustrates practical examples related to the development of defensible present levels of performance. The first section of the chapter provides a rationale for the importance of this component of the IEP. The second section of the chapter introduces a set of guiding principles that, in our opinion, should be used to shape all PLAAFP statements, including those for diverse learners. The third section provides examples of well-written present levels of performance statements across four major areas: academic, behavioral, social, and functional, with specific attention to culturally and linguistically responsive PLAAFP features. The last section of the chapter further examines a step-by-step process for the development of appropriate PLAAFP statements, highlighting additional considerations to ensure cultural and linguistic responsiveness for English language and other diverse learners.

WHAT ARE PLAAFP AND WHY ARE THEY IMPORTANT?

As stated, present levels of performance are the foundation upon which measurable annual goals are developed (Twachtman-Cullen & Twachtman-Bassett, 2011). Granted, general goal area(s) might be initially considered as a reaction to the identified needs of a particular student; for example, the IEP team might note that a goal in the area of reading comprehension is needed. However, the actual measurable features of the goal are best derived from the well-constructed present levels of performance in either or both academic and functional areas.

The reason that present levels of performance are so important is that everyone who works with the student needs to have a clear understanding of what the student can and cannot do at the time of IEP development. That is, not only do the present levels inform educators of specific skill sets, but they also provide insight about conditions that most and least contribute to effective learning. Knowing this information, and stating it properly, allows for the development and delivery of a meaningful IEP.

The concept of present levels of performance has been a required component of IDEA since the law was first enacted in 1975. The most recent regulations of IDEA (2004) include specific wording on what the IEP requires:

(1) A statement of the child's present levels of academic achievement and functional performance, including

    (i) how the child's disability affects the child's involvement and progress in the general education curriculum (i.e., the same curriculum for students who are nondisabled);

or

    (ii) for preschool children, as appropriate, how the disability affects the child's participation in appropriate activities [(Sec. 300.320(a)(1)].

It is extremely important that accurate and meaningful present levels be generated for all students in order to create appropriate educational programs that allow meaningful access to the general-education curriculum. This includes teaching and learning features that reflect the culturally and linguistically diverse demographics seen in today's schools and classrooms.

IDEA does not define what is meant by "academic achievement" and "functional performance" (Pennell, 2011); therefore, the interpretation of these concepts is left up to personnel at the school or district level. However, the following designations can be inferred from the meaning of these distinctions.

Academic achievement: reading, writing, mathematics, language, and study skills

Functional performance: social skills, self-direction skills, life skills (including self-care, home living, use of community, safety/health, career/vocational skills), motor skills (fine and gross), and mobility skills

It is important to note that the 2004 authorization of IDEA is the first time that these two terms have been used. Previously, the more generic term, "present levels of performance," was used. To a great extent, the introduction of these two terms provides an emphasis that both areas are important and should be considered for every student. However, the law does not require that goals be written for both areas. Moreover, many students who qualify for special education services may need goals written in only one of these areas. It is safe to say that in the past, the functional needs of students whose primary educational needs resided in academic areas (e.g., students with learning disabilities) were often overlooked, thereby leading to their inclusion in the newest legislation. Similarly, academic areas of students whose primary needs were in the functional area were typically not considered at all.

In reference to English learners, consideration of both academic and functional areas is essential given their integrated nature in English language development. Without question, the academic language demands of English learners with special needs, discussed in the previous chapter, will often be a centerpiece of their IEPs. Therefore, developers of IEPs for English language and other diverse learners must consider and, when necessary, attend to functional areas as well academic content and language needs. For example, certain social-emotional behaviors may clearly reflect cultural teachings or be directly associated with the learner's stage of second language acquisition. Educators must make certain to draw upon and refer to these qualities when developing PLAAFP statements, while avoiding misinterpreting them as contributors to the disability.

CREATING MEANINGFUL PLAAFP STATEMENTS USING THE CRISEN PRINCIPLES

Development of meaningful PLAAFP statements that value cultural and linguistic diversity is a cornerstone of the IEP process for all learners, especially for English language and other diverse students with special needs. In our opinion, many PLAAFP statements that we have seen do not meet a minimum set of criteria that we believe should be reflected in useful and meaningful PLAAFP. Courts and due process proceedings have wrestled with this issue of what is appropriate PLAAFP. For the most part, these decisions have focused on PLAAFP that were imprecise and not objective. Furthermore, as will be discussed below, the presentation of broad test scores is insufficient only as a basis for providing meaningful PLAAFP.

For the purpose of providing a structure to guide the development of meaningful PLAAFP statements, we have developed an acronym, CRISEN (Culturally and linguistically responsive; Reflect current performance; Instructionally meaningful assessment; Sufficient detail; Educationally relevant; Needs and accomplishments), to reflect the key elements that go into the development of PLAAFP statements. Each of these components is described below.

Culturally and Linguistically Responsive

As is evident in the heading statement, this criterion focuses on making certain that the present levels are written in consistent and relevant ways, valuing the cultural and linguistic qualities of the student. The key challenge here is to frame the academic and functional needs of the learner within a relevant cultural and linguistic context informed by home, school, and broader community contributions. Reference to academic and functional behaviors associated with stages of second language acquisition and WIDA Can Do Descriptors introduced in Chapter 2 provide an excellent beginning point to frame culturally and linguistically responsive PLAAFP.

Reflect Current Performance

The key point of this particular criterion, current performance, highlights the fact that the data and information obtained and used in the development of PLAAFP statements reflect current functioning. Sole use of information that is old or dated fails to provide an up-to-date sense of what the student can and cannot do at the time of IEP development. In most cases, data that are more than two or three months old should not be used to depict current present levels of performance. For instance, adaptive behavior information may be highly descriptive and precise, yet if it is over a year old, it may not be relevant in the present context.

We recognize, however, that in some situations the use of older data, coupled with more recent evidence, may be appropriate especially if trends over time are important to document. For instance, it might be possible that the current levels of performance may not have changed much from levels that were determined at an earlier point of time exceeding two or three months, or perhaps one academic school year. In such cases, use of both previous and current data may best inform educators of a learner's present performance levels and of associated learning conditions.

Instructionally Meaningful Assessment

This "linking assessment to instruction" criterion pinpoints the fact that most of the information that will be useful for the development of meaningful PLAAFP statements will come from assessments that deliver evidence that is instructionally meaningful with sufficient detail to begin teaching. That is, the overall result of properly written PLAAFP statements is application to teaching and learning. And for English language and other diverse learners, this includes attention to culturally and linguistically responsive ESL and bilingual education instructional best practices (see Echevarria, Vogt, & Short, 2008; Hoover, Hopewell, & Sarris, 2014). As emphasized, the listing of broad test scores, without supporting evidence, limits the value of the PLAAFP statements in establishing what a student can do and cannot do relative to the disability need area.

For the most part, much of the assessment that is conducted during the eligibility process does not lend itself directly to the development of IEPs to be used as effective instructional tools. Furthermore, the formal, standardized instruments that are required or important to determine special education eligibility often do not provide the type of assessment information that is needed for instructional programming purposes. For CLD learners, an added dimension is the lack of validity in the assessments typically used for non-CLD learners, as discussed below.

Most standardized tests provide a range of derived scores. Derived scores (e.g., standard scores, percentile ranks, grade equivalents, age equivalents, stanines, normal curve equivalents) provide "ballpark" performance levels yet do not provide the type of detail needed for instructional purposes. For instance, it is common to see the use of grade equivalents in the present levels in many IEPs (e.g., reading at a 3.2 grade level based on the *Wechsler Individual Achievement Test*). Though educators would possess a very general idea as to where to begin instruction based on grade level, this grade-level number provides little in the way of informing instructional practice.

Consider the following: Would a teacher really know how to approach instruction if all she/he had in the statement of present levels of performance was that the student was comprehending reading materials at a 6.5 grade level, without other supporting evidence clarifying the grade level? The answer to this question would be "no." A teacher would need to have additional information not typically provided by standardized testing to develop the type of present level performance necessary to create a meaningful IEP for instructional purposes.

Issues in use of standardized test results in PLAAPF development become more pronounced for students who represent diverse cultural and linguistic backgrounds, especially English learners. Assessment of diverse learners requires significantly more information than what is typically gathered for English-speaking, mainstream learners (Basterra, Trumbull, & Solano-Flores, 2011; Hoover, Baca, & Klingner, 2016). Specifically, assessment devices that have been standardized and normed to English speakers provide little useful information about the academic and functional skill sets of English language and other diverse learners. Researchers cited above also discuss further the importance of using multiple forms and data sources to best assess diverse learners for both special education eligibility and instructional purposes. Consideration of these assessment concerns and suggestions is essential to best develop present levels of performance for diverse learners.

Teachers need to have proper tools and resources to be able to generate appropriate present levels of performance for culturally and linguistically diverse students. A comprehensive list of assessment techniques that provide the kind of information necessary for determining where to begin instruction across a range of academic and functional areas is presented in Table 4.1. Each measure identified in the table provides valuable information for English language and other diverse learners when used in the proper context and in consideration of cultural and linguistic diversity.

Table 4.1 Assessment Tools to Inform Development of Present Levels of Performance Statements

Area	*Contributions From Other School Personnel*	*Assessment Tools*[1]
Academic/ Language Achievement	• Diagnostician • Bilingual speech/language therapist/ pathologist • English language development (ELD) specialist	**Reading:** • Brigance Comprehensive Inventory of Basic Skills II—Reading/ELA • Dynamic Indicators of Basic Early Literacy Skills • Reading Observational Scale (ROS) • Curriculum-based measures (CBM)[2]

(Continued)

Table 4.1   (Continued)

Area	Contributions From Other School Personnel	Assessment Tools[1]
		• Bilingual Verbal Ability Tests (BVAT) • Development Reading Assessment–2nd ed. (DRA2) • Reading A-Z • Fountas and Pinnell Literacy (levels) • Scholastic Reading Inventory (SRI) • Running record • Reading Response Journals **Math:** • Brigance Comprehensive Inventory of Basic Skills II—Math • Curriculum-based measures (CBM) • Performance-based • Measures of Academic Progress (MAP) **Writing:** • Informal writing sample • 6+1 Trait Writing Model of Instruction and Assessment • Written Language Observations Scale (WLOS) • Curriculum-based measures (CBM) • Performance-based **Language proficiency:** • WIDA ACCESS Language Proficiency • English Language Proficiency Assessment for the 21st Century (ELPA21) • Family questionnaire/input
Behavioral	• Behavioral specialist • School counselor • Social worker • Mental health professional	**Externalizing/internalizing behaviors:** • Observational techniques[3] • Basic Assessment System for Children—3rd ed. (BASC-3) • Behavioral Intervention Planning—3rd ed. (BIP-3) **Self-regulatory behaviors:** • Observational techniques

Social	• School psychologist	**Social awareness and perception:**
		• Observational techniques
		Social interaction skills:
		• Observational techniques[4]
		• *Adaptive Behavior Planning and Instruction Guide*
		Pragmatic language skills (receptive and expressive language):
		• Observational techniques
		• Pragmatic Language Observation Scale (PLOS)
Functional	• School social worker	**Life skills (self-care, home living, community use, health, safety, leisure)[5]:**
		• Adaptive Behavior Planning Inventory (ABPI)
		• Informal Assessments for Transition Planning: Independent Living and Community Participation
		• Informal life skills inventories/check-lists
		• Family questionnaire/input
		Study skills:
		• Study Skills Inventory
		Career/vocational skills:
		• Informal Assessments for Transition: Employment and Career Planning

[1]Some of the tools listed in this table serve as a means to get to specific data that should be included in well-written PLAAFP statements—the instruments in and of themselves do not provide the precision that will be needed.

[2]Curriculum-based measurement includes techniques that measure performance on content that comes directly from the content that is being covered—for example, a sample of grade-level vocabulary.

[3]This section focuses on the language abilities of English learners. Other important areas related to culture and background must also be assessed; however, these other areas do not typically result in the development of goals.

[4]Observational techniques include frequency counts, interval data, or duration/latency data. We make the assumption that teachers have obtained the necessary knowledge and skills to perform these observational techniques.

[5]Life skills are frequently referred to as adaptive skills or activities of daily living. Information on current performance levels in some of these areas may have to be obtained from parents or other persons at the home.

Table 4.1 houses a variety of informal and formal techniques that teachers will find useful in establishing meaningful PLAAFP. As indicated, the instruments can be used with any student for whom an IEP needs to be developed including English language and other diverse learners. All of the Table 4.1 commercially available instruments are listed and briefly described in the Appendix ("Commercially Available Instruments for Determining Present

Levels of Performance"), which can be found at end of the book. Readers are encouraged to examine specifics associated with commercial instruments to make certain the selected and used tests are reliable and valid for both (a) the academic or functional skill area in question (e.g., reading fluency, social skills development, motor skill abilities) and (b) cultural and linguistic responsiveness to reflect learners' diverse backgrounds and languages.

Sufficient Detail

As has been noted, many PLAAFP statements provide only a very general indication of where a student functions, based primarily on test scores (e.g., grade equivalents or standard scores). Well-written PLAAFP statements include sufficient detail so anyone who examines the data/information will be able to know where to begin instruction (e.g., single-digit addition) and under what conditions (e.g., when presented a set of problems on the computer). Sufficient detail implies that the information included in the PLAAFP statements is measurable, observable, and informing. For instance, note the difference in the following statements.

Vaguely written: "The student is able to do some simple addition problems yet has trouble with more advanced problems."

Clearly written: "When presented single-digit addition problems on a computer, student is able to solve correctly 19 of 20 problems. When presented double-digit problems without regrouping, the student is able to answer correctly 8 of 20 problems."

The point being made is that PLAAFP statements need to have a level of specificity that enable (a) teachers to know exactly where a student is functioning, going beyond grade-level scores; (b) IEP teams to develop reasonable and measurable annual goals and associated objectives; and (c) IEP teams to establish appropriate techniques and monitoring procedures for measuring student progress toward these goals, including accommodations.

Educationally Relevant

An overarching criterion in any IEP developmental process is assurance that whatever is developed is educationally relevant, which reflects different aspects of education required within IDEA (e.g., least restrictive, curricular access, responsive instruction). Thus, even though this guideline is not the first one addressed in the CRISEN process, it is one that needs to be considered initially and throughout IEP development as the other criteria are put into action. Specifically, this PLAAFP development criterion implies that key areas of need leading to student access to the general-education curriculum have been thoughtfully considered. For culturally and linguistically diverse students who are struggling in school, this guideline is especially important (i.e., educational relevance is dependent on context and purpose based on cultural perspective and stage of second language acquisition).

The comprehensive needs of every student should be examined, discussed, and assessed so that informed decisions about IEP development best occur. Too often, it is just the "obvious" areas that receive the attention of the IEP team. For example, often students with learning disabilities have an abundance of academic goals (e.g., reading, writing, language); students with serious emotional disorders are likely to have a majority of their goals focused on behavior change (e.g., social skills development, self-management); students with a significant intellectual disability have goals that emphasize functional issues (e.g., motor skills; basic self-help).

However, learners with each of these types of disabilities may also have related functional or academic performance needs that, when addressed, will further advance progress toward the more obvious areas of development. Therefore, certain related skills areas such as important social skills, background academic language, or requisite study skills are often overlooked in the process of determining the most instructionally relevant skills to address. Often, these other areas, though challenging to a student, if mastered would provide increased access to the general-education curriculum, positively impacting the more obvious areas of need. The underlying message is to ensure that all relevant academic and functional areas are considered and incorporated into the PLAAFP statement to create the most meaningful IEP possible.

Another key point that must be made is that critical PLAAFP information should come from the parents or others who might be advocating for the student, a practice previously emphasized in Chapter 2. Often, knowledge of important aspects that will contribute to the student's ultimate success and access, especially functional performance skill sets, may come only from persons who see the student outside of school or beyond the specific classroom.

The need to identify instructionally relevant areas of need and subsequently develop appropriate PLAAFP is heightened for students who are learning English and adjusting to new cultural demands in and outside of school. For English language and other diverse learners, it is incumbent upon school personnel to consider needs associated with a variety of factors including second language acquisition, acculturation, and associated cultural teachings (e.g., social interactions, ways of knowing, funds of knowledge, class participation) to best shape an IEP to be educationally relevant. The diversity that parents and other family members bring to the IEP development process is essential to draw upon and value throughout the development process.

Needs and Accomplishments

The intent and language of the 2004 reauthorization of IDEA explicitly states that the strengths of students should be identified and considered in the development of the IEP. For this reason, well-written PLAAFP statements should include information detailing three items: (1) what a student *can do*,

(2) what a student *cannot do*, and (3) under what conditions learning best or least occurs. Clearly, the IEP is designed to address needs that a student has in order to benefit from the educational experiences to be provided. However, building instruction based on learner strengths best facilitates teaching to advance those identified skill areas in need. Simply knowing only what a learner cannot perform or do (i.e., deficit perspective) provides little insight into (a) selection of best practices, (b) accessing prior knowledge, or (c) ways of tapping into other related skill strengths necessary to educate the whole child.

In summary, application of CRISEN features provides an easy-to-use structure for developing PLAAFP, which in turn drive the development of the remaining IEP components. Properly developed PLAAFP statements adhering to the CRISEN principles will clearly and with specificity describe current levels of knowledge acquisition and skill development in those areas that have been determined to be instructionally relevant by the IEP team. For English language and other diverse students with special needs, the PLAAFP statements must go beyond that which we typically include for any learner by incorporating accurate information pertaining to second language acquisition and cultural values relative to the academic and functional needs.

EXAMPLES OF MEANINGFUL AND INSTRUCTIONALLY RELEVANT PLAAFP STATEMENTS

Building on the background information provided above, this section includes several practical examples demonstrating appropriate PLAAFP for a variety of learners in both primary and secondary grades. The examples illustrate the types of important features necessary to create responsive and defensible PLAAFP statements for any learner, with particular emphasis on cultural and linguistic diversity. For each topical area, two examples are provided. The first represents an example that best fits learners who are fluent English speakers and highly acculturated to US schools and classrooms. The second provides an example in which direct attention to culturally and linguistically diverse languages, teachings, and perspectives is necessary. Readers are encouraged to examine each example, keeping in mind that material in any example is applicable for all learners who have a disability depending on context, English language proficiency, and related cultural perspectives. Boldface material indicates CLD features.

Personal Interests and Supports

Personal interests and supports provide a snapshot of the learner's personality and learning style in order to provide teachers an understanding of learner needs. This includes the learner's interests, hobbies, strengths, dislikes, or supports necessary to succeed in the classroom:

PLAAFP for a first-grade student:

- Adam is an active first grader who enjoys playing soccer with his friends at recess, and PE is his favorite subject in school. His favorite color is blue, and he likes math centers because he gets to use the math blocks to build. Adam does well when he is given physical hand cues or mnemonics to help him memorize information. When prompted with the hand cue or mnemonic, Adam is able to easily retrieve necessary skills to complete a task. Adam does well when given a little extra wait time.

PLAAFP for a first-grade English language or other diverse learner:

- Santiago is an active first grader who enjoys playing soccer with his friends at recess, and PE is his favorite subject in school. His favorite color is green, and he enjoys center time because he can color pictures. Santiago works best when given cues or mnemonics and ample wait time. **He is in the process of acquiring English as a second language and performs well when given prompts followed by extra time to process information.** When he is in whole group, **providing Santiago a visual to process questions, opportunity to ask a peer, and wait time to work through the request before answering are effective teaching practices. He does best when he is able to receive his question and spend time considering his response then reporting back to the class when he is ready.** Santiago does not do well with the teaching practice that demands an immediate response to questions.

Academic

Academics are typically the area that gets the most coverage in the development of goals in many IEPs, especially in reading, writing, mathematics, and language. There are a variety of tools to utilize to capture academic information for both the primary and secondary grades, including those necessary for culturally and linguistically diverse learners:

Reading

PLAAFP in reading for a first-grade student:

- Maria is able to recite the alphabet and name letters in random order: capital letters: 22/26 (85% accuracy) and lowercase letters: 21/26 (81% accuracy). Maria is able to name consonant letter sounds 17/21 (81% accuracy) and long and short vowels 7/10 (70% accuracy). With consonant-vowel-consonant (CVC) and vowel-consonant (VC) words she is able to read 18/24, which is 75% accuracy. Maria's current performance on consonant diagraphs is 18/24 (75% accuracy) and vowel diagraphs 17/24 (71% accuracy). Based on the Dolch Sight Words Assessment, she reads, List 1: 15/20, List 2: 15/20, and List 3: 15/20, which yields an overall 75% accuracy. When assessed on the Reading A-Z, she reads at a level C, which is her instructional level, at 93% accuracy. Maria learns best in small reading groups and struggles to remain on task in whole-class instruction.

PLAAFP in reading for a ninth-grade student:

- Rachel was assessed with the Scholastic Reading Inventory (SRI) and received a Lexile score of 821. When reading a passage at the sixth-grade reading level, she is able to answer comprehension questions with 75% accuracy. She retells five-part sequence of events within stories 4/5, 80% accuracy. Rachel is able to identify cause and effect relationships 7/10, 70% accuracy. She often rereads material in class to help her with comprehension, recalling details, or sequencing events.

PLAAFP in reading for a first-grade English language or other diverse learner:

- Santiago, who **is a second language learner,** is able to recite the English alphabet and name letters in random order: capital letters: 20/26 (77% accuracy) and lowercase letters: 21/26 (81% accuracy). Santiago is able to name consonant letter sounds 17/21 (81% accuracy) and long and short vowels 2/10 (20% accuracy). **He is at the stage of second language development in which phonological differences between Spanish and English cause confusion, and he consistently mixes up the letter sounds and the letter names between both languages.** When provided visual cues, he is able to more accurately identify sounds. With CVC and VC words, he is able to read 15/24 (63% accuracy). Santiago's current performance with consonant diagraphs is 18/24 (75% accuracy) and vowel diagraphs 8/24 (33% accuracy). When assessed on the Dolch Sight Words Assessment, he reads from the pre-primer list: 10/20, primer list: 10/20, and Grade 1 list 3: 5/20, yielding an overall 42% accuracy rate. Based on existing current data from Reading A-Z, collected from the classroom teacher, Santiago performs at level C, which is his instructional level, at 90% accuracy.

PLAAFP in reading for a ninth-grade English language or other diverse learner:

- Nadia, **who is at the Expanding Level (i.e., Level 4) of English proficiency based on the WIDA ACCESS Language Proficiency,** was assessed with the Scholastic Reading Inventory (SRI) midyear and received a Lexile score of 821. When reading a passage at the sixth-grade reading level, she is able to answer comprehension questions with 75% accuracy. She retells five-part sequence of events within stories 3/5, or 60% accuracy. However, she is able to consistently retell three-part sequence of events at 95% accuracy. When reading passages, Nadia is able to draw conclusions and make generalizations based on the context clues within the story 6/10 (60% accuracy). Nadia is able to identify cause and effect relationships 6/10, or 60% accuracy. **She is at a stage of second language development where confusion with higher-level concepts (e.g., compare-contrast, synthesis) is evident, and she consistently needs to use both Spanish and English to best examine and understand more detailed concepts. When provided the combined uses of visual cues or illustrations along with increased wait time, she is able to more accurately respond to comprehension items.**

Writing

PLAAFP in writing for a first-grade student:

- Adam is able to write his first name without a guide at 100% accuracy and his last name 7/10 (70% accuracy). Based on a visual prompt, Adam uses phonetic spelling in his writing and is able to create and write one-line sentences, "My bruthr play vid gams," based on the teacher created writing rubric, punctuation: 4, capitalization: 4, grammar: 3, content/ideas: 2, spelling: 3, total 16/20, or 80% accuracy.

PLAAFP in writing for a ninth-grade student:

- Rachel is able to write a five-paragraph persuasive essay on a topic of her choice. The essay was graded based on the 6+1 Trait Writing rubric, ideas: 3, organization: 2, voice: 3, word choice: 3, sentence fluency: 2, conventions: 3, presentation: 3, total 19/35. Rachel is able to type her essay into a word processor and make edits on the computer rather than on paper. She struggles with how to use feedback to revise and improve sentence fluency and word choices based on instructor input.

PLAAFP in writing for a first-grade English language or other diverse learner:

- Santiago, **an English as a second language learner,** is able to write his first and last name by copying his name tag on his desk. He writes his first name without a guide 5/10 (50% accuracy) and is unable to accurately write his last name (0/10) without copying from his name tag. His most **common type of miscue is the spelling of his name of Santiago as "Sonteego," reflecting typical phonological errors seen in second language learners when attempting to negotiate between letter sounds and names in first and second languages.** Santiago practices phonetic spelling in his writing and is able to create and write one-line sentences, "The cat climd up the tri." Though spelling requires improvement, the statement clearly illustrates that Santiago is grasping the meaning of what he is attempting to write. When using the word wall posted in the classroom, Santiago is able to create additional one-line sentences using different English vocabulary, further demonstrating written comprehension, even though spelling is less than perfect. **The ESL instructional practices of making connections and building background knowledge assist Santiago to more accurately write his name as well as recall how to begin to write his last name.**

PLAAFP in writing for a ninth-grade English language or other diverse learner:

- Nadia writes a five-paragraph persuasive essay on a topic of her choice once she studies a visual or illustration to identify ideas. The essay is graded based on 6+1 Trait Writing rubric, ideas: 2, organization: 2, voice: 2, word choice: 3, sentence fluency: 2, conventions: 3, presentation: 3, total 17/35. Nadia dictates her writing to a teacher or paraprofessional to record her ideas on an iPad or computer where she can make her edits. **The teacher/paraprofessional helps Nadia with spelling during the dictation. This allows for Nadia to more clearly focus on formulating her thoughts in English, rather than being distracted by spelling issues, which will be addressed at a later time. The ESL instructional practices of making connections and building background knowledge are highly effective at helping Nadia recall vocabulary and generate five-sentence paragraphs.** Also, making certain that her writing is connected to the task of reading provides additional instructional support to ensure success in writing.

Mathematics

PLAAFP in mathematics for a first-grade student:

- Adam is able to count to 100 with 95% accuracy and identifies numbers to 20 with 90% accuracy. With single-digit addition problems, he is able to complete 15/20, 75% accuracy, and single-digit subtraction 12/20, 60% accuracy. Adam is able to compare two numbers to determine greater than, less than, and equal to 15/20, 75% accuracy. He struggles with completing mathematics assignments that contain many problems on a computer screen or worksheet, achieving greater success when assignments are broken into two to three smaller segments. He also achieves greater success when provided manipulatives to complete mathematics problems.

PLAAFP in mathematics for a ninth-grade student:

- Rachel's MAPs math RIT score is 220, which is the equivalence of a sixth grader midyear, 13th percentile. Within MAP, key areas are identified:

  number sense—low average

  algebraic methods—average; data analysis and probability—low average geometric concepts—average; measurement—low average; computation—low average

- Based on a teacher-generated curriculum-based algebra probe completed two weeks ago, Rachel scored 30/50, 60% accuracy. Rachel uses a calculator on assignments and tests so that she is able to focus on the concepts unless computation is being measured. Rachel is also more successful when she verbally restates what the mathematics problems are requesting prior to completing them.

PLAAFP in mathematics for a first-grade English language or other diverse learner:

- Santiago, **an English learner,** is able to count to 100 in English with 95% accuracy and **in Spanish to 20 with 100% accuracy.** He identifies numbers to 20 in English with 85% accuracy and in Spanish at 50% accuracy. **Santiago will object count in Spanish for quantities under 20, but he performs math computations in English.** With single-digit addition problems, he is able to complete 10/20, 50% accuracy, and single-digit subtraction 7/20, 35% accuracy. Santiago is able to compare two numbers to determine greater than, less than, and equal to 15/20, 75% accuracy. **When provided visuals or manipulatives, he is able to more quickly and easily complete the above mathematics problems, yet he requires extended wait time to think through even the most basic word problems. Building academic language associated with the mathematics problems prior to asking him to respond is essential to ensure success.**

PLAAFP in mathematics for a ninth-grade English language or other diverse learner:

- Nadia was assessed at the beginning of the school year on the MAPs math and received a RIT score of 220, which is the equivalence of a sixth grader at midyear, 13th percentile. Within MAP, key areas are identified:

  number sense—low average

  algebraic methods—low average; data analysis and probability—low average

  geometric concepts—average; measurement—low average; computation—low average

- Based on a teacher-generated curriculum-based algebra probe completed two weeks ago, Nadia scored 35/50, 70% accuracy. **When solving word problems, Nadia utilizes a bilingual dictionary that includes definitions and translations from Spanish to English, which the family provides. Also, when provided visuals or manipulatives, she is able to more quickly and easily complete** the above mathematics problems, yet she requires extended wait time to think through word problems. Building academic language associated with the mathematics problems prior to asking her to respond is essential to ensure success.** Nadia also uses a calculator on mathematics assignments and tests, allowing her to focus on concepts over computation.

Language Proficiency

Though English language proficiency cannot be used as a reason for placement with a disability for special education, English language or other diverse learners require continued language development, especially academic language, along with special services provided for disabilities most evident in reading and writing. Therefore, PLAAFP statements for diverse learners should include statements about English language proficiency to incorporate into the special education programming.

PLAAFP in language development for a first-grade English language or other diverse learner:

- **Santiago is a bilingual student and an English learner. Based on existing current data assessed at the middle of the school year, Santiago is functioning at the Developing Stage of English proficiency (i.e., Level 3) based on the WIDA. Family reports that at home he speaks only Spanish though he has not received any formal schooling in Spanish. At school, he predominantly uses English yet will periodically code switch when he is unable to determine the appropriate word in English. He will often ask the teacher to model the translated word in English when possible, which is an effective instructional practice to use with Santiago. He displays frustration when he is not able to determine the word or phrase in English and when the teacher is unable to identify what he is trying to say. In these situations, use of a Spanish-speaking peer provides necessary support to identify the appropriate vocabulary. He speaks in short and simple phrases and is working on expanding his social and academic vocabularies. He continues to work on ways to improve his answering how and why questions, currently at 5/10 (50% accuracy). His accuracy improves when the teacher builds the English academic language needed to understand what the questions are asking.**

PLAAFP in language development for a ninth-grade English language or other diverse learner:

- Nadia is **a bilingual learner who is fluent in Spanish, based on a Spanish language proficiency test, and at the Expanding Stage (Level 4) in English proficiency, based on the WIDA. Nadia just recently tested at Level 4, making the move from Developing to Expanding within the past six months. For the past four school years, prior to entering high school, she has been educated in** dual language and ESL programs in a US school, having moved from Mexico after Grade 4. Her acculturation to the US schools has been smooth, with only a few instances periodically arising that relate to completing independent work, since she is most familiar with cooperative and paired methods of learning used in her school in Mexico.

Family reports that Nadia predominantly speaks Spanish at home, yet she will use English when helping siblings with homework. At school, Nadia speaks Spanish with her friends and completes all her schoolwork in English. Nadia utilizes an English/Spanish bilingual dictionary in all of her classes. As often seen in second language acquisition, Nadia becomes confused with English idioms and slang, frequently requiring explanations. English skills are more proficient in social situations when compared to academic language situations. She is more proficient and near grade level with receptive skills, as compared to below grade level with expressive skills. Based on performance analysis of WIDA Can Do Descriptors, Nadia still periodically functions at the Developing Stage, which is one level below Expanding. She makes key grammatical errors in writing and has trouble finding the appropriate vocabulary in Spanish or English in expressive academic situations, thereby demonstrating skills significantly below her grade-level bilingual peers. Nadia completes a weekly vocabulary and idiom assignment that requires her to provide the definition, illustration, and an example of how the vocabulary or idiom is used in a sentence, averaging 5/10 (50% accuracy). Continued emphasis on use of WIDA Can Do Descriptors at the Expanding Stage is necessary to assist her progress toward English academic language proficiency and content area achievement.

Behavioral

Most often, the classroom teachers and parents/family members will provide input about behaviors that require interventions. Behaviors vary from internal to external as well as self-regulatory. They are typically identified as those that inhibit the students' ability to learn, inhibit the student's ability to participate in the daily activities, or interfere with others' learning in the classroom.

PLAAFP for behavior skills for a third-grade student:

- Sammie is able to stay on task 9 minutes within a 20-minute interval sampling as compared to her peers who are on task an average of 15 minutes within a 20-minute time frame. Her off-task behaviors that include looking around, talking with the person next to her, or reading something unrelated to the assigned tasks lead to incomplete assignments. Sammie raises her hand when she has a question or something to share with the class 6/10 times as compared to her peers who raise their hands to speak 8/10 times. Sammie and her teacher have developed a hand cue between each other to remind Sammie to raise her hand and wait for her turn, if it is not an appropriate time to share, or to remember her story for later. Planned ignoring of Sammie's off-task behaviors was unsuccessful; however, use of a simple behavioral contract has assisted her to remain on task, complete more assignments, and raise her hand prior to speaking in class.

PLAAFP for behavioral skills for a third-grade English language or other diverse learner:

- Malia is able to stay on task 7 minutes within a 15-minute interval sampling as compared to her classroom peers who are on task 11 minutes of 15-minute intervals. Her off-task behaviors lead to incomplete assignments and include looking around, discussing the assignment with the person next to her, or reading something unrelated to the assigned task. **Upon further examination, it was determined that during many of the apparent off-task times, Malia was engaging in personal thought or peer interaction to acquire a greater understanding of the assignments. This process is highly cultural for Malia as from a very young age she has been taught to be thorough in her work, to think through something prior to responding, and to discuss ideas with a peer if unsure of the expectations.** Typically, the structure of the assignments and time allotments do not allow for Malia to engage in these tasks, due to the need to quickly complete tasks and move on to the next assignments. **Providing Malia time to engage in more in-depth study of the required tasks prior to completion usually leads to more complete and accurate task completion, while simultaneously valuing cultural preference in learning. And her classroom teachers have found that use of these interactive and peer instructional practices often leads to improved and more complete assignments from other classmates as well.**

Social

This area encompasses social awareness and perception, interaction with peers and adults, and pragmatic language skills. Social skills are lifelong skills that learners need to operate in their daily lives in and out of the academic setting. It is particularly important to understand and respect cultural teachings that influence and shape learners' social behaviors.

PLAAFP for social skills for a second-grade student:

- Thomas enjoys interacting with his friends and making them laugh throughout the day. However, Thomas's efforts in seeking his friends' attention are often inappropriate, such as engaging in hitting, pinching, or interrupting. When Thomas ignores assistance from adults, he forgets to use his words and reverts to physical actions to gain attention. Instructional practices that help Thomas properly engage in social interactions include use of brief social stories to help remind him of the appropriate ways to interact with friends and teachers throughout the day. Thomas must learn to gain his peers' attention by tapping their arm gently or saying their name and waiting for a response. When Thomas wants to work independently, he tells the teachers "No thank you" or "I would like to try this by myself" 5/10 times. When a behavioral contract was used, Thomas increased his appropriate interactions with peers to 7/10 times and his appropriate interactions with his teachers concerning independent work 8/10 times as measured through direct observation and use of positive social reinforcement.

PLAAFP for social skills for a second-grade English language or other diverse learner:

- Sasha enjoys interacting with his peers throughout the day and is always offering to help. He is very engaging, often to the point that he frequently disrupts the work of others (e.g., disruptive to others 9/10 times on average based on daily observations for three consecutive school days). **His home teachings include use of hugs, verbal praise, and "playing around" as forms of positive social interaction. However, to his surprise— being unfamiliar with US school expectations—his peers tend to push him away, and he does not understand why they do not like his ways of interacting. In his culture, peers are affectionate with each other as a part of their daily interactions to show they are friends. Sasha is working on alternate ways of interacting with his friends that are more acceptable in US schools, while still respecting his cultural values, such as saying hello with no physical contact, avoiding touching, hugging, or "high fiving" unless approved by the peer and then waiting for a response prior to continuing with the interaction.** Use of planned ignoring by peers has been helpful in changing Sasha's behavior, yet more is needed to reduce negative interactions. **Positive systematic teacher approval or use of a behavioral contract incorporating positive social reinforcement has been shown to help Sasha interact in more socially acceptable ways, consistent with peer and teacher approval.**

Functional

The family assumes a crucial role in guiding educational professionals to determine which functional skills are important and those that require attention and training to be documented on the IEP. Similar to social interactions just presented, the family's cultural background, traditions, and religion influence the level of independence and dependency of the learner considered appropriate for family dynamics. Functional skills can be addressed separate from or in complementary ways to academic learning and typically include the components of life skills, study skills, and career and/or vocational skills.

PLAAFP for functional skills for a tenth-grade student:

- Under certain conditions, Anthony is able to navigate his way around the school to his various classrooms, such as the general education content classrooms, resource room, school library, or other classroom, throughout the day. However, he must return to the resource room in between each class in order to find his way to the next class, which frequently results in being tardy to classes. With verbal prompts and daily guidance, Anthony is able to navigate entering and exiting the school from the bus stop and move to his class periods without first returning to the resource room for a total of eight passing periods per day. However, Anthony independently travels to only 3/8 transitions (38% accuracy) when he does not have daily verbal prompts/support from others or does not first return to the resource room. Anthony has a tendency to stop and talk with others along his route and often forgets the location of his next class. Anthony carries his class schedule with him, will ask teachers for help when he is lost, and typically needs to be escorted to class. A behavioral plan was established in which Anthony begins from the resource room and then successfully moves directly to three classes in a row without returning to the resource room (i.e., he would be allowed to return to the resource room twice each day following attendance in three classes in a row). The blocks of three transitions each, followed by returning to the resource room, was successful in that his tardiness was reduced and his dependence on always needing to begin class transitions from the resource room was minimized, leading to an increase to 6/8 (75% accuracy) successful transitions within the first three weeks.

PLAAFP for functional skills for a tenth-grade English language or other diverse learner:

- Evan is able to navigate his way around the school to attend his eight classes per day. However, he is frequently late to his classes, experiencing difficulty moving from one class to the next within the specified few minutes of time allotted. On most days, he successfully enters his next classroom without being tardy only 4/8 (50% accuracy) times when transitioning independently. However, when moving with a peer, he is infrequently late for class. **Family reports that his difficulty with time is cultural in that in his home culture time does not take on the rigidity seen in US schools (i.e., approximation in use of time is preferred and practiced). Evan also prefers to not ask for help when lost, continuing to wander around the school until he locates the classroom. In Evan's culture, seeking advice from others is important, so his reluctance to seek directions to his next classroom is not culturally based, though, as stated, difference in how time is viewed is a culturally based teaching.** His family and teachers agree that Evan needs to be more reliable and self-sufficient in transitioning to classes. A behavioral plan was established in which Evan would transition from one class to the next with a peer for four of the eight classes daily—and independently for the remaining four classes, provided he asks for assistance if he is unsure of the next class location. The behavioral plan was revised as successes occurred to where Evan was able to successfully arrive on time on a more independent basis. Over a four-week period, his on-time attendance improved to 6/8 classes then to 100% over a 6-week period. Behavioral contracting is successful in improving his ability to independently transition between classes.

DEVELOPING RESPONSIVE AND DEFENSIBLE PLAAFP

This section presents a way to incorporate the CRISEN framework and principles into a set of step-by-step procedures to develop defensible PLAAFP statements. These statements should be current, instructionally relevant, and precise enough to lead to development of annual goals and associated instructional best practices. The example of Santiago from above will be referred to in each step to demonstrate this process for a learner who brings culturally and linguistically diverse values and teachings to the IEP developmental process.

Step 1. Determine educationally relevant areas needing attention.

The IEP team has the responsibility of identifying the academic and functional areas central to what a student needs to possess to benefit from special education and to gain access to the general-education curriculum. It is important to note that needs change over time due to the emergence of new challenges in school (e.g., using study skills, increased independence in learning, relating socially in more mature ways). It is also essential to recognize the important PLAAFP contributions of parents by sharing their knowledge concerning interests and relevancy to their children's lives.

Critical Question. What evidence confirms that the areas of emphasis on the IEP are instructionally relevant to the learner's long-term academic and functional progress?

Santiago: The IEP team identified needs in reading, writing, and math.

Step 2. Locate and gather existing current data.

Current data that relate to the areas of need should be accessed and used in the development of the PLAAFP statements and other IEP components. For example, if the annual IEP meeting approaches, where measurable annual goals for the next year are going to be determined, data that might be available from recent progress monitoring activities should be useful in establishing current levels of performance.

Critical Question. What evidence confirms that the IEP's present levels and associated annual goals, related services, and accommodations are based on current assessment and results of monitoring instructional progress?

Santiago: In the area of reading, a classroom teacher had recently administered the Reading A-Z. The information acquired from this tool contributes to the other teacher-generated reading data to be used in framing the PLAAFP and other IEP components.

Step 3. Assess key areas to determine specific current levels of performance.

The collection of new data reflecting current performance levels and responsiveness to the learner's linguistic and cultural features and qualities should be gathered in a timely and consistent way. Various instructionally appropriate data-collection practices, as introduced earlier in the chapter (see Table 4.1), can be used for this purpose. In reviewing the examples presented in the previous section of the chapter, many different tools are appropriate for use in the development of PLAAFP statements. Table 4.2 summarizes the various assessment techniques appropriate for use with English language and other diverse learners when identifying PLAAFP and associated IEP components, such as those created for Santiago.

Table 4.2   Assessment Techniques Used With the CLD Students in Above Examples

Example	*Informal Assessment*	*Formal Assessment*
Personal Interests and Supports		
Santiago—1st grade	• Classroom teacher input • Family questionnaire and interview	
Reading		
Santiago—1st grade	• Teacher-created curriculum-based measurement (CBM) • Dolch Sight Words	• Reading A-Z* • Running Records
Nadia—9th grade	• Teacher-created CBM	• SRI*
Writing		
Santiago—1st grade	• Teacher-created writing rubric • Teacher-created CBM	• WIDA Writing
Nadia—9th grade		• 6+1 Trait Writing rubric
Math		
Santiago—1st grade	• Teacher-created CBM	
Nadia—9th grade	• Teacher-created CBM	• MAP*
Language Proficiency		
Santiago—1st grade	• Teacher-created CBM • Family questionnaire and interview	• WIDA*
Nadia—9th grade	• Teacher-created CBM	• WIDA*
Behavioral		
Malia—3rd grade	• Interval sampling—20 minutes • Observation • Frequency count	

Social		
Sasha—2nd grade	• Observation • Frequency count	
Functional		
Evan—10th grade	• Observation • Frequency count	

* indicates data/information that currently exists on students.

It should be noted that competence in using the assessment practices depicted in Table 4.2 requires various levels of training and practice, and educators should plan accordingly prior to their use (e.g., formal standardized devices require more training than use of curriculum-based measurement). Teachers should be exposed to these assessment tools and practices in coursework completed during undergraduate- or graduate-level educator preparation. Newer evidence-based techniques that emerge over time should be introduced to teachers as part of ongoing professional development in schools.

Critical Question. What evidence confirms that properly prepared educators gather contemporary data in a timely manner using culturally and linguistically responsive assessment devices and practices?

Santiago: As can be seen in Table 4.2, the most commonly used tools for generating useful data for Santiago are curriculum based as teacher-developed (e.g., teacher-created CBM) or teacher-accessible (e.g., Dolch sight words list) tools. The suggested curriculum-based measurements (CBMs) were either constructed by the teacher or obtained from commercial sources. Select nationally normed standardized measures were also considered along with formally developed standards-based tools.

Step 4. Generate detailed information.

The goal of using instructionally appropriate and culturally and linguistically responsive assessments is to generate present levels that are accurate, within context, and precise in detail to lead to development of an IEP as a useful instructional tool. The examples provided in this chapter adhere to the CRISEN guideline of providing "sufficient detail" so that a teacher would know what a student can do, under what conditions, and more precisely where in the scope and sequence instruction needs to begin.

Critical Question. What evidence confirms that the PLAAFP are based on appropriate assessments and detailed to the extent that an educator would know what the learner can and cannot do within best learning conditions?

Santiago: In all three areas for which present levels of performance were developed for Santiago, detailed information was generated. For example, in the area of reading, specific numerical data are presented in all of the identified areas of need: letter naming (e.g., 20 of 26 capital letters); sounds (e.g., 2 of 10 long and short vowels); CVC/VC words (e.g., 15 of 24 words); and sight word recognition (e.g., 5 of 20 words on list 3). Additionally, specifics connected to his second language acquisition are provided to guide delivery of appropriate instruction.

Step 5. Review PLAAFP statements to make certain they are written in a concise, organized fashion, focusing on what the student can presently do and what needs to be addressed, while valuing cultural and linguistic qualities and strengths.

Overall, once developed and prior to final acceptance, review the present levels to make certain they are written in a manner that is informative, clear, and concise. The statements need to have sufficient detail so that it is clear where instruction needs to begin and under what conditions the student best learns in order to generate SMART annual goals.

Critical Question. What evidence confirms that the completed PLAAFP statements clearly delineate learner strengths, areas of need, and known effective practices sufficient for immediate use for further IEP development?

Santiago: Reviewing Santiago's present level of performance in the area of reading, we see that the statement is clearly stated and organized. After reading the present level, educators have sufficient information to begin developing annual goals and associated instructional practices in those areas needing academic attention. Also, all three statements of present levels (reading, writing, mathematics) include attention to Santiago's English as a second language development with suggested supports and ESL/bilingual best practices provided.

CONCLUSION

IEPs for English language and other diverse learners require content that specifically informs classroom teachers, interventionists, and related service providers about students' cultural and linguistic qualities, strengths, and contributions to best deliver equitable teaching and learning. That is, in order to deliver culturally and linguistically responsive instruction to meet measurable goals and objectives, various skill sets, preferred ways of learning, experiential backgrounds, family teachings, and other features that diverse learners bring to the school setting must be recognized and incorporated into the IEP, beginning with the development of the present levels of academic achievement and functional performance (i.e., PLAAFP).

Throughout this chapter, numerous suggestions and examples were provided for developing meaningful PLAAFP statements for students with disabilities in Grades K–12. However, for CLD learners, the PLAAFP must go beyond that which is typically developed for non-CLD students, since diverse students bring an added dimension to the IEP that non-CLD students do not bring (i.e., cultural and linguistic diversity, qualities, second language acquisition). Therefore, in addition to the important aspects necessary to create a relevant PLAAFP statement for any learner, cultural and linguistic features must be included to best inform service providers of ways to deliver English language and other diverse learners sufficient opportunities to achieve IEP goals and objectives.

IEPs and the Development of Measurable Annual Goals Using SMART Principles

5

By Molly Betty

Practitioner's Perspective . . .

What are the key components of a SMART goal? How is material documented in the PLAAFP statement relevant to the development of a SMART goal? What features should be considered to make a SMART goal culturally and linguistically responsive?

INTRODUCTORY CONSIDERATIONS

Caroline is an itinerant special education teacher who works with elementary students in Grades K–5. A new fourth-grade learner with an Individualized Education Program (IEP), Daniel, transferred into her school and was added to her caseload. Caroline reads over his IEP, which includes the following annual goals:

> **Goal 1**: *Daniel will read for meaning with 75% accuracy in four out of five trials.*

> **Goal 2**: *Daniel will improve his writing stamina by writing for extended periods of time with 80% accuracy in four out of five trials.*

> **Goal 3**: *Daniel will engage in appropriate social interactions with peers four out of five days per week.*

While the language in these goals is probably familiar to most educators with experience reading IEPs, Caroline is perplexed as she considers how she will measure these three annual goals and report on Daniel's progress to his classroom teachers and family. For example, what does it mean to "read for meaning" with 75 percent accuracy? What kinds of texts should Daniel be reading? How long is an "extended period of time"? How should she measure writing accuracy? What does an "appropriate social interaction" look like?

As Caroline unpacks the language of these annual goals, she finds that they offer little guidance in determining (a) the skills Daniel needs to master, (b) progress monitoring procedures, (c) types of supplemental supports or needed accommodations, and (d) types of data to collect to chart progress. Unfortunately, many existing IEPs contain these types of vague and subjective annual goals leading to IEP delivery and monitoring problems. Fortunately, the issues are resolvable through the use of a research-based structure for developing measurable annual goals and associated short-term objectives through the SMART goal set of features.

WHAT IS A SMART GOAL?

SMART is an acronym outlining best practices for developing management goals and objectives discussed by Doran (1981) that are highly appropriate for shaping learners' IEPs. Embedded within a SMART goal is a clear description of the skill being addressed, as well as specific criteria for measuring student progress. Over time, SMART items have remained similar, with some variation in how each letter is represented. For example, some variations of SMART include the original terms of *specific, measurable, attainable, relevant,* and *time-bound* while others refer to *specific, measurable, achievable, results-focused,* and *time-bound.* And still others use the terms *specific, measurable, achievable, realistic,* and *time-bound* to frame a SMART goal. As can be seen, though slight variations exist, a SMART goal focuses on similar features to best develop meaningful goals.

Wright and Wright (2006) discussed the practice of making IEPs SMART by including specific and measurable goals framed by action words that are realistic and relevant and achieved within a specific time frame (see LDOnline .org). Building on the above ideas, we adhere to the original terms associated with SMART to guide development of IEPs for English language and other diverse learners.

Specific

Specific goals address only one skill or behavior at a time. Daniel's first goal, *"Daniel will read for meaning with 75% accuracy in four out of five trials,"* is not specific because it offers no information about the reading skill being addressed. Reading for meaning is a very broad notion and involves multiple skills, so this goal needs more precise language. For example, is Daniel working on decoding grade-level texts and/or understanding what he has read? Does he struggle more with nonfiction texts or with fiction? Does he need additional support with literal or inferential questions? A more effective goal for Daniel would use a variety of assessments to determine the specific reading skills Daniel needs to master. An appropriately written specific goal requires educators to be familiar with the student's present levels of academic achievement and functional performance (PLAAFP), and use this information to generate IEP annual goals, along with reasonable sequences for skill acquisition to meet the goals. For example, if Daniel is not yet able to decode grade-level texts, it does not make

Table 5.1 Vague/Specific Comparison Chart

Vague Skill	*Specific Skill*
Read for meaning	Identify the main ideas in a nonfiction text at Fountas and Pinnell level R
Improve writing stamina by writing for extended periods of time	With the use of a graphic organizer, produce a minimum of 10 sentences within 20 minutes without prompting
Engage in appropriate social interactions with peers	Participate in reciprocal conversations with peers that last at least 2 minutes

sense for him to work on answering inferential questions about grade-level texts he reads independently. A more realistic sequence of skill sets should be identified and delivered through the IEP such as those identified in Table 5.1.

As illustrated, with additional clarity, an annual goal is easily transformed into a *specific* goal by identifying expected behaviors related to the content area.

Measurable

Measurability is not just best practice when writing IEP goals; it is also a legal requirement under the Individuals with Disabilities Education Improvement Act (IDEA, 2004). According to IDEA, Sec. 300.320(a)(2)(i), IEPs must include

> a statement of **measurable** annual goals, including academic and functional goals, designed to meet the child's needs.

In addition, for a goal to be measurable it must contain an *observable* indicator of success (Bateman, 2007). In other words, a goal must explicitly state what the student will do when demonstrating the skill. The observable behavior is something that is directly seen, rather than inferred, by others. For example, *independently gathering materials for an activity* is observable, while *approaching work with enthusiasm* is inferred and less observable.

A measurable goal must also include *objective* criteria for determining whether or not a student is able to successfully demonstrate a skill. These criteria outline how often or how well a behavior must be performed, and because they are objective, anyone reading the IEP should draw the same conclusions about how success will be measured. Measurability for academic goals is often based on grade- or age-level standards, rate, standardized assessments, criterion-referenced tests, or progress monitoring (Wright, Wright, & O'Connor, 2010). Functional behavioral goals should include the context in which the behavior occurs. For example, a student's behavior might be measured "when given a one-step direction" or "when interacting with peers at recess."

While the phrase "with __ accuracy" is a common criterion in IEP goals, it is not always appropriate. For example, in Daniel's second goal, "*Daniel will improve his writing stamina by writing for extended periods of time with 80%*

accuracy in four out of five trials," accuracy is not an appropriate unit of measurement because writing is not measured according to a yes/no scale (unless a specific rubric is being used), and different evaluators could draw different conclusions about what 80 percent accuracy means (Rowland, Quinn, & Steiner, 2015). For example, one evaluator might decide that Daniel must spell 80 percent of the words correctly, while another might decide he needs to score 80 percent on a writing rubric. A properly written and measurable goal should define specifically what the evaluator would look for to determine whether or not the goal has been met. In addition to or instead of accuracy, other criteria for success might be measured in terms of duration (*for ___ minutes*); quantity (*will write ___ sentences* or *will solve ___ problems*); independence (*will ___ independently/without prompting*); or frequency (*___ times per period/day/week*). When developing IEP goals, educators must determine which criterion makes the most sense based on the skill being measured and then include that term in the stated goal.

Measurable goals also include *meaningful* criteria for success. The goal should state the frequency or success rate for a skill, as well as outline how educators will know when the child has mastered that skill and met the goal (McWilliam, 2009). For example, Daniel's third goal, *"Daniel will engage in appropriate social interactions with peers four out of five days per week,"* does not include a meaningful unit of measurement. In this situation, it is insufficient to simply state the frequency with which interactions should occur. Rather, for this goal to be meaningful, it must explicitly outline the indicators to be used to determine whether the interactions are appropriate and the duration of these interactions. An improved, measurable Goal 3 for Daniel with a meaningful unit of measure could state that *Daniel will engage in reciprocal conversations with peers for at least two minutes, four out of five days per week.* With the addition of the meaningful criteria for measurement, educators will know what to look for to determine whether or not Daniel has met this goal.

Overall, though it is appropriate for a goal's criteria to include factors such as a percentage (*with ___ percent accuracy*) or a fractional measure of success (*___ out of ___ times*), these measurements are often used improperly in IEPs. Prior to including these and similar criteria, educators should examine the outcome for a student who meets a goal less than 100 percent of the time (Bateman, 2007). For example, if a student has a behavioral goal regarding not hitting other students and the criterion is 80 percent of the time, this would erroneously imply that it is permissible for the student to hit others 20 percent of the time! This behavioral expectation does a disservice to all the students and requires a 100 percent success rate expectation, even if difficult to achieve. On the other hand, in some cases 100 percent accuracy may be unnecessary to demonstrate mastery and may also be unrealistic. For example, even an expert reader will not decode every word in every text with 100 percent accuracy. In this context, it is appropriate to set the criterion for success at less than 100 percent (however, it should still be set at a high enough level to demonstrate mastery based on grade level and content area). Other examples of measurable goals with appropriate criteria are provided in Table 5.2.

Table 5.2   Immeasurable/Measurable Comparison Chart

Immeasurable Criteria	*Measurable Criteria*
Solve math problems with 90% accuracy	Solve 90% of single-digit addition problems correctly
Participate in reciprocal conversations with peers that last at least 2 minutes with 75% accuracy	Participate in reciprocal conversations with peers that last at least 2 minutes, 4 out of 5 days
Understand a text she has read	Correctly answer 9 out of 10 multiple-choice questions about a Developmental Reading Assessment level 10 text

Providers must carefully consider the most appropriate level of accuracy or frequency to demonstrate mastery given the context of the skill prior to setting the measurable criterion at less than 100 percent.

Attainable

Attainable or achievable goals are appropriately challenging for a student. A goal should set high expectations for a student's growth and achievement, yet it should also be reasonable given the student's current skill levels. Setting an appropriate goal requires up-to-date (not more than a few weeks old) progress monitoring data to accurately determine a student's present level of performance. Writing an appropriately challenging goal is a balancing act: the goal should not be so close to the student's current skill level that the student will meet it within a short time span, yet it should be something the student can realistically accomplish with intensive, effective instruction in a realistic annual time frame (Bateman, 2007).

For students with disabilities at mild to moderate levels, one year of growth using intensive interventions is often insufficiently ambitious, particularly since the goal should seek to close the achievement gap between the student with a disability and grade- or age-level peers. In this situation, a year of growth will only maintain the gap at a constant rate and therefore should be more rigorous. That is, appropriately ambitious goals should strive for more than a year's growth (e.g., 1.2 years; 1.5 years). Properly written PLAAFP statements lead to effective and realistic annual goals, which when addressed through appropriate intensive, high-quality instruction makes more ambitious growth possible. For students with more significant disabilities, such as cognitive delays or severe autism, appropriately attainable goals will be realistically less ambitious, yet they should still be as challenging as possible. Additionally, for these students, goals may address adaptive skills in addition to academic progress.

If a student does not achieve a goal within the given time frame, that goal should not simply be carried over to the student's next IEP. For some reason, the goal was not attainable for that student; therefore, it should be modified, revised, or eliminated. When educators begin to see that a goal is not or will not be mastered, several questions should be posed with updated responses:

1. Has the learner been provided the instruction recorded on the IEP with fidelity?

2. In retrospect, is the PLAAFP statement properly written, detailing both quantitative and qualitative content or functional skills?

3. Has the learner exhibited skill deficits not originally seen at the time of the IEP development?

4. For diverse learners, is the English language proficiency level commensurate with the instructional language and expectations?

5. Are the procedures and devices used to monitor progress appropriate for the (a) content area taught, (b) methods of instructional delivery, (c) learner's English proficiency level, (d) learner's accommodation needs?

These and similar questions challenge educators to revisit the IEP and disability classification, should lack of progress be evident, prior to automatically assuming that additional deficits exist within the learner (i.e., determine quality of instruction). This type of information is highly useful when making instructional adjustments based on lack of progress with annual IEP goals and associated short-term objectives. In some instances, making certain that the goals are consistent with the PLAAFP may be necessary, as illustrated in Table 5.3 showing attainable goals based on students' PLAAFP statements.

Attainment criteria for challenging, yet realistic, annual goals are stated in the IEP and used as a basis for selecting and implementing progress monitoring and necessary instructional adjustments.

Table 5.3 PLAAFP Comparison Chart

PLAAFP	*Attainable Goal*
Reads text at independent level at a rate of 85 wpm with 95% accuracy	Reads text at independent level at a rate of 120 wpm with 95% accuracy
Skip counts by all single-digit numbers	Solves 3-digit by 1-digit multiplication problems using the standard algorithm
Uses one-word utterances to request assistance or support from adults	Uses complete sentences phrased as questions to ask for support

Relevant

A relevant IEP goal is an individualized goal that is realistic and results driven, based on the student's unique academic, behavioral, and functional needs, while also addressing the gap between the student's present level of performance and his/her long-term educational and social goals. According to IDEA (2004), the purpose of an IEP is

to ensure that all children with disabilities have available to them a free appropriate public education that emphasizes special education and related services designed to meet their unique needs and prepare them for further education, employment and independent living. [Sec. 300.1(a)]

In other words, the IEP should be educationally meaningful (i.e., relevant) and not only a legally mandated document. To be educationally relevant, it should support the learner's progress toward mastery of the general-education curriculum as well as independence in real-world settings (Yell & Stecker, 2003).

A relevant academic goal for students with mild to moderate disabilities takes into account the skills that increase a student's access to state standards and associated curricula based on the learner's strengths. Additionally, a relevant goal requires educators to perform a task analysis of the student's long-term academic goals to determine deficits in standards-related skills that may be preventing the student from successfully accessing the general-education curriculum, leading to the development of appropriate IEP goals building on strengths to address areas of weakness. For example, if Daniel struggles conceptually with basic multiplication facts, it may not be appropriate at this time for him to work on the fourth-grade state mathematics standard that stresses *"Multiply a whole number of up to four digits by a one-digit whole number"* (see Corestandards.org/Math). However, his teachers should task analyze those mathematics skills that Daniel currently possesses and those he needs to develop in order to more realistically engage in a sequence of tasks associated with the above state standard example using multiplication with a multi-digit number. That is, based on his present level of performance, it may be more appropriate for Daniel to initially focus on making equal groups or skip counting by single-digit numbers. These skills incrementally support progress toward the above stated general education mathematics standard, while also targeting current levels of performance and individual needs. For students with more significant disabilities, goals addressing grade- or age-level state academic standards require careful consideration, task analysis, realistic sequencing, and highly short-term progress indicators. Relevant goals for these students will also focus on adaptive skills to maximize appropriate levels of independence in learning and daily living.

Additionally, when considering relevance, educators must ensure that the student's goals do not comprise highly detailed, irrelevant subcomponents of basic skills (McLaughlin & Nolet, 2004). Consider the following two examples:

Narrow Goal With Irrelevant Tasks: *Daniel will get out a pencil and eraser during independent writing time without prompting in 9 out of 10 writing periods.*

Unless Daniel particularly struggles with bringing a pencil for writing it should not be a stated goal. Rather, the revised broad goal is more beneficial and relevant due to its focus on organizational issues as a whole, not just on one or two discrete aspects of writing.

Relevant Broad Goal: *Daniel will gather all needed materials for independent work without prompting in 9 out of 10 independent work times.*

As can be seen from the above discussions, determining relevance in IEP goals is challenging and requires educators to use thoughtful professional judgment about which skills will support a student's broader academic, functional, and behavioral needs. Grade-level standards may act as guidelines, while relevance is determined by the child's unique long-term needs, present levels of performance, and existing skill sets that contribute to how the student best learns. Since IEP goals determine the type and intensity of interventions required, if the goal does not have a long-term benefit for the child, the intervention services will not maximize his/her educational opportunities (Shinn & Shinn, 2000).

Time-Bound

The final component of SMART IEP goals specifies a time limit within which goals should be attained. Typically, annual goals have a time frame of the academic school year. However, variations may exist. For example, the IEPs of students who take alternate assessments will include short-term objectives, outlining sequential steps that will measure the child's incremental progress toward the annual goal in the IEP (Wright et al., 2010). A time-bound IEP annual goal uses a student's present level of academic, functional, or behavioral performance as the basis for determining what the student should accomplish by the end of the academic school year or other relevant time frame. The IEP also includes a component outlining the plan and time frame for monitoring progress toward the goal at regular intervals (see Chapter 8 for discussion about progress monitoring).

EXAMPLES OF SMART GOALS

There is no requirement about the number of goals to include in an IEP, and the "more is better" concept does not apply to IEP goals. In fact, including too many goals may water down the effectiveness of interventions for the student. Educators and parents must work together to prioritize the most relevant goals that will have the greatest positive impact on a student's academic, functional, or behavioral performance based on results from the comprehensive special education evaluation and present levels of performance. An IEP may include any combination of academic, functional, and behavioral goals depending on the student's disability. For example, a student whose disability primarily impacts his/her academic performance may have no functional or behavioral issues, and so the IEP would include only academic goals. Conversely, a student may struggle with social or functional skills yet have few academic issues. In short, the types of goals included in the IEP are determined by the child's unique needs (Wright et al., 2010).

Within the parameters of making certain to identify the most necessary type of goal(s) (i.e., academic, functional, behavioral), we provide examples of SMART goals for each of the three categories along with analysis of how each incorporates SMART features:

ACADEMIC GOAL EXAMPLE

Jeremy, a third grader:

Within one year, Jeremy will demonstrate understanding of place value by independently solving 20 addition problems with numbers up to three digits (with and without regrouping) within 5 minutes with 95% accuracy.

Specific: This goal is specific because it clearly outlines how Jeremy will demonstrate mastery of the skill. After reading the goal, educators and parents will be able to articulate or write an example of the kind of problem Jeremy is working on.

Measurable: The criteria for measurement are clear: Jeremy must solve at least 19 of the 20 problems correctly to meet the goal. The behavior is observable, objective, and meaningful. The accuracy rate of 95% reflects mastery but does not require absolute perfection.

Attainable: Based on his present level of math performance, Jeremy can attain this goal within one year. At the same time, the goal is ambitious and addresses the gap between Jeremy's PLAAFP and grade-level expectations.

Relevant: This goal relates to the state standards: the third-grade standard for Numbers and Operations in Base Ten states that students should be able to *"fluently add and subtract within 1000 using strategies and algorithms based on place value, properties of operations, and/or the relationship between addition and subtraction"* (see Corestandards.org/Math). Place value is also a foundational math concept, and mastery of this concept will help Jeremy better access the general education mathematics curriculum.

Time-Bound: This goal clearly states that Jeremy is expected to meet the goal within one year.

FUNCTIONAL GOAL EXAMPLE

Thomas, a first grader:

By May 2016, Thomas will play with peers during independent play times by sharing play materials, such as blocks, toys, and physical space, for at least 5 minutes four times per week.

Specific: While the overarching goal of playing appropriately with friends is broad, the indicators of sharing blocks, toys, and so on make this a specific goal.

Measurable: The context is explicit (during independent play times) and the criteria for success are outlined in terms of what Thomas's behavior should look like, the duration of the behavior, and the frequency of the behavior.

Attainable: This goal is based on Thomas's present level of functioning in the classroom and should be attainable within one year.

Relevant: This goal will support Thomas's functioning both in and out of school. Thomas's ability to play appropriately with peers will support his social interactions and also his interactions with peers and adults in academic settings. It will improve his independence in a variety of contexts.

Time-Bound: The goal clearly states that it is attained at the end of the school year in May.

BEHAVIORAL GOAL EXAMPLE

Maya, a fifth grader:

Within one year, Maya will independently use strategies to calm herself down, such as getting a drink of water, counting backward from 10, and using positive self-talk, as demonstrated by her ability to return to the class activity within 2 minutes when directed to take a break in 9 out of 10 instances.

Specific: While "use strategies to calm herself down" could be a vague goal, in this case the indicators that educators must look for are clearly specified. Maya will rejoin the class activity within the given time period by demonstrating mastery of one or more self-calming strategies.

Measurable: The criteria for success are embedded within the goal. The goal outlines the precipitating event (when she is asked to take a break), the duration (2 minutes), and the success rate (returning to class activity successfully in 9 out of 10 instances).

Attainable: Based on Maya's present level of participation, this goal is ambitious, but it should be attainable within one year.

Relevant: Successfully employing self-regulating strategies to calm herself down will help Maya to participate appropriately in many classroom activities and in her daily life. If Maya is able to master this skill, it will have a long-lasting positive impact on her lifelong learning abilities.

Time-Bound: Maya should achieve this goal as stated within one year.

DEVELOPING SMART GOALS

Writing a SMART goal may take more time and effort at the outset yet over time will ultimately facilitate greater efficiency in IEP development and implementation. SMART goals improve outcomes for students by offering specific guidance about the skill being taught and mastered and the progress monitored. After reading a well-written SMART goal, educators obtain a clear understanding of (a) exactly what the student is working on, (b) the performance context in which the skill should be demonstrated, and (c) the teacher's role in supporting the student.

When writing a SMART goal, the first step is to examine and review the student's present levels of academic achievement and functional performance. This review process frames for educators the skills students must develop, under what conditions learning best occurs, and potential, appropriate supplemental supports or accommodations. Once clarity about skills for development is established, educators systematically consider each of the five components of the SMART goal.

Examining Present Levels of Academic Achievement and Functional Performance

As discussed in Chapter 4, a properly developed PLAAFP statement includes use of a combination of formal and informal assessments to develop a comprehensive understanding of a student's strengths, weaknesses, cultural values, and preferred ways of learning. These assessments typically include a combination of standardized tests, curriculum-based measurements, work samples, observations, and interviews. Collectively, the comprehensive assessment results identify the student's skills, attitudes, and behaviors relative to the area of disability. It is essential that the PLAAFP focus on both learner strengths as well as areas of need.

Once the areas for growth are identified, educators generate annual goals, short-term objectives, and progress monitoring plans to address those needs. In many instances where multiple needs emerge, professional judgment is required to prioritize the extent to which different skills are emphasized through the IEP, relative to learning that will have the most impact on the student's access to the general-education curriculum and success in real-world settings. Educators should incorporate student input (if appropriate) as well as the student's family perspectives during the IEP development process to ensure that everyone's voice is heard and valued in the goal writing. Overall, the IEP will be of most benefit for the student if everyone understands, contributes to, and agrees upon the annual goals and associated short-term objectives.

Generating a SMART Goal

Specific. Once the educators and the student's family have selected a general area of focus, the next task is to ensure that the goal is specific, adhering to the suggestions presented above (Rowland, Quinn, Steiner, & Bowser, 2013). First, each goal should focus on one and only one skill. If the goal's focus is too broad or contains multiple skill demonstrations, progress toward the goal will be difficult to monitor and assess, and its benefits for the student may be limited. After development, when others read the goal, it should be easy to pinpoint exactly what the student will do to accomplish the goal. Those reading the goal should also be able to picture the context in which the skill will be demonstrated, as well as the teacher's role in providing support. Finally, when choosing a specific skill upon which to focus, it is important to consider and emphasize the skill that best fits the learner's needs to initially address. Also, as discussed, a student will be more successful if goals follow a logical developmental sequence.

The following questions may be helpful for educators and parents to ask during goal development to ensure specificity:

- What specific skill is the student working on?
- Is this skill broad (e.g., *writing with stamina*) or focused (e.g., *independently writing 10 sentences in a 20-minute time frame*)?
- Does this skill make sense given the student's present level of performance?
- What will the teacher's role be in supporting the student?
- In what context should the student demonstrate this skill?
- How will we monitor the progress?

Measurable. The next task in SMART development is to consider how the goal will be measured. When choosing appropriate criteria for monitoring, it is helpful to think through the most important aspects of the skill or behavior and then determine how these can be best assessed. The measurable factor should be stated within the content of the goal, thereby clearly showing how the skill will be demonstrated in observable, objective, and meaningful ways. For English language and other diverse learners, the measurable factor must be culturally and linguistically responsive. Additionally, when identifying the measurable feature of the goal, educators must decide on expected levels of accuracy, duration, quantity, frequency, and/or some other relevant unit specific to the skill being demonstrated. As noted above, the criteria should be ambitious enough that attaining the goal will have a real positive outcome for the student. The following questions may be helpful for educators and parents to ask to ensure measurability:

- Is the behavior described in this goal observable?
- Is the language objective?
- Will other educators reading this goal take away the same understanding?
- Do the criteria outlined for mastery accurately indicate mastery of the skill?
- Are the criteria rigorously sufficient to benefit and challenge the student?

Attainable. Once specificity and measurability are developed, goal developers move into the step that pertains to attainability. Determining the extent to which the goal is attainable is based on a student's present level of performance as well as the steps necessary to acquire the skill. It may be helpful to complete a task analysis to determine necessary prerequisite skills that the student currently possesses and must develop in order to successfully demonstrate the skill. For example, if a student's annual goal is to organize writing into several paragraphs that include topic sentences, supporting details, and a concluding sentence, important prerequisite skills are knowledge of a paragraph's structure and ability to write in complete sentences with accurate syntax (Lloyd, Kameenui, & Chard, 2014). In addition, knowledge of a hierarchical understanding of concepts (i.e., from big picture to more focused concepts) must exist to distinguish the main idea from supporting details. Though the above writing example is only one of many, the idea of performing a task analysis will help educators decide whether the skill is realistically attainable within one year, based on existing and needed prerequisite skills. Also, as noted above, if the student's performance falls below grade or age-level expectations, the goal should be written so as to challenge the student to strive for more than a year's growth to address the achievement gap. The following questions may be helpful for educators and parents to ask to ensure attainability:

- How does this annual goal connect to the student's present level of performance?
- Is this goal appropriate as an annual target, given the prerequisite skills currently possessed by the learner?
- With proper instruction, will the student meet the goal within a too short time frame?
- Will achieving this goal help to close the achievement gap between the student and peers?

Relevant. The next step in the development process is to make certain the goal is relevant by being student centered while addressing specific learner needs. A relevant goal is a goal that once attained ultimately benefits the student in one or more ways including (a) academic learning, (b) settings outside the classroom, and/or (c) generalization to other contexts. Conversely, if a goal addresses a specific subskill, or focuses too much on minutiae, it is unlikely to have much relevance to the student's academic, social, or personal life (e.g., overemphasis on phonemic awareness abilities with little connection to comprehension). Given the significant amounts of time spent developing the IEP, delivering the instruction, and monitoring the progress, it is important for IEP goals to be challenging, worthwhile, and relevant. Overall, the most relevant IEP goals will simultaneously help students with disabilities improve skills while maintaining successful access to the general-education curriculum. The following questions may be helpful for educators and parents to ask to ensure relevance:

- Will mastering this goal benefit the student in other academic and/or social contexts?
- Will mastering this goal move the student toward achieving long-term educational and social goals?
- If this is an academic goal, have the state's grade-level performance standards been considered and incorporated?
- How certain are we that the skills within the goal are not too simple or discrete to lead to meaningful importance to the learner?

Time-Bound. Determining a time frame for goal completion completes the SMART development process. By their design, annual goals typically have a time frame of one year or close to one year, with intermediate progress monitored through completion of short-term objectives (i.e., quarterly, monthly). Since IEP meetings often take place near the end of the school year, annual student goals are generated for the following year. Time-bound parameters are closely related to each of the previous SMART features, with attainability being of particular relevance to establishing realistic timelines for goal completion.

The material in this chapter presented thus far has focused on the development of SMART IEP goals for any learner with a disability. Though some cursory references to issues specific to English language and other diverse learners were made in the above discussions, the development of SMART goals requires special considerations in order to ensure a culturally and linguistically responsive IEP.

MAKING SMART GOALS CULTURALLY AND LINGUISTICALLY RESPONSIVE

An effectively developed IEP occurs through a partnership between school professionals and families. When families are active participants in the IEP process, students benefit by receiving family support for and reinforcement of learning at home. Unfortunately, many special education programs are not culturally and linguistically responsive due to limited consideration of diverse values and beliefs of the students and the families they serve.

> Though an IEP lacking diversity may be the result of many factors, the most significant is the misperception that culturally and linguistically diverse language and values have little or no role in the delivery of special education. As discussed in Chapter 2, nothing could be further from the truth.

Family members of diverse learners bring a variety of important contributions to the IEP and special education process including (a) cultural funds of knowledge, (b) home teachings, (c) community values grounded in ethnicity, (d) perceptions about the most significant aspects of education based on cultural values and English language proficiency, and (e) cultural views about disability, to name a few (Hoover, Baca, & Klingner, 2016; Hoover & Klingner, 2011). Too often, families are assigned a secondary role in the IEP process, and goals are written with limited or no parent input. The situation of developing an IEP that lacks diverse input is compounded when school professionals make little or no effort to ensure that parents understand the goals their child will be working toward once special education begins (Zhang & Bennett, 2003). In many cases, the first time the family sees the IEP or hears about their child's goals is in the IEP meeting when they are expected to agree to and sign the IEP document with little or no time for reflection or input (Yell & Stecker, 2003). Additionally, IEP development with families that speak a home language other than English challenges educators to convey important information in a non-English first language. And though interpreters are required by IDEA in these situations, the greater concern is to make certain the family members actually understand the contents of the IEP, specifics about special education, and ways in which the school is best designing instruction for the benefit of their child. Oftentimes, making certain parents truly understand what is occurring regarding the IEP and special education requires additional time and consideration that go beyond simply translating information into a language other than English at the IEP meeting.

As stressed in the literature, family participation should begin during the referral process, continue during the special education comprehensive evaluation process, and extend into the development of the IEP, leading to ongoing progress monitoring updates and home supports. Specific to the topic of this chapter and book, parental input and involvement should begin long before the actual IEP meeting is convened. School professionals must take strides to demystify the special education and IEP process for culturally and linguistically diverse families by considering at minimum two important realities when writing responsive IEP goals: (1) *accessibility* and (2) *meaningful family involvement*.

Accessibility

Consider terms like *present levels of academic achievement and functional performance, behavioral intervention plan, Individualized Education Program,* and *least restrictive environment.* Though these terms are meaningful to special education professionals, they are not exactly transparent to a layperson. IEPs are typically written in jargon-heavy language that makes them inaccessible to the general public (Rowland et al., 2013). It is easy for service providers, who are used to speaking in a language of acronyms, to forget that this terminology can be confusing and overwhelming for parents and other family members. This is particularly true for families whose first language is not English.

While much of the language found within the IEP is established by school districts or delineated by law, educators must strive to write IEP goals that are language accessible and meaningful for families. An accessible IEP goal should be written in clear language that nonschool professionals are able to understand. The goal writer should try to avoid specialized diagnostic or educational terminology as much as possible (Zhang & Bennett, 2003). Periodically, however, it is necessary to include specific terminology that may be confusing to noneducators. In these situations, educators should share several examples of the task or skill that the goal addresses, discussing it in terms understandable to noneducation professionals, thereby allowing families to see exactly what is expected of their child.

For example, if a child has a math goal designed to master solving division word problems with dividends up to three digits, educators should share several examples of this type of problem with the family prior to and/or during the IEP meeting. For culturally and linguistically diverse learners and families, it will take extra effort to ensure that (a) goals are written in clear language, (b) sufficient interpretation is provided if necessary, and (c) some task examples are provided to the family to ensure understanding. Engaging families in these positive ways empowers and enables them to better support their child's IEP goal acquisition. Meaningful involvement is further explored in the next section.

Meaningful Family Involvement

IDEA outlines many legal requirements for schools to ensure that parents have a voice in the IEP process. The school or agency in charge of scheduling a child's initial or annual IEP meeting must make certain that a child's family has the opportunity to attend and participate. It is also required to ensure that parents understand the proceedings, which may mean the services of a translator are needed for families that speak a language other than English. As discussed previously, although schools usually follow the letter of the law, school professionals often fall short when it comes to ensuring that families are meaningfully involved. Cultural beliefs influence a family's goals for their child, and these beliefs may generate differences between families and school professionals, creating barriers to family participation (Zhang & Bennett, 2003). A culturally and linguistically responsive IEP takes into account the family's cultural norms, particularly the academic, behavioral, and social skills valued by their community (Garcia, 2014). For example, if a family comes from a culture that believes children should listen to adults and follow directions quietly, a goal around active classroom participation may not be culturally responsive.

It is important for educators to recognize their own cultural beliefs and biases in these interactions rather than adopting a deficit view of families with different beliefs and values (Hoover, Baca, & Klingner, 2016). For example, *disability* is a subjective term that is laden with cultural assumptions. Baxter and Mahoney (2016) wrote, "Different cultures have different views of disability and treat children with developmental disabilities in different ways" (How Do Different Cultures View Developmental Difficulties section). Some cultures view disability (a) as a shameful situation that is not disclosed to others, resulting in reluctance to seek outside support such as from a school, or (b) as a stigma resulting in outcasting or isolating the member (Baxter & Mahoney,

2016). Depending on their cultural lenses, school professionals and families may disagree about the kinds of services a child should receive or even about the existence of a disability at all (Zhang & Bennett, 2003). In these situations, an educator or community support person who is familiar with the language and culture of the family can help both the family and school professionals to navigate each other's values and points of view (Barrera, 1996). It is crucial for school professionals to keep in mind that their status as professionals does not mean that their perspective is objectively correct. No matter how different views may appear, school professionals have a responsibility to ensure that families have an equal voice in crafting the IEP.

As stipulated in IDEA, school professionals have a responsibility to take the time to gather family input before any goals have been written to ensure that everyone's voice is reflected in the IEP. Some questions that may be helpful in guiding an initial conversation with diverse families about potential IEP goals include these:

- What are your child's greatest academic strengths? Social strengths?
- What are your child's interests?
- What do you see as your child's greatest academic challenge? Social challenge? Behavioral challenge?
- How does your child react to frustration?
- What skills do you think would be the most beneficial for your child to focus on during school?
- What do you value most for your child during daily school participation?
- What goals beyond formal schooling do you have for your child?

Throughout the IEP process, educators should listen to families' voices and provide them with objective information about their child's eligibility for services and available programming options (Rowland et al., 2015). In summary, open channels of communication, ongoing dialogue, and clearly stated information may require additional effort to best meet the needs of culturally and linguistically diverse learners with disabilities; however, these efforts are well worth the time as they will lead to the best possible outcomes for all students.

CONCLUSION

A major component of any IEP is the development of annual goals stated in measurable terms within a defined time frame. The use of SMART goal procedures and principles facilitates the development of meaningful, specific, and attainable IEP goals for all learners. In regard to English language and other diverse learners, the IEP needs to reflect cultural and linguistic diversity consistent with the student's second language acquisition stage of development, cultural values and teachings, as well as family input, perspectives, and expectations. Numerous examples were provided to guide readers in the development of annual goals, including culturally and linguistically responsive IEP annual goals, to ensure the most meaningful and measurable IEPs for all students.

Delivering Appropriate IEP Services 6

Practitioner's Perspective . . .

How are English language development and IEP implementation interconnected? What are examples of specialized services, related services, and supplemental supports? How are IEP related and supplemental services best delivered for English language and other diverse learners?

The overall purpose of an Individualized Education Program (IEP) is to document a plan for providing effective specialized instruction to students with a disability in the least restrictive environment. That is, our emphasis is to take an IEP beyond *compliance* only and situate it as a useful *instructional* tool. As a brief review, the following should exist on IEPs for all students, including English language and other diverse learners, requiring special education:

NOTE: All material in the items below is directly relevant to identified academic or functional behavioral area(s) of need underlying the disability diagnosis.

- Present levels of academic achievement and functional performance specifying current strengths and needs, while also incorporating cultural and linguistic considerations that support diverse learners' effective instruction
- Extent to which student continues to receive instruction with general education peers through access to the curriculum, including English language development
- Annual goals detailing measurable expected levels of knowledge and skills connected to state standards adhering to SMART procedures
- Instructional objectives (*note: these are not required by IDEA [2004] regulations yet highly preferred by most professionals in the field*) reflecting intermediate progressions toward achieving the annual goals, including identifying and developing specific academic language necessary to successfully master IEP taught skills

- Assessment procedures to monitor progress toward annual goals and/or instructional objectives
- Instructional and assessment accommodations reflecting both disability needs and cultural and linguistic diversity considerations to best improve learning
- Specialized services and related supplemental supports
- Parent/guardian input, concerns, or related information reflecting cultural and linguistic diversity and teachings

IEPs developed for use as instructional tools require educators to utilize documented material for each of the above items in their unit and lesson plan development. Therefore, the more the IEP content informs selection of curricula, methods, group settings, management techniques, or progress monitoring, the more connected the IEP will be to actual classroom instruction, which in turn more directly connects with measurable progress. In regard to English language and other diverse learners, the IEP should include opportunities for continued English language development in addition to academic or functional behavioral development. This chapter provides coverage of the implementation of IEP components creating an instructional tool that incorporates cultural and linguistic considerations and practices. We begin with the topic of building English language development into IEP implementation, followed by discussion of strategies for operationalizing the various required IDEA (2004) IEP components.

ENGLISH LANGUAGE DEVELOPMENT AND IEP IMPLEMENTATION

One of the most misunderstood practices for instructing English learners who receive special education services is that their English language development becomes secondary to the instruction documented on the IEP. The perception is that once an English learner (EL) is placed into special education, the IEP services supersede or override English language development, even though the learner is still in the process of acquiring English as a second language. In some instances, school staffs reduce the amount of time devoted to English language development (ELD) to provide time for special education services. Although the need for English language development cannot be used as a basis for placement into special education, responsibility for providing this service is not relinquished once the student has been identified with a disability.

ELD and IEPs

A learner's IEP documents programmatic aspects necessary for assisting students to master the documented goals and objectives. Necessary related and supplemental services are recorded to facilitate such growth. In regard to ELs, continuation of ELD services is essential to achieving satisfactory progress with IEP goals and objectives. Therefore, all ELs with identified disabilities must continue to receive ELD instruction on a regular basis. Along with the monitoring of progress toward mastery of IEP goals, progress toward English proficiency should be measured on a periodic basis (e.g., WIDA ACCESS), since progress toward language proficiency directly relates to progress toward achieving IEP goals. That is, a direct connection exists between continued English language development and achievement toward academic content goals, particularly in reading (Hoover, Baca, & Klingner, 2016).

When developing the IEP and considering the most appropriate services for English learners, identifying the intersection between level of English language proficiency and severity of disability is a critical piece of information to obtain. One framework to use to consider this intersection is illustrated in Figure 6.1, developed from discussions found in several sources (see Hoover, Baca, & Klingner, 2016; Hoover & Klingner, 2011). Illustrated are four different classification types providing educators with a general perspective of language proficiency and disability relative to levels and severity, respectively. Knowledge of where the EL best fits at the time the IEP is developed assists to clarify instructional need. Each of the four classifications pairs the level of English proficiency with relative severity of disability as determined by the special education comprehensive assessment body of evidence. IEP team members should know in which classification type the learner most situates, to select and deliver appropriate instruction sufficient to master IEP goals and objectives.

As shown, four general classification levels are identified. These are not all-inclusive yet represent most diverse learners with disabilities and are not in any order of importance or significance, since clarifying the most accurate level for the learner is critical to best provide IEP services that integrate ELD and special education instruction.

Knowing the English learner's severity of disability relative to English language proficiency level informs best practices to document on the IEP necessary for delivering appropriate services. The more significant the disability, the more intensive the interventions required; the less developed the English proficiency, the more English language development required. The challenge to educators developing the IEP is to balance the intensive intervention needs with English language development opportunities and supports. The recommended practice

Figure 6.1   English Language Proficiency and Disability Intersect Classifications

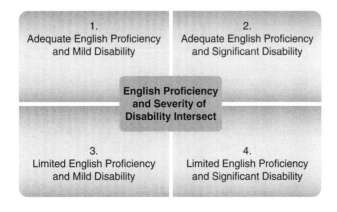

Classification 1. Adequate English Proficiency and Mild Disability: At this level, the English learner possesses higher-level English development and proficiency (e.g., Level 5 or 6 based on WIDA ACCESS assessment) and portrays, based on the multiple assessment body of evidence, a mild-moderate disability.

Classification 2. Adequate English Proficiency and Significant Disability: At this level, the EL possesses higher-level English development and proficiency (e.g., Level 5 or 6 based on WIDA ACCESS assessment) and portrays, based on the multiple assessment body of evidence, a severe or significant disability.

Classification 3. Limited English Proficiency and Mild Disability: At this level, the EL possesses English proficiency at the developing or expanding stage (e.g., Level 3 or 4 based on WIDA ACCESS assessment) and portrays, based on the multiple assessment body of evidence, a mild-moderate disability.

Classification 4. Limited English Proficiency and Significant Disability: At this level, the EL possesses English proficiency at the developing or expanding stage (e.g., Level 3 or 4 based on WIDA ACCESS assessment) and portrays, based on the multiple assessment body of evidence, a severe or significant disability.

NOTE: Under extreme conditions, ELs who exhibit little or no English language proficiency (e.g., Level 1 or 2 based on the WIDA ACCESS assessment) may exhibit evidence of a disability. However, placement of a non-English-proficient learner for special education should rarely occur due to the need for more extensive English language development prior to being able to adequately separate language acquisition from disability. However, in rare instances, this situation may exist, and the same IEP requirements are addressed as those for second language learners in the developing or higher stages of proficiency (e.g., WIDA ACCESS Stage 3 or higher).

> Failure to provide continued ELD for English learners with a disability often results in lack of progress with IEP content goals and objectives due to reduced English language instruction essential for academic success.

for schools is to provide a regular block of ELD (e.g., forty-five minutes daily or three times per week), along with ELD embedded into both the general education instruction and special education services.

Therefore, continued ELD instruction should be included on an IEP as this is a necessary service to facilitate adequate progress with IEP content goals and objectives. For example, in the Los Angeles Unified School District, "all EL students with disabilities must have an IEP that addresses any goals and/or supports needed to make progress toward (language) reclassification" (Regan, 2013, p. 6). Additionally, IEP team members should be familiar with existing English language proficiency levels or stages (see Table 2.2) to best inform the development and implementation of IEP goals relative to English language proficiency. When designing IEPs for ELs, team members should consider and include supports needed based collectively on disability severity and English proficiency level, providing access to ELD both in and outside of the general classroom instruction.

ADDRESSING LANGUAGE AND CONTENT DURING INSTRUCTION FOR ENGLISH LEARNERS

Chapter 3 of this book presented the topic of academic language development in teaching and learning for ELs. The reader is encouraged to revisit that chapter to review the principles and practices for incorporating academic language into instruction for ELs in the delivery of an IEP through both general and special education instruction. Specifically, essential components of ELD include emphasis on vocabulary, background knowledge, and other features related to academic language in classroom instruction discussed in Chapter 3. Therefore, though an IEP clearly includes content goals and objectives, it should also include academic language provisions necessary to provide ELs with sufficient language skills to be successful with those content goals or objectives. IEP developers should respond to one simple question for each measurable goal and associated objective:

> *What vocabulary and English language abilities are necessary for ELs to possess in order to successfully master the goal and objective?*

Responses to this question should be incorporated into the IEP to best inform educators of how to meet English learners' disability needs while simultaneously improving English language proficiency. Inclusion of the academic language required for success with each IEP goal or objective is also essential to making an IEP a useful instructional tool. It is important to note that

> *by incorporating academic language into IEP goals/objectives, we are in no way implying that we view language as a disability. Rather, incorporation of academic language development into the IEP is viewed as a necessary strength-based approach complementing methods used to help English learners with disabilities best achieve their IEP content goals and objectives.*

Educators of ELs are encouraged to (a) make certain that required academic language is incorporated into IEP development, (b) attend to the academic language recorded on the IEP in the instructional delivery of the IEP, and (c) view development and mastery of academic language as a necessary component to helping ELs achieve the IEP content goals and objectives. Within the parameters of providing necessary and sufficient ELD, the overall IEP can be properly delivered meeting culturally and linguistically diverse needs of students with disabilities.

IMPLEMENTING THE IEP

The developed IEP should frame instruction for students, providing sufficient information succinctly and in a manner for easy use in unit and lesson plan development. Though IEPs generally do not specify or name individual methods, materials, or curricula, it should document the conditions under which the student best learns, thereby leading educators to select appropriate methods, materials, and curricula. Consider the following examples for an EL or other diverse learner placement in special education:

> Documented Strength: *The learner's present level of reading performance indicates that the student learns well within paired or small-group settings with teacher direction.*

> Instructional Implication: *Select a teaching method that facilitates paired or small-group learning, such as reciprocal teaching, cooperative learning, or language experience approach.*

> Documented Strength: *The learner's present level of performance indicates that the student requires additional "wait time" in order to grasp the necessary English language vocabulary needed to understand a question or task.*

> Instructional Implication: *Methods selected for this student should avoid practices that require quick, on-the-spot responses until the learner becomes more proficient with English academic language.*

> Documented Strength: *One instructional accommodation documented to be successful with the culturally and linguistically diverse CLD learner is use of reading material that reflects the student's cultural teachings.*

> Instructional Implications: *When completing a reading or writing task, allow the student to select material of cultural relevance to further develop academic skills and associated academic English language.*

These and similar examples provide direction and clarity to educators responsible for delivering instruction framed by the IEP. Also, as previously emphasized throughout this book, the reader should note that when implementing instruction based on an IEP for ELs, that instruction must be culturally and linguistically responsive or the learner will have little chance of mastering the IEP goals and associated objectives. For example, simply providing reading instruction used with non-ELs without considering English language development proficiency, cultural perspectives, or home teachings is insufficient as it would not provide cultural and linguistic responsiveness necessary to situate that instruction into a meaningful learning context for an EL.

Other IEP-required components needing documentation and implementation include (a) service delivery settings, (b) selecting and using evidence-based interventions, (c) selecting and using curricular materials, (d) special education related services, and (e) supplemental aids and services.

Service Delivery Settings to Operationalize IEP Goals (*Push-In, Pull-Out*)

One of the cornerstones of the IDEA (2004) legislation is the practice of providing education in the "least restrictive environment (LRE)," which requires making certain that all students with disabilities are educated with peers as much as possible (Siegel, 2014). LRE reflects a continuum of services ranging from general education through residential placement based on learner needs. Though education in and access to the general classroom and curriculum is the legally mandated and preferred practice, other delivery settings may be appropriate and warranted as possible options for IEP team developers. Determination of best instructional settings has significant implications for the development of an IEP for any student, with unique considerations required for English language and other diverse learners due to the cultural and linguistic diversity brought to the teaching and learning environment. Therefore, every IEP must include documentation of the specific setting(s) in which the learners will be instructed. For English language and other diverse learners, this setting should be the general education classroom as much as possible, limiting use of other settings that isolate CLD learners from peers in the general school population. Once the proper settings have been identified and clarified, the task of operationalizing the IEP to deliver effective instruction ensues. In order to effectively deliver an IEP for diverse learners in a school setting, two types of service delivery options must be considered and used to frame comprehensive instruction (i.e., pull-out, push-in).

Pull-Out Instruction. Providing special education services outside of the general education classroom is considered the last option for students with disabilities; however, a pull-out situation may be very appropriate and necessary to meet some learning needs and is therefore a viable option:

Pull-Out Concerns

- Learners are removed from instruction with general class peers.
- Pulled-out students may miss important instruction delivered in their absence.
- Instruction delivered in a pull-out setting may be disconnected from instruction received in the general classroom.

Pull-Out Strengths

- Learners from different classrooms or grade levels are provided targeted instruction specific to identified learning needs in small groups with other learners who have similar needs (i.e., all students require reading fluency supports).
- When structured properly, pull-out services provide necessary supports to general education instruction (i.e., general and specialized instruction are connected).

Push-In Instruction. A primary goal of push-in delivery is to facilitate learners on IEPs to continue to be instructed with grade- and age-level peers as much as possible.

Push-In Concerns

- Push-in educators may be unable to satisfactorily deliver necessary instruction leading to increased maintenance rather than improved learning (e.g., improper use of paraprofessionals).

- If not properly structured, push-in services may stigmatize learners by presenting the appearance of tracking due to low abilities.

Push-In Strengths

- Students remain in their own classroom setting and are not removed from peers.
- Instruction is easily integrated into the overall classroom instruction.
- Co-teaching is facilitated (i.e., push-in and general class teachers work together).
- Student groupings are easily changed based on learner needs.
- Learners' general classroom teachers are actively involved in the delivery of IEP instruction.

Cultural/Linguistic Pull-Out and Push-In Considerations. Using the guidance provided in the previous chapters about culturally and linguistically responsive instruction, the delivery of IEP services in both pull-out and push-in situations requires specific considerations for English language and other diverse learners.

- Quality English language development must be embedded into IEP instructional delivery for ELs.
- Peer instruction for ELs requires interactions with students who have similar English language proficiency and/or cultural experiences (i.e., true peers) as well as other grade-level peers.
- Materials should reflect diverse cultures and values.
- Methods selected and used should be researched and validated with English language and other diverse learners.

Use of push-in and/or pull-out settings when instructing ELs is based primarily on disability needs and not English proficiency, since ELD is a general education service provided to all ELs. Consideration of the above strengths and concerns along with efforts to provide culturally and linguistically responsive instruction will serve to frame the best use of these two types of IEP service delivery options.

Aligning Learner Strengths With Evidence-Based Intervention Selection

As discussed previously, though an IEP does not identify specific evidence-based interventions, programs, or materials, to be a useful instructional tool it must identify learning characteristics that reflect conditions under which the student best learns and those most suitable for progress. This information, in turn, is used to select best methods or programs for implementing IEP goals. The following statements provide examples of learning qualities that could be included in the present levels of academic achievement and functional performance (PLAAFP), reflecting student characteristics that inform intervention selection:

- Works best in small group or pairs
- Prefers a cooperative learning group

- Infrequently attends to tasks in whole- or large-group settings
- Requires additional wait time to think about and respond to a question
- Prefers to respond orally rather than in writing
- Is able to maintain his/her own behavior for five to seven minutes at a time
- Requires instructions to be provided in segments (e.g., give one direction and when task is complete provide a second direction for subsequent task)
- Works best when using manipulatives and visuals
- Completes tasks best when provided the opportunity to restate the directions prior to beginning the assignment
- Lacks self-management abilities in large-group instruction
- Requires tasks to be broken into two to three segments (e.g., provide first three rows of math computation problems and when completed introduce the next set of rows)
- Requires opportunity to build academic language and background knowledge to make connections to previous experiences prior to beginning and completing new tasks

These and similar statements clarify or define the conditions under which the student best learns, and when considered in the selection of methods or programs to use during instruction, the IEP becomes a functional instructional tool (i.e., methods used align with a student's best ways of learning). The methods selected for teaching should include practices that complement student strengths in learning. Stated differently,

> *If the student best learns through direct instruction, then the method or program selected to help that student meet IEP objectives should be grounded in direct instruction methodology.*

The selection of methods aligned with a student's best ways of learning should frame implementation of any IEP academic content or behavioral goal or objective to provide sufficient opportunities to learn. A few examples, illustrating alignment between learner characteristics and appropriate methods or programs, are provided in Table 6.1.

The suggestions are not all-inclusive and many other examples could be provided. However, whichever methods are selected, what is of most importance is that they are grounded in and use procedures that align with specific student learning strengths.

Conversely, these and similar learning qualities illustrated in Table 6.1 provide information as to which methods to avoid. For example, learners who struggle when working independently with computer programs should not be provided extensive instruction using Read 180, since this method relies heavily on independent computer skill sets. Or if the student is not proficient with decoding, then use of the collaborative strategic reading (CSR) method should be delayed until decoding skills are further developed, since CSR is designed for use with learners who already possess decoding skills. Or if a learner in math does not function well working in pairs, then PALS-Math may not be the best

Table 6.1   Evidence-Based Interventions That Align to Learning Characteristics

Learning Characteristic	Sample Intervention That Aligns With LC
Prefers small-group instruction with teacher direction	Reciprocal teaching
Prefers active engagement in small groups	Classwide peer tutoring
Works best when using visual material or diagramming in writing tasks	Graphic organizing/Venn diagrams
Learns best when using his/her own vocabulary in acquiring basic reading skills	Language experience approach (LEA)
Is able to work independently to record impressions about reading or written material	Reading/writing response journaling
Responds appropriately to behavior management that teaches personal responsibility/ownership	Self-monitoring method
Is proficient with decoding yet struggles with reading comprehension	Collaborative strategic reading (CSR)
Prefers to work in pairs rather than small or large groups	Peer-assisted learning strategies (PALS)
Performs best when prompted to access prior knowledge by reflecting on her/his own prior experiences	Self-questioning methods
Is able to learn via independent computer programs	Read 180

method of choice, since it requires paired learning to be effective. As can be seen, if properly documented on the IEP, student learning strengths and areas of concern provide educators with valuable information necessary to make informed intervention and programming decisions to meet IEP goals and objectives.

Cultural/Linguistic Evidence-Based Interventions. Emphasized throughout this book is the notion that cultural responsiveness is compromised if we deliver to ELs only instruction that was developed primarily for and validated with non-English learners. The preferred intervention-selection practice is to use methods researched and validated for use with diverse learners (e.g., CSR, LEA, reading response journals, graphic organizers; see Boele, 2016; Hoover, 2013; Hoover, Baca, & Klingner, 2016, for additional methods). Absent use of culturally and linguistically responsive research-based methods (e.g., district-mandated method or curriculum validated for use with primarily non-CLD learners) is the challenge to differentiate providing ELs sufficient opportunities to acquire knowledge and skills. Fortunately, research provides guidance into effective practices that assist educators to differentiate classroom instruction

Table 6.2 Thematic Practices for Culturally and Linguistically Responsive Instruction

Theme	*Description (Selected Examples)*
Connections	Helping students connect existing vocabulary and experiences to the learning of new knowledge and skills
Relevance	Incorporating and valuing students' diverse cultural teachings and practices into classroom instruction to strengthen engagement, motivation, and relevancy in teaching and learning
Native Language Use	Providing ELs with instructional supports and classroom opportunities to use their first language in completing academic tasks as well as in the acquisition of English
English Language Development	Instructional use of a variety of effective supports (e.g., word walls, sentence stems, visual illustrations) to help—for example, ELs in their (a) use of academic language, (b) development of English, and (c) use of English in classroom instruction
Materials	Incorporating a variety of classroom materials (e.g., visuals, graphic organizers, cultural stories, diagrams) to help ELs connect the concrete to the abstract, develop academic language, make connections to prior learning, or develop background knowledge
Differentiations	Varying instructional practice to incorporate research-based methods addressing differentiated ways of learning among ELs (e.g., explicit instruction, scaffolding, flexible groupings, sheltered instruction)
Assessment to Inform Instruction	Employing formative and summative progress monitoring in unit and lesson instruction to make timely and informed instructional adjustments based on achievement and affective data

for English language and other diverse learners (see August, Shanahan, & Shanahan, 2006; Gay, 2010; Hoover, Hopewell, & Sarris, 2014; Hoover, Klingner, Baca, & Patton, 2008; Hoover, Sarris, & Hill, 2015; Saunders, Goldenberg, & Marcelletti, 2013; Tharp et al., 2004; Valle, Waxman, Diaz, & Padrón, 2013; Zainuddin, Yahya, Morales-Jones, & Ariza, 2011). An example of one contemporary perspective and tool categorizes research-based instructional practices for delivering culturally and linguistically responsive instruction into seven instructional themes, as illustrated in Table 6.2, developed from the research of Hoover et al. (2015) and Hoover et al. (2014).

As shown, the seven themes incorporate different practices for educators to use in the delivery of culturally and linguistically responsive IEPs, especially when using methods or curricula not specifically designed for or validated with English language or other diverse learners. A research-based tool titled Core ESL Instructional Practices (CEIP) developed by Hoover et al. (2014) guides practitioners to self-examine use of each of the seven themes in their teaching and learning. The reader is referred to the CEIP tool for over forty research-based practices situated within the seven themes that will assist teachers to provide culturally and linguistically responsive IEP delivery for English language and other diverse learners.

Selecting and Using Curricular Materials (General and Specialized Curricula)

Similar to the selection and use of evidence-based interventions and research-based practices is the need to use curricular materials that provide a relevant context to learners. A relevant context exists when materials incorporate vocabulary, illustrations, diversity, and practices with which learners identify based on experiences, interest, and English language proficiency. A most important practice in the education of diverse learners is the selection of curricular materials meaningfully based on cultural and community teachings, heritage, and values. Increased motivation, interest, task completion, and other positive outcomes to daily teaching and learning occur best when students are able to identify with the topics, individuals, events, and/or story lines reflected in the curriculum materials. Therefore, a culturally and linguistically responsive IEP includes student strengths that identify the types of curricular materials that would best provide English language and other diverse learners sufficient opportunities to master the goals and objectives. Of critical importance is one's ability to make certain that the selected curricular materials do not present barriers to learning due to the study of material that lacks relevancy to diverse students. Selection of curriculum requires an understanding of both general and specialized curricular options for diverse learners with disabilities.

General Curriculum. Curricular materials, methods, and differentiations used in the delivery of core (Tier 1) or supplemental (Tier 2) instruction represent general education curricular practices typically implemented with all learners to meet diverse learning and behavioral needs in the classroom. As stated, English language and other diverse learners with IEPs are required to be educated within the general curriculum with peers as much as possible, based on disability needs. For ELs, this includes use of English language development methods and materials delivered in the general education settings (i.e., general education classroom; ELD instructional setting usually as a forty-five-minute block per day). Of particular note is that ELD is *general curriculum* and not specialized or special education curriculum, which is discussed next. ELD instruction is required of all ELs in general education classrooms delivered by highly prepared ELD, second language acquisition educators. As discussed throughout this book, attention to English language proficiency, academic language, and experiential background or vocabulary are just some of the many important features that represent culturally and linguistically responsive instruction to be continued in the general curriculum, once the student has been identified and placed for special education or specialized curriculum. The IEP should document access to, delivery of, and progress monitoring of both language and content growth in conjunction with instruction to meet stated IEP annual goals and objectives within general curriculum as much as possible.

Specialized Curriculum. Specialized curriculum (i.e., methods and materials) includes a range of practices designed to be (a) highly specific (i.e., targets a specific academic or behavioral need) and (b) intensive (i.e., requires additional support beyond general education Tiers 1 and 2 instruction) associated with the identified special education disability. The IDEA (2004) legislation identifies special education as specially designed instruction necessary to meet teaching and learning needs due to a disability. It refers to instruction, materials, or other supports "not part of the general-education curriculum" (Vaughn & Boss, 2012, p. 6). That is, curriculum that goes beyond that which is delivered through the general class instruction, as described above, falls into the broad category of specialized curriculum and may include these features:

- Fluency instruction five days per week, thirty minutes per day in addition to general class Tier 1 and Tier 2 fluency instruction
- Use of a specific, individualized multisensory method (e.g., Fernald method) to teach reading skills
- Extensive one-on-one instruction to remain on task and to self-manage learning
- Use of a highly specialized academic curriculum (e.g., Wilson Reading System)
- Need for participation in the use of an intensive social skills curriculum

These and similar practices become specialized since they are in addition to or replace materials and methods delivered through the general-education curriculum.

However, much confusion exists about instruction delivered to diverse learners concerning the category of best fit: general or specialized. Practices listed below fall within *general curriculum* and are often misunderstood as specialized for English language and other diverse learners and thereby are misunderstood as evidence of the need for special education:

- Daily ELD in the general classroom
- Daily ELD instruction in a pull-out setting
- Differentiations that accommodate English language proficiency and cultural diversity (e.g., increased wait time; cooperative rather than competitive learning; allotting extra time to build background knowledge, access prior knowledge, make cultural connections, use native language)
- Use of reading and other learning materials that depict or present diverse cultures
- Differentiations necessary to provide culturally and linguistically responsive instruction when using a curriculum not specifically developed or validated with diverse learners and/or lacking culturally relevant perspectives
- Use of alternate assessments to supplement normed tests to best provide ELs opportunities to demonstrate knowledge and skills based on current English academic language (e.g., multiple assessments, dynamic assessment, performance-based)

These and related educational practices (a) should be incorporated into delivery of general-education curriculum and assessment, (b) do not constitute *specialized* instruction or curriculum, and (c) are not acceptable reasons for requiring special education as defined by the IDEA (2004) regulations. Keep in mind that in many school systems, over 50 percent of the student population represents diverse cultures and/or languages. The reality that many established curricula and assessment devices do not account for diversity or different levels of English language proficiency does not provide justification for making use of the above practices as specialized, requiring a special education classification. Greater differentiation in the selection and delivery of needed educational supports in Tiers 1 and 2 for English language and other diverse learners, such as the above examples, provides increased opportunities for students and their teachers to deliver more appropriate general curriculum, while also reducing the misperception concerning need for specialized curriculum.

Special Education and Related Services

In addition to curriculum delivered through general or special education, other services may be required to best meet the learners' needs. These types of services support the instructional aspects of the IEP and include related assistance in a variety of areas including, but not limited to, (a) speech and language, (b) psychological, (c) occupational, (d) nursing, (e) mobility, (f) transportation, (g) technology, (h) social work/counseling, (i) transition, or (j) interpreting. When used with English language and other diverse learners, the selection and implementation of these services should be made within a cultural and linguistic context to be meaningful and relevant. Additionally, parental input should be sought and valued when one or more of these services is to be provided. The IEP contains a required item that specifically documents parental input, concerns, and supports, and these are especially relevant to the selection of related services for diverse students.

Supplemental Aids and Services

"Supplementary aids and services are intended to improve children's access to learning and their participation across the spectrum of academic, extracurricular, and nonacademic activities and settings" (Center for Parent Information and Resources [CPIR], 2013, Would You Like to Read About Another Component of the IEP section). Though this includes athletics, school clubs, and other extracurricular/nonacademic activities, this provision also includes "accommodations and modifications to the curriculum under study or the manner in which that content is presented or a child's progress is measured" (National Association of Special Education Teachers, 2006/2007, para. 1). The IDEA (2004) legislation specifically addresses this aspect of an IEP, providing wide latitude in implementation covering supplements related to both academic and nonacademic tasks, which have significant implications to IEPs for English language and other diverse learners. Discussing special considerations, Gibb and Dyches (2007) wrote:

If the student has limited English proficiency, the IEP team will consider the student's language needs as these needs relate to his or her IEP. (p. 72)

Addressing cultural diversity and English language development for learners with disabilities has been emphasized throughout the previous chapters and is appropriately addressed in the (a) PLAAFP statements, (b) measurable annual goals/short-term objectives, (c) accommodations, and (d) modifications included as supplemental aids or services. Researchers and advocacy educational organizations have provided examples of acceptable academic-related supplemental aids and services (e.g., CPIR, 2013; Gibb & Dyches, 2007; see also The Arc Greater Twin Cities website, Arcgreatertwincities.org). Many of these are relevant to the appropriate education of English language and other diverse learners, for example,

- preferential seating;
- necessary program modifications (e.g., culturally responsive materials);
- breakdown of directions into step-by-step instructions;
- primary language usage (e.g., first language use in addition to English);
- paired learning, cooperative grouping;
- wait time: extended time to complete tasks and assessments;
- shortened assignments (e.g., tasks broken down into multiple segments);
- use of multiple assessments to capture accurate knowledge and skill sets.

When considering the supplemental aids component of the IEP, it is important to again emphasize that attention to cultural diversity and language needs of diverse learners is integral to successful IEP development and implementation. These and similar types of supports listed above should be clearly identified on the IEP and be provided to English language and other diverse learners with disabilities as critical supplements to deliver culturally and linguistically responsive IEP instruction.

CONCLUSION

An IEP for English language and other diverse learners requires documentation of present performance, annual goals, modifications, related services, supplemental supports, accommodations, and general education participation that accounts for *both* English language proficiency and disability needs. The continued emphasis on English language development serves as a necessary foundation for developing and delivering an appropriate IEP for diverse learners. Operationalizing the suggestions and items presented in this chapter, along with others presented throughout this book, provides educators the best framework for delivering appropriate services to all diverse learners with disabilities, while simultaneously meeting the IDEA and IEP mandates.

7 Special Considerations and Diversity

By Le M. Tran, James R. Patton, and John J. Hoover

Practitioner's Perspective . . .

What are special considerations in an IEP? How are special considerations situated into a proper culturally and linguistically responsive context? How do functional behavioral assessments and associated behavioral intervention plans inform IEP development? What are some important factors that shape the selection of IEP special considerations for English language and other diverse learners?

The IDEA (2004) legislation stipulates that team members describe necessary special and/or related services by addressing certain required Individualized Education Program (IEP) components as discussed in the previous chapters. In addition to the core foundational components (e.g., PLAAFP, measurable annual goals), IEP services are supported by several other essential features, referred to as *special considerations*, which are addressed in this chapter: (a) supplemental aids/services, (b) accommodations and modifications, (c) assistive technology and services, (d) functional behavioral assessment and behavioral intervention plans, and (e) high stakes testing. While each of these topics might warrant separate chapters, our intent is to introduce the topics, providing sufficient detail for immediate application, with specific emphasis on their use with English language and other diverse learners.

SUPPLEMENTAL AIDS/SERVICES FOR DIVERSE LEARNERS

All too often, families from diverse cultures do not adequately participate in their child's IEP process due to factors such as lack of understanding, language differences, limited reaching out by educators, or various diverse cultural features and expectations about special education. However, there are ways in which school staff may empower the child and the family to be active and meaningful participants in the IEP process. One highly successful practice is to provide families with an opportunity to review a draft of the proposed IEP prior to the official annual meeting. This allows the family ample time to review and discuss with others and understand the key components of the IEP. In addition to displaying educator interest in accommodating parents and families, once the IEP is understood, parents are better equipped to contribute, generate questions, and assist with implementation at home. A second important practice is to keep the language simple and avoid technical jargon without an explanation. Also, stop and check for understanding, encourage families to ask for clarifications, and provide opportunities for families to contribute. In some instances, another family member or a member in the community may accompany the family to the IEP meeting. In other situations, families may rely on others who have more experience and knowledge with the education system to accompany them to the IEP meeting to ensure that appropriate services are being considered and provided to the child.

Translation

Use of physically translated content material and assessments for English learners or their family members may be necessary, going beyond the services of an interpreter, which is discussed in the next section. These efforts may be challenging and time-consuming to educators as they often follow a different set of guidelines and considerations than other resources. There are several cautions educators need to consider when using translation. Prior to translating the content materials or assessments, educators must first determine the level of language proficiency the English learner has in the native language by conducting informal interviews with the family and learner or by providing them with a questionnaire to complete. Use of English proficiency scores (e.g., WIDA ACCESS) usually provide educators with sufficient information about the English learner's language abilities commensurate with the content instruction received in the native language. The language proficiency level will determine whether or not it is appropriate for the student to receive translated materials to be incorporated into the IEP. However, a key consideration is that translation into the native language is only effective for those learners who have a solid foundation of that content in their native language (Kieffer, Lesaux, Rivera, & Francis, 2009).

Additionally, research informs us about the negative effects in the use of translations when there is a mismatch between the language of instruction and assessment (Kieffer et al., 2009). Since it is often difficult for some English learners to learn a new language and acquire content simultaneously, there must be a strong foundation of language to overlay with content (Goldenberg, 2013). Another possible constraint with the use of translation with English learners is the lack of resources to obtain high-quality translations for less common languages (Alt, Arizemendi, Beal, & Hurtado, 2013). To be most effective and appropriate, translations take into account the linguistic and cultural equivalence to elicit the same critical thinking and responses as in English, to ensure the same functional outcome (Alt et al., 2013). In some situations, similar concept or term equivalences do not exist in the English learner's native language.

Similarly, the language and method of communication with the family follow translation guidelines: (a) determine the family's preference of language and method by providing them with a questionnaire or conducting an oral interview, (b) provide families access to the IEP and all communications regarding their child in the language preferred and best understood, and (c) once the family language preference is determined, translate all important IEP documents and components (e.g., IEP, prior written notice, PLAAFP, goals, accommodations and modifications, related services, consent for services, e-mails) into that language. For phone calls and all scheduled meetings, the district is responsible for providing a translator. It is also essential to keep in mind that diverse learners' families' language preference for written and verbal communication may differ, depending on English knowledge levels and native language preference.

Interpreters

In addition or complementary to written translation is the service of providing interpretation of verbal discussion at IEP meetings. When utilizing district-provided interpreters during an IEP meeting or any other related verbal communications with the families, we recommend following a few key guidelines.

Briefing Prior to IEP Meeting. Schedule the interpreter well in advance once the IEP meeting time and date have been confirmed. Arrange for the interpreter to arrive at least ten minutes before the meeting to meet members of the team. At this time, the IEP team leader briefs the interpreter about the IEP meeting, clarifying various aspects such as the purpose of the meeting, agenda, any technical terms that will be used, and seating arrangements to facilitate discussion. This initial interaction provides the interpreter an opportunity to determine the appropriate vocabulary that should be used to convey conceptual meanings and topics in the parents' native language. The team leader and interpreter will also decide on the most appropriate style of interpretation (e.g., consecutive or simultaneous) as well as pace. The interpreter briefs the team, clarifying the role as one of providing direct translations of all verbal communications among and between the family and school members. Additionally, it is important to remember that interpreters interpret only what others verbally state and that they are not allowed to actively participate in the IEP meeting by providing any opinions or guidance to the family or school members.

Interactions During IEP Meeting. At the start of the meeting, introduce the interpreter along with all members present and acknowledge those who were unable to attend. All information discussed is confidential and everything said will be translated including any side conversations among the school and family members. Participants should keep sentences short, simple, and to the point. Speak one at a time in a slow and clear tone and allow the interpreter opportunity to translate every few sentences. Incorporate extra time for clarifications and questions throughout the meeting. Maintain eye contact with the family while speaking and listening, even though the communication is going through the interpreter (i.e., speak directly to the family members, not the interpreter).

Though a district-provided interpreter is typically used, instances exist in which someone other than a district person provides interpretation. For instance, the family may speak a language for which interpreters are not readily available in the district, or the family may elect to bring its own interpreter who might be someone from the community, another family member, or in some situations the student. In these types of situations, the interpreter guidelines discussed above may require adaptation due to the fact that the family interpreter may also be an active participant, as well as interpreter, in the IEP meeting. In these situations, speakers must balance the amount of eye contact displayed between the interpreter and family members. Any questions or concerns brought to attention by the interpreter must be addressed unless the family explicitly denies responses to these issues. In many cases, the adaptations necessary for these situations cannot always be preplanned and will therefore occur at the beginning and/or during the meeting. Additionally, other dynamics may exist when someone other than a district person provides interpretation or if the district is required to use an interpreter for a less frequently spoken language:

- The family of the learner may have differing opinions from that of a relative or community member providing the interpretation.
- When the student is the interpreter, English proficiency may not be sufficient to fully comprehend and interpret the concepts.
- Districts may not always have the highest quality interpreters, especially for less frequently spoken languages.
- Frequent checks for understanding may be required to ensure that the correct concepts are being conveyed to and understood by the family.
- There may be issues that arise that the family may not be comfortable discussing through the interpreter whether district provided, another family member, community member, or in front of the learner.
- Reluctance to discuss or accept school staff concerns about the child may surface.
- Conceptual equivalence of ideas or vocabulary may not exist in the native language to adequately convey meaning to the family.
- Differences between home/community and school structures and systems may exist, leading to insufficient background knowledge to build conceptual understanding of IEP concepts with family members, thereby requiring additional time and supports.
- Cultural philosophical differences especially in regard to disabilities and the way they are conceptualized and/or addressed may become evident.

ACCOMMODATIONS AND MODIFICATIONS

This section examines effective and realistic accommodations and modifications for documentation on IEPs when working with culturally and linguistically diverse learners. Accommodations and modifications identified on an IEP are distinct features yet are related, given that each is typically discussed within the "Special Education/Related Services and Supplemental Aids/Services" section of the IEP. The effectiveness of selected accommodations and modifications for diverse learners with disabilities is influenced by several factors including (a) cultural beliefs and teachings, (b) native and English language proficiency levels, and (c) most proficient language of instruction (Pennock-Roman & Rivera, 2011). For these reasons, IEP teams need to be aware of these factors when making decisions on which techniques to use. While "accommodations" and "modifications" are often interconnected in practice, these terms actually have key differences and are therefore presented separately since each reflects a unique set of skills.

Accommodations

According to the IDEA regulations "special education" is referred to as "specially designed instruction" [§300.39(a)(1)]. This particular term is further defined as "adapting, as appropriate to the needs of an eligible child under this part, the content, methodology, or delivery of instruction" [§300.39(b)(3)]. Providing an appropriate education to students with disabilities implies not only the implementation of evidence-based interventions to address needs (e.g., reading) but also the utilization of accommodative tactics and strategies that allow students to gain access to the general-education curriculum—whether the students are in special education or in general education.

Accommodations pertain to techniques that involve *how* students access the content being studied or assessed and, in turn, demonstrate that learning. An "accommodation is intended to help the student to fully access and participate in the general-education curriculum without changing the instructional content and without reducing the student's rate of learning" (Skinner, Pappas, & Davis, 2005, as quoted in Wright, 2011, p. 1). Various accommodative practices involve making changes to (a) the way teachers design instruction (i.e., present information), (b) ways to assist learners better interact with material (i.e., accessing learning), and (c) how students respond to instruction (i.e., demonstration of learning). Accommodations provide learners with resources and tools that level the playing field; however, students are still expected to learn the same content at the same proficiency level as their peers.

Table 7.1, developed from several sources (see Abedi, 2006; Kieffer et al., 2009; Klingner, Artiles, & Barletta, 2006; Pennock-Roman & Rivera, 2011), illustrates different types of accommodations, organized according to five general areas that are considered effective and appropriate for English language and other diverse learners with disabilities. Table 7.1 expands upon the accommodations summarized in Table 2.5, providing examples often used when constructing IEPs, including culturally and linguistically responsive (CLR) considerations. Each of the five general areas is discussed in more detail following the table.

Table 7.1 IEP Assessment and Instructional Accommodations

Area	Description	Accommodations	CLR Considerations
Setting	Changing the location for learning in the classroom or school provides the learner with increased motivation and confidence in abilities to attend to and complete the assessment and instructional tasks	• Separate and/or quiet setting • Small group • Preferential seating	Classroom arrangement varies across cultures such as where students prefer to be situated (e.g., rows, desks, small clusters, by gender). Ways in which learning occurs within a culture (e.g., all facing the teacher, through interpersonal interactions with extended dialogue) should be valued, often leading to the need to change from large to small group or to pairs when acquiring new skills to best motivate and elicit meaningful interactions and confidence.
Presentation	Changes to presentation of assessment or instructional material provide the learner with increased opportunities to acquire and/or demonstrate knowledge and skills	• Graphic organizer • Outline • Notes provided • Visuals • Audio • Read aloud • Simplified language • Lower-level reading texts • Accessing prior knowledge	If not already included in daily instruction, use of effective ESL best practices may be considered accommodations in some classroom situations (e.g., extended time for building background knowledge, incorporation of WIDA Can Do Descriptors, visual labeling, realia, manipulatives, simplified language, extended wait time) to directly accommodate equal access through presentation for students acquiring English as a second language. Also, providing notes or PowerPoint slides ahead of time allows learners to focus on the content and meaningful dialogue rather than on taking notes during the lectures or small-group discussions.
Response	Allowing the learner to respond in an alternate or different manner (e.g., oral vs. written, using computer vs. paper-pencil, portfolio) results in increased attention in learning and accuracy in demonstrating knowledge and skills	• Oral, written, portfolio • Dictation • Speech to text • Word processor • Alternative projects	Cultural preference and second language acquisition stage of development guide most appropriate or preferred response methods (e.g., some cultures adhere to oral tradition while others prefer a more visual method); emergent English speakers may be more successful providing oral responses over written or prefer to demonstrate knowledge through a performance-based project over multiple-choice test.

(Continued)

Table 7.1   (Continued)

Area	Description	Accommodations	CLR Considerations
Scheduling/ Assignments	Adjusting the format facilitates task completion (e.g., breaking task into three segments), and providing resources (e.g., dictionary, spell checker) allows the learner a fairer opportunity to demonstrate true abilities and skills	• Chunk • Scaffold • Dictionary: bilingual or English • Spell checker • Reduced multiple choice • No true/false • Word bank provided • Adjusted schedule • Alternative knowledge assessment	Use of bilingual dictionaries, English dictionaries, or spell checkers may benefit diverse learners who receive instruction in their native language and/or need additional support in English. Also, ways in which assignments and assessments are scheduled can be reformatted to allow diverse learners increased access to content knowledge and skills, reducing issues often associated with navigating ambiguity of instructions, questions, answers, and so on, frequently experienced in teaching and learning.
Time	Providing additional time facilitates increased task completion or greater accuracy in demonstrating knowledge and skills	• Extended time • Frequent breaks • Adjusted or no due dates	Students in the process of acquiring English as a second language often require extended wait time to successfully think through a question or issue prior to responding, and some cultures teach that taking more time to think about an issue is preferred over quick, immediate, or timed responses.

As shown, the various accommodations adjust how the learner receives, interacts with, and demonstrates learning while keeping the same proficiency level expectations as other students. It is also important to note that though the five accommodative areas are distinct, each is often implemented in integrated ways by addressing more than one area simultaneously (e.g., assessment presentation, setting, and response mode all implemented in the same testing situation). Supporting effective teaching and learning for diverse students is best achieved by attending to and valuing culturally and linguistically diverse backgrounds, family teachings, and other features brought to the school setting that must be recognized and incorporated into the IEP to provide appropriate education and curricular access. Though not all-inclusive, Table 7.1 provides a select list of specific accommodations. However, caution must be exercised when deciding which practices are most appropriate for diverse students, given different IEP situations, learning environments, English language proficiency, and cultural backgrounds relative to each of the five accommodation areas.

Setting. The setting reflects the environment and arrangement of the classroom within which the learner best works, with limited distractions, while fostering confidence and increased motivation. This may periodically include use of a separate workspace in or outside of the general classroom to complete tests and/or assignments because a quiet space is needed to allow for the student to work at her/his own pace without the pressure of time or other distractions. It is also important to recognize when establishing seating accommodations that in some cultures it is not customary for opposite genders to interact or sit near each other in the classroom. With this in mind, the ways in which the classroom is arranged can reflect cultural preference as well as facilitate positive peer interactions (e.g., rows, small groups, U-shape).

Presentation. The ways in which instructional content, assignments, and assessments are presented will have significant effects on the academic progress of English language and other diverse learners with disabilities. Some of the more effective methods for educating diverse learners that may be used as effective accommodations to ensure proper presentation, include the best practices of scaffolded English language development, establishing appropriate wait time, or use of visuals, concept maps, and instructional diagrams commensurate with English language proficiency level (Abedi, 2006; Hoover, Baca, & Klingner, 2016; Hoover, Sarris, & Hill, 2015; Kieffer et al., 2009; Pennock-Roman & Rivera, 2011). The complexity of language often presents unique challenges to both students and educators, requiring accommodations to address diverse learners' cognitive load to best facilitate processing of material to reduce misinterpretations of concepts and skills (Abedi, 2006). In addition, when provided word walls, sentence stems, or visual aids, diverse learners more effectively attend to content instruction, increasing comprehension and generalization. Similarly, use of graphic organizers provides a strategy to assist English language and other diverse learners to task analyze academic work, enabling them to identify, comprehend, and master key points of reading, writing, language, and mathematical concepts.

Response. Allowing English language and other diverse learners some variation in multiple preferred and appropriate methods of demonstrating knowledge and understanding of content material (e.g., oral, short answer, multiple choice, dictation, speech to text, word processor, performance based, curriculum based) is essential to reducing instructional and assessment bias needed to improve accuracy in learning (Hoover & Klingner, 2011). For example, assessment and learning norms vary among cultures and depend on educational experiences in the native community, thereby contributing significantly to determining appropriate classroom expectations in teaching and learning (e.g., speaking only when called on, increased observation over speaking, refraining from asking questions, responding to open-ended items to form his/her own interpretation rather than memorizing isolated facts, thinking through an idea for an extended period of time over quick response). These and similar cultural and linguistic variations have important effects on diverse learners' academic progress and associated demonstration of knowledge unless methods for response are accommodated as necessary.

Scheduling/Assignments. When determining the best accommodations for a particular task, educators must decide if altering the schedule to best complete assignments is necessary. For example, determining to what extent it is beneficial for the student to (a) receive extended time to complete the task in its entirety, (b) receive extra practice, or (c) be provided two-part shorter assignments to complete the entire task represent typical scheduling features that should be documented on the IEP when appropriate. Also, ways to alter test formats should focus on providing tools or eliminating ambiguous or unique wording if unfamiliar to the learner (e.g., negation, true/false, reduced multiple choice, academic language). Use of these types of scheduling adjustments assists diverse learners to focus more directly on the essentials of the task within the complexities of language acquisition rather than on negotiating complex schedules of which they may be unfamiliar.

Time. The amount of time one should provide diverse learners to complete a task or provide a response whether orally (e.g., class discussion) or written (e.g., assignments, activities, assessments) is highly cultural, requiring specific consideration when accommodations are included in IEP development. The concept of time may vary considerably for some learners from culturally and linguistically diverse backgrounds, especially when time approximations are preferred over strict time allotments typically seen in US schools (Hoover & deBettencourt, in press). Therefore, to best accommodate learning, some English language and other diverse learners will need increased time considerations to process language, respond to requests, engage in reading comprehension topics, or complete similar instructional and assessment demands. The challenges associated with processing a second language, building background knowledge, or addressing unfamiliar vocabulary may require the allotment of additional time for many diverse learners, and this should be documented on the IEP as a necessary accommodation.

In summary, as illustrated in Table 7.1 and brief discussions, English language and other diverse learners often require culturally and linguistically responsive instructional and assessment accommodations to best perform in today's classrooms. Closely related, yet distinctly different, is the use of modifications in teaching and learning to further benefit the education of culturally and linguistically diverse exceptional learners.

Modifications

Modifications differ from accommodations in that these reflect adjustments to the expectations associated with the level and amount of content and skills to be acquired and mastered by the learner. "A modification changes the expectations of what a student is expected to know or do—typically by lowering the academic standards against which the student is to be evaluated" (Wright, 2011, p. 1). Therefore, modifications refer to changes to curricular topics that ultimately alter the anticipated outcomes for the learner. When used appropriately for students with disabilities, modifications of *what* the student learns facilitates increased success by more accurately matching expectations with instructional level. However, modifying curricular expectations and content requires careful thought and planning since the student may not be receiving the same level of content or subjected to the same performance expectations as other students in a particular grade or class.

Distinguishing Between Modifications and Accommodations

As discussed above, modifications pertain to adjusting or modifying the *what* of learning and accommodations adjust the *how* of learning. Therefore, the same instructional situation and content may simultaneously include both accommodations and modifications. However, it is essential that educators be clear as to which type of instructional change is being considered and documented on a learner's IEP to provide the most accurate education. Table 7.2 illustrates an example of modifications and accommodations for the same instructional activity, demonstrating their integrated uses.

As shown, the modifications directly affect the amount (i.e., reduction of 20 percent of number of topics to master) and level of expectation (i.e., focus on knowledge, comprehension level questions only), based on disability, while the accommodations maintain the same level of expectation (i.e., response to synthesis, evaluation level questions) with some adjustments made to provide better access to the material (i.e., use of video in addition to reading story) and demonstration of knowledge and skills (i.e., permitted to orally respond to items rather than in writing). Therefore, modifications are important educational practices to appropriately refine specific aspects of instruction and assessment to best meet the instructional level needs of diverse learners with disabilities, whereas accommodations maintain the same level of expectation seen for all students through adjustments to how the material is acquired and skills demonstrated. It is up to educators to make certain that instruction is culturally and linguistically responsive, supplemented by meaningful and relevant accommodations and modifications to provide sufficient opportunities to learn as noted in the previous chapters of this book.

Table 7.2 Modifying and Accommodating a Sample Instructional Activity

Instructional Activity/ Evaluation	*Select Modifications*	*Select Accommodations*
Activity Read in small groups *Romeo and Juliet* and respond to higher-level comprehension questions for ten topics found in the material **Evaluation** Students respond in writing with 90% accuracy to synthesis and evaluation questions, demonstrating comprehension of key topics in the reading material	• Reduce the number of reading topics for mastery by 20% (i.e., 8 versus 10) • Focus initially on responses to understanding and remembering level skills and questions followed by applying, analyzing, and evaluating level items in reading • Set accuracy level to 80% rather than 90%	• Alternative textual materials (e.g., culturally relevant topics) • Bilingual peers use first language to help second language learners understand concepts in English • Use of media (e.g., films, cartoons) to engage with story • Specially designed questions, in both first and second languages, to increase access to material • Alternative assessment techniques (e.g., oral versus written responses) to accurately demonstrate knowledge and skills

ASSISTIVE TECHNOLOGY AND SERVICES

Different types of technologies are available in today's world, such as (a) personal technology (i.e., technology we use to enhance our everyday lives—e.g., GPS directions), (b) workplace technology (i.e., technology required to perform certain work activities—e.g., barcodes to track inventory), (c) instructional technology (i.e., technology used to enrich learning for students and teachers—e.g., polling apps), or (d) assistive technology (i.e., technology that certain individuals "require" to be able to perform certain daily activities—e.g., voice-input software for someone who has difficulties with writing). While each of these and similar technologies mentioned above have merit for all students, the IDEA legislation requires only that IEP consideration be given to the assistive technology (AT) needs of students with disabilities.

What the Law Requires

The IDEA legislation requires that the IEP team consider whether a student with a disability requires use of a technological device and/or service in order to (a) best access curriculum and (b) receive sufficient opportunities to receive an appropriate education. If educators or parents believe that a student would benefit from the use of an AT device or service, an evaluation of the need for AT should be conducted to best inform IEP development.

According to IDEA 2004, an AT device is defined as "any item, piece of equipment, or product system, whether acquired commercially, off the shelf, modified, or customized that is used to increase, maintain, or improve the functional capabilities of children with disabilities" (34 CFR §300.5). An AT *device* is a specific piece of equipment used in school and, possibly, at home. AT *services* are more general in nature and, as Siegel (2014) notes, may include one or more of the following:

- Evaluating how the child functions in his/her customary environment
- Leasing or purchasing assistive technology devices
- Using and coordinating other therapies, interventions, or services in conjunction with such technology
- Training and technical assistance for the child, the child's family, and the educational staff. (pp. 31–32)

The need for an AT device is determined on a case-by-case basis (Norlin, 2009), and a predetermined list of devices for a particular disability is not allowed. If an AT device is found to be needed, it is possible that the student can use this device inside and/or outside of school.

AT Considerations for Diverse Learners

Use of assistive technology with diverse learners adheres to the same parameters, guidelines, and purposes as with all students. One area of consideration, however, is cultural perspective in use of technology within diverse communities.

In some instances, CLD learners may lack exposure to or experience with even the most basic forms of technology (see Colorincolorado.org) and will therefore require some added supports when initially using assistive technology. Additionally, similar to other instructional aspects discussed throughout this book, any use of assistive technology should be consistent with language proficiency for English learners so the assistive technology properly supports, rather than deters, the student's academic, language, or social-emotional development.

One particular type of assistive technology that may be of significant value to English learners is use of a text reader, which allows for audible output of the reading material. This feature allows the student to hear the material read while simultaneously reading the printed page. This practice facilitates increases in comprehension and should be considered during IEP development and implementation.

Another potentially beneficial assistive tool is use of "word prediction" to assist with writing (see National Center to Improve Practice online, www2.edc.org/NCIP), especially with second language learners who know what they wish to say yet may be unable to access the proper English language vocabulary to best express themselves in writing. This feature is now commonly found on smartphones and is also available on tablets that are often used in classroom settings. Similarly, success may also be found when using assistive tools to visually illustrate a picture along with the written language to further develop English academic vocabulary and related language skills.

Overall, use of assistive technology to support academic and language development of diverse learners with disabilities provides increased opportunities to learn as progress toward mastery of IEP goals and objectives is made.

FUNCTIONAL BEHAVIORAL ASSESSMENT AND BEHAVIORAL INTERVENTION PLANS

The underlying concepts shaping a functional behavioral assessment (FBA) and a behavioral intervention plan (BIP) have been used in the field of special education for many years. However, it was only with the 1997 amendments to the IDEA regulations that a mandate for performing FBAs and BIPs began. Initially, much of the focus on the use of FBAs and BIPs was in relation to change of placement as a reaction to disciplinary concerns. Over time, however, use of these techniques evolved into a more generalized set of practices used to understand, clarify, and address behaviors that interfere with learners' progress both academically and socially.

A functional behavioral assessment is a systematic method for observing and clarifying behavior, particularly undesirable behavior, leading to plausible hypotheses for why that behavior exists and is maintained (i.e., reinforced). The behavioral intervention plan, is a document that contains suggested behavior management procedures to address the challenging behavior analyzed and clarified during the FBA process. As McConnell, Patton, and Polloway (2006) assert, "Teachers and other professionals involved in changing behavior must identify the underlying causes and functions of the behavior and analyze the existing context that contributes to the behaviors that are of concern" (p. vii).

Behavioral Intervention Plans and the Law

IDEA 2004 requires that the IEP team develop a behavioral intervention plan for any student whose behavior interferes with his/her own learning or the learning of others [34 C.F.R. §300.324(a)(2)(i)]. Additionally, though the IDEA legislation does not explicitly require completion of an FBA, completion of an FBA is necessary to properly develop the behavioral intervention plan. Therefore, expertise with the two-stage FBA and BIP development process is essential to meeting the IEP demands of learners who exhibit significant behavioral disorders. The BIP becomes part of the IEP once it is developed for a student who is served under IDEA.

McConnell et al. (2006) suggest that when a behavioral concern arises, educators should attend to the connected uses of an FBA and associated BIP in several situations:

- As part of the prereferral intervention process
- When writing behavior plans for students served under Section 504
- To positively support students whose behavior impedes their learning
- To positively support students whose behavior impedes others' learning
- When required by IDEA 2004, because of long-term removal, including an interim alternative educational setting (IAES)
- When required by IDEA 2004 to conduct a manifestation determination (pp. x–xi)

Key Components

Presented in this section are key elements of FBAs and BIPs. Initially, some of these elements such as the "manifestation determination" (i.e., determination of whether the behavior in question is related to the student's disability) will be needed in certain situations (e.g., a major disciplinary action that involves a change of placement). Our intent is to provide an overview of these two important techniques, sufficient to understand their uses in IEP development. Readers are referred to several other sources (for example, Cipani & Schock, 2010; McConnell et al., 2006; Steege & Watson, 2009) for more detailed coverage of these topics.

Functional Behavioral Assessment. The basic function of an FBA is to determine plausible explanations for a behavior's occurrence. To accomplish this, school-based personnel must have a set of skills and tools to effectively arrive at hypotheses clarifying why a behavior is potentially occurring. In essence, as McConnell and colleagues (2006) point out, the FBA "provides a structured way to analyze the contextual aspects of a behavior by asking for an exact description of the behavior in question along with information regarding precipitating conditions, consequences that follow the behavior, and a hypothesis about the purpose or purposes the behavior serves" (p. xii). The major elements necessary to complete an FBA are

- general identification of the behavior in question;
- listing of specific techniques used to analyze the behavior—this would include interview notes, observation records, rating scale data, or any other type of evaluation that contributes to an understanding of the behavior;
- description of precipitating conditions (setting, time of day, and other descriptor information);
- description of the specific behavior;
- description of the consequences (events that typically follow the behavior);
- hypotheses as to the function of the behavior;
- review of related information/considerations such as cultural/linguistic features, academic, social/peer, or family/community factors.

Once information and evidence are gathered, recorded, and summarized, educators examine the material generating hypotheses about the behavior in question. The development of the BIP is subsequently completed if the behavior is considered significant to the detriment of the education of the learner and/or peers.

Behavioral Intervention Plan. Although IDEA requires a behavioral intervention plan for learners whose behavior significantly interferes with teaching and learning, it provides little guidance as to what an actual BIP should look like and include. However, the fundamental essence of this document is to provide a plan of action for addressing the problematic behavior(s) based on the hypotheses for why the behavior exists and is reinforced. The development of an effective BIP depends greatly upon the knowledge and skill sets of the professionals who are involved in its development and that of the FBA upon which the BIP is based.

Once developed, the behavioral intervention plan must be shared with all school personnel who will have contact with the student whose behavior is at issue. According to McConnell and colleagues (2006), an effective BIP should include the following elements:

- Statement of overall behavioral goals to be achieved
- Specific interventions intended to change the student's behavior
- Persons responsible for implementing the proposed interventions
- BIP evaluation methods and timelines

In addition, periodic meetings among educators most involved with the learner should occur to evaluate progress and discuss the need for BIP adjustments for best behavior results. Also, documentation of the most appropriate reinforcers for the learner should be included (Hoover, 2017), along with attention to ways in which the BIP connects with the school-wide positive behavioral interventions and supports (PBIS) program.

Considerations for Diverse Learners

Exhibited school behavior is often a direct function of a diverse learner's cultural and linguistic context and background (Hoover, Baca, & Klingner, 2016; Hoover, Klingner, Baca, L. M., & Patton, 2008); therefore, it is essential that school personnel incorporate responsive practices when conducting an FBA and developing a BIP. Specifically, Moreno, Wong-Lo, and Bullock (2014) emphasize the significance of making certain that the behavioral clarification process incorporate an "understanding of the social/behavioral needs of students from CLD backgrounds as a means to differentiate cultural differences from disability indicators" (p. 59). Drawing on research and literature discussing the topic of behavior and cultural/linguistic diversity, the following suggestions and cautions are provided to guide educators in their decision making when examining the behaviors of English language and other diverse students in IEP development:

- Recognize that some behaviors may not be seen as problematic in certain cultures or family situations (i.e., the spectrum of what is considered "normal" is broader in some communities than others; Harry & Klingner, 2014).
- Understand the potential cultural stigma of having a child labeled with a disability (e.g., problematic behavior that some families go to great lengths to shelter).
- Interview family members by incorporating a culturally responsive functional interview into the process (e.g., "view the student and family's culture as foundational rather than superficial" [Moreno et al., 2014, p. 63]).
- If necessary, consult with and include individuals who are from the student's culture to more clearly understand the diverse context shaping a behavior.
- Follow the guidelines provided in the first section of this chapter on using interpreters if school personnel are not fluent in the language used by family members. For example, if school personnel are involved in interviewing family members, it is extremely important that the interviewer "is a professionally competent speaker (i.e., proficient in speaking, reading, writing of the family's native language" [Moreno et al., 2014, p. 66]).
- Incorporate culturally and linguistically responsive behavioral interventions and practices (see Hoover, Hopewell, & Sarris, 2014; Hoover et al., 2015) into BIPs to value cultural teachings and norms, being consistent with home and community heritages while accessing and using learners' funds of knowledge.

The sample FBA and BIP at the end of this chapter provides an example of a culturally and linguistically responsive functional behavioral assessment and behavioral intervention plan for a tenth-grade student currently residing in the United States whom we identity as Amir. The example demonstrates the behaviors that clearly interfere with learning, which require specific attention, while also respecting the learner's home cultural context. The example demonstrates the key components of the behavioral intervention process, the identified problematic behaviors, and how these behaviors are being addressed in culturally responsive ways.

HIGH STAKES ASSESSMENT, DIVERSITY, AND IEPs

One of the more controversial issues regarding IEPs is the use of high stakes testing to determine achievement of annual goals. At issue is that "state policies commonly assume that high stakes assessments are appropriate for judging whether students have met the standards established by the state" (Duran, 2011, p. 118). High stakes refers to large-scale assessment that leads to significant or *high stakes* decisions about students, educators, and schools including (a) grade promotion, (b) identifying learners at risk, (c) individual school accountability, (d) secondary school graduation, (e) need to continue or discontinue special education services, (f) high standards accountability for students with disabilities, or (g) overall school system effectiveness (Goh, 2004; Iris Center for Training, 2011). This is in contrast to *low stakes* assessment from which important decisions are made yet which lack the significant, longer-term impactful effects seen in high stakes assessments (Duran, 2011).

Educators who rely on high stakes assessments to monitor annual outcomes documented on IEPs assume that the test results accurately show the extent to which the student has met the standard, or part of a standard, from which the annual goal is derived. Unfortunately for many English language and other diverse learners, results from high stakes assessments completed in English may misinform educators about students' true progress, due to cultural bias and/or second language acquisition levels (i.e., the English language vocabulary required to successfully take a high stakes test is beyond the level possessed by the English as a second language learner; Basterra, Trumbull, & Solano-Flores, 2011). See Table 2.3 in this book.

What the Law Requires

The most recent version of the IDEA (2004) legislation states that students with disabilities are to be included in general state and district assessment programs and, where appropriate, as documented on the IEP, accommodations and/or alternative assessments may be used (Yell, Katsiyannis, Collins, & Losinski, 2012). Federal legislation also prohibits states and school districts from limiting or denying accommodations, which should be clearly documented on the learners' IEPs (Wright & Wright, 2016). The use of high stakes assessments initially increased in necessity due to mandates found in the previous law, No Child Left Behind (NCLB), which was replaced in 2015 by the Every Student Succeeds Act (ESSA). Though ESSA continues to require state assessments, greater flexibility exists to allow each state to determine its own process and tests to determine district accountability with student progress. States must continue to measure progress in reading and mathematics annually in Grades 3–8 and once during the secondary grades and in science three times between Grades 3 and 12.

Though high stakes assessment continues for all learners, many educators question use of standardized, large-scale tests in educational decision making due to their limited scope—lacking sufficient comprehensiveness to be of value in making critical educational decisions (Darling-Hammond, 2002; Goh, 2004).

Considerations for Diverse Students

In addition to the general concerns described above, high stakes assessment use with English language and other diverse learners provides other unique challenges such as the following issues as discussed in several sources, including Basterra et al. (2011), Duran (2011), Goh (2004), and Hoover et al. (2008):

- High stakes assessments often lack sufficient reliability and validity for use with English learners.
- High stakes results may erroneously lead to remediation recommendations for English learners that may be less than appropriate or necessary in their teaching and learning.
- Use of one annual high stakes assessment score, rather than the preferred multiple forms of assessments, often underestimates the true academic progress of English learners.
- Unless sufficient opportunities to learn are provided to English learners by delivering culturally and linguistically responsive instruction, use of many high stakes assessments may be inappropriate.

Overall, of critical concern is the extent to which the high stakes assessment accurately reflects the (a) standard(s) to which IEP annual goals and associated objectives are connected, (b) use of research-based instructional methods that provide English language and other diverse learners with culturally and linguistically responsive learning experiences, and (c) knowledge and skills directly taught in the classroom.

In summary, if use of a high stakes test is incorporated in the IEP, it should also include necessary assessment accommodations, along with culturally and linguistically responsive instructional modifications to ensure accurate results as discussed in other chapters in this book.

CONCLUSION

A variety of special considerations requires educator attention to best develop and implement an IEP for English language and other diverse learners. These include supplemental aids and services, accommodations and modifications, uses of assistive technology, and completion of functional behavioral assessments and behavioral intervention plans, along with special considerations when using high stakes assessments to measure learner progress. Adhering to the principles, practices, and recommendations relevant to delivering culturally and linguistically responsive IEPs discussed throughout this chapter and book, diverse learners are provided increased opportunities to appropriately access curriculum and demonstrate learning in general and special education environments.

Behavioral Intervention Planning–Third Edition

BIP-3

Functional Behavioral Assessment (FBA)

Steps for completing this form can be found on pages 9 through 13 in the manual.

Student's Name: _Amir   10ᵗʰ grade_

Background Information

The following sources of background information were considered for this FBA.

✔ Parent information/interview (see Parent Contact form) Attached? ✔Yes ☐No
Summary of parent information: _Has no prior experiences working with female teachers or students. He exhibits verbal aggression towards his mother and sisters_

Behavior checklist or rating scale Attached? ☐Yes ☐No
Summary of checklist or rating scale:

✔ Recent observation data (see data collection forms) Attached? ✔Yes ☐No
Summary of observations: _frequency data per class period, teacher reports and observations of verbal aggressions towards females._

✔ Discipline records Attached? ✔Yes ☐No
Summary of discipline records: _5- In-school suspensions (ISS) 2 - out of school suspension (OSS)_

✔ Assessment information Attached? ✔Yes ☐No
Summary of assessment information: _Amir has ADHD and bipolar disorder_

Information from other agencies or service providers Attached? ☐Yes ☐No
Summary of other information:

Review of prior BIP (see Reasons and Review form, Section Three) Attached? ☐Yes ☐No
Summary:

✔ Student interview/conference Attached? ☐Yes ☐No
Summary: _Amir reports that in his culture he does not have to use respectful language when speaking to females_

Video- or audiotape Attached? ☐Yes ☐No
Summary:

✔ Teacher/administrator interview(s) Attached? ☐Yes ☐No
Summary: _ESL teacher - believes part of his behavior is due to cultural differences, but part is related to his bipolar disorder_

Additional copies of this form (#12258) may be purchased from
PRO-ED, 8700 Shoal Creek Blvd., Austin, TX 78757-6897
800/897-3202, Fax 800/397-7633, www.proedinc.com
ISBN-13 978-1416401889
ISBN-10 1416401881

Student's Name: _Amir_

Analysis of Behavior

Prioritized Behavior # 1   verbal aggression

Antecedents (Events or conditions occurring before or triggering the behavior)	Behavior* (Exactly what the student does or does not do)	Consequences (Actions or events occurring after the behavior)	Function of Behavior (Hypothesized purpose of the behavior)
✓ Setting, subject, or class: *female teacher or seated next to a female peer* Time of day:	Behavior in observable, measurable terms: *verbal aggression towards females*	Behavior is ignored ☐ Planned ☐ Unplanned ☐ Peer attention	✓ Avoidance or escape ✓ Avoid a directive or request ☐ Avoid an assignment ✓ Escape a situation or a person
✓ Person(s): *female teacher/ students* Interruption in routine:	Baseline measures of behavior Frequency of behavior: *2 per class*	✓ Adult attention ☐ Reminder(s) ✓ Repeated directive or request ✓ Private meeting or conference ✓ Reprimand or warning ☐ Change in directive or request	Attention Gain peer attention Gain adult attention ✓ Self-control issue ✓ Express frustration ☐ Express anger ☐ Vengeance ✓ Power or control ✓ Intimidation
✓ Directive or request to: *complete task, any directives* Consequences imposed:	Duration of behavior: *5 - 10 mins per incident*	Loss of privilege:	Sensory or emotional reaction Fear or anxiety Sensory relief or stimulation
Lack of social attention:	Intensity of behavior: *escalates to loud yelling and leaves the classroom*	✓ Time out in classroom ✓ Administrative consequences: *ISS → OSS*	✓ Other(s): *cultural habits*
✓ Difficulty or frustration: *interactions with females*			
✓ Other(s): *group work with mixed gender*		✓ Parent contact Other(s):	

* Observation forms for collecting data are available in Appendix D.

Behavioral Intervention Planning–Third Edition

BIP-3

Behavioral Intervention Plan (BIP)

Steps for completing this form can be found on pages 15 through 19 in the manual.

Student's Name: _Amir_

Behavior # 1

Behavior To Be Decreased: Verbal Aggression

Replacement Behavior: Uses respectful language to express feeling

Specific Behavioral Objective	Interventions*	Person(s) Responsible	Evaluation Method(s)/Timeline
Amir will: use respectful language to express feelings under these conditions: when interacting with female teachers & classmates To meet these criteria: improve to 100% of time	Positive environmental supports: assigned seating away from female peers, no mixed gender group work Instructional strategies: agression management strategies Positive reinforcement: 15 mins of free time on Fridays with ESL teacher Reductive consequences:** In-school suspension call to parents	Amir will: practice new ways to express feelings, ignore female classmates and uses respectful language with teachers teachers will: model appropriate language, provide visual & verbal cues counselor/social worker will: provide aggression management strategies	Method(s): check teacher reports, discipline referrals, observation, conference with Amir Timeline: teacher check-in/referrals weekly observations - monthly conference - bimonthly

Additional information:

* Interventions must include positive behavior supports (positive environmental supports and positive reinforcement). The BIP may not contain only reductive consequences.

** All students are subject to the student code of conduct (SCC). Short-term disciplinary consequences that do not involve a change of placement may be imposed for any SCC violation.

Additional copies of this form (#12259) may be purchased from
PRO-ED, 8700 Shoal Creek Blvd., Austin, TX 78757-6897
800/897-3202, Fax 800/397-7633, www.proedinc.com

ISBN-13 978-1416401896
ISBN-10 1416401896-X

8 IEP Progress Monitoring and Diverse Needs

Practitioner's Perspective . . .

What are essential skills for implementing progress monitoring with English language and other diverse learners? Why is curriculum-based measurement an effective process for monitoring IEP progress toward annual goals and objectives? What are special considerations when monitoring and interpreting academic and functional behavior progress of diverse learners?

PROGRESS MONITORING DEFINED AND OVERVIEW

Fundamental to all Individualized Education Programs (IEPs) is documentation of how progress toward annual goals and short-term objectives is measured, charted, and results interpreted. When considering the monitoring of IEP progress for English language and other diverse learners, it is essential to consider the issues previously presented in Chapters 1 and 2, along with effective measurement strategies documented over time in the literature (e.g., Basterra, Trumbull, & Solano-Flores, 2011; Gottlieb, 2006; Hoover & Klingner, 2011), to ensure that valid and reliable progress-monitoring procedures are used. The three Multi-Tiered System of Supports (MTSS) assessment methods of screening, monitoring, and diagnostic are important in measuring progress toward IEP annual goals and objectives. However, of particular concern in IEP development for English language and other diverse learners is the use of culturally and linguistically responsive monitoring tools and procedures to measure ongoing progress.

Progress monitoring refers to the task of systematically gathering assessment data to determine the extent to which a student responds to evidence-based instruction by monitoring progress on a frequent basis (e.g., monthly, weekly, daily; Hoover, 2009). Progress-monitoring tools typically include a variety of criterion-referenced measures, such as running records, Dynamic Indicator of Basic Early Literacy Skills (DIBELS), Academic Improvement Measurement System based on the web (AIMSweb), Development Reading Assessment (2nd ed.; DRA2), or select educator-developed curriculum-based measurement procedures.

Key to the effective monitoring of progress for diverse learners is use of multiple tools or procedures validated for use with culturally and linguistically diverse (CLD) students. Though a variety of features are important to consider when implementing IEP monitoring procedures for diverse learners, four are highlighted in these discussions: (1) culturally responsive monitoring competencies, (2) multiple monitoring procedures, (3) curriculum-based measurement, and (4) special considerations when interpreting monitoring results for diverse learners.

CULTURALLY RESPONSIVE MONITORING COMPETENCIES

Two prominent issues that challenge both educators and diverse learners if not properly considered in the IEP progress-monitoring process are (1) academic language factors (see Chapter 3) that influence progress-monitoring performance, which, in turn, influence educator perceptions about progress; and (2) English learners' (ELs') English proficiency levels situated at the developing or emerging stages, being especially vulnerable to misinterpretation of progress-monitoring results due to second language development needs that may appear to be indicative of lack of progress or a disability. Educators conducting monitoring of an EL's IEP progress must keep in mind several general assessment characteristics as summarized by Hoover (2016b):

1. English learners often perform lower than non-ELs on content-based monitoring measures (i.e., reading, math, science, social sciences), even though they might not actually know less than their non-EL peers.

2. Lower levels of English language proficiency (i.e., WIDA ACCESS Levels 2, 3, 4) impact both instruction and progress-monitoring results.

3. Progress-monitoring tools and processes (e.g., DRA2, DIBELS, AIMSweb) typically used with ELs often have lower validity and reliability than when used with non-ELs, especially for those at the lower end of the English proficiency spectrum (Abedi, 2004), that is, WIDA ACCESS Levels 1–4.

4. Limited English academic language proficiency reflects measurement error, thereby affecting validity and reliability of the progress monitoring (Basterra et al., 2011).

Table 8.1 provides a checklist of select competencies to assist educators in developing and implementing effective IEP progress monitoring for diverse learners by addressing the assessment characteristics discussed above.

Classroom teachers and other educators of diverse learners should self-assess abilities with the competencies listed in Table 8.1 to ensure they possess these needed skill sets prior to engaging in the development and implementation of progress monitoring of diverse learners' IEP annual goals and objectives.

Table 8.1 Knowledge and Skills Checklist for Effective IEP Progress Monitoring of Diverse Learners

Instructions: Educators completing IEP progress monitoring for English language and other diverse learners should possess the following competencies (*Check each item once confirmation exists in the progress-monitoring situation*). ***Educators who conduct IEP progress monitoring for diverse learners possess . . .***
___ Knowledge of the appropriate use of progress-monitoring instruments and procedures commensurate with English language proficiency and first language abilities
___ Knowledge of the principles needed to select a progress-monitoring device or process designed for use with diverse students, including but not limited to consideration of reliability, validity, and sources of cultural or linguistic bias
___ Knowledge of limitations of various progress-monitoring devices and practices due to student English language proficiency levels and cultural background and teachings
___ Ability to apply progress-monitoring results to identify (a) growth from baseline skills and comprehension levels, (b) conditions under which skill acquisition occurs best, (c) the proper gradual-release sequence for instructional activities, and (d) needed instructional adjustments reflecting culturally and linguistically responsive teaching
___ Knowledge and application of appropriate collaboration skills necessary for conducting IEP progress monitoring toward annual goals and associated objectives
___ Ability to develop or adapt existing progress-monitoring instruments for English language and other diverse learners, which may include (a) accommodating academic language, (b) valuing cultural perspectives, (c) developing new normative data appropriate to the diverse population in the district or school, and (d) developing curriculum-based measurements appropriate to the population and content area of instruction
___ Knowledge of second language acquisition stages and factors that influence second language development including motivation, attitude, cognition, and first language; apply this knowledge in progress monitoring
___ Ability to analyze progress-monitoring devices and procedures for needed English academic language, and compare with English learners' English academic language proficiency, using only those devices in which an acceptable match exists
___ Knowledge of cultural factors and influences, including ways of learning and teaching, as they relate to the progress-monitoring environment
___ Knowledge of the dynamics of progress-monitoring procedures, including but not limited to strategies for (a) establishing rapport, (b) using appropriate nonverbal or native language communication, or (c) providing methods and techniques of needed language interpretation
___ Ability to plan and execute progress-monitoring conferences with colleagues, parents/guardians, and students to use in the formative teaching and learning process

Source: Adapted by permission from Hoover (2016b).

PROGRESS-MONITORING PRACTICES

Once the competencies described in the checklist in Table 8.1 are confirmed, the task of selecting progress-monitoring practices and associated devices begins. A most fundamental principle in the assessment of English language and other diverse learners is the need for using multiple forms of monitoring to make certain that language and cultural diversity are recognized and valued (Hoover, Baca, & Klingner, 2016). That is, frequently a diverse learner may be able to best demonstrate performance in some skill areas through one type of monitoring device or practice and other skills through other practices (Basterra et al., 2011). When developing the IEP for English language and other diverse learners, educators should consider the need for using different practices for monitoring the same skill sets (i.e., one size of monitoring does not fit all monitoring needs). In particular, selection and use of progress-monitoring practices and associated tools require consideration of cultural and linguistic responsiveness, to ensure validity leading to accurate results, appropriate instructional decisions, and responsive adjustments.

> Progress monitoring that fails to reflect culturally and linguistically diverse features the student brings to the teaching and learning environment contributes to misinterpretation of results as lack of progress when in reality results reflect use of biased or invalid practices or tools.

Table 8.2, developed from several sources (see Hoover, 2009, 2013; Hoover & Klingner, 2011; O'Malley & Pierce, 1996), provides select practices and examples of associated tools that educators may draw upon to deliver appropriate IEP progress monitoring for diverse learners. Also provided to guide practitioners are statements illustrating how the practices and associated devices may reflect culturally and linguistically responsive assessment for diverse learners.

As shown, a variety of practices and tools are readily available for use in monitoring the IEP goals and objectives of English language and other diverse learners. Each monitoring method may contain an established quantitative rubric (e.g., 1–4 scale), or one may be developed, that is used to score and quantify student performance through data collection procedures. When used over time, rubric scores are charted to illustrate learning progress toward IEP goals and objectives. As will be discussed in subsequent sections, for each monitoring practice and device, the combination of using a curriculum-appropriate monitoring measure with a scoring rubric, along with adhering to a standard process for administering the monitoring device each time it is used, provides highly relevant curriculum-specific, progress-monitoring results.

The need for using multiple measures and practices for diverse learners cannot be overstated. Use of only one measure may not accurately capture all the content knowledge and related skills that a diverse learner possesses relative to a specific IEP goal or objective (e.g., fluency, comprehension, high-frequency word usage, problem solving). Therefore, to best reflect cultural and linguistic diversity, more than one means for measuring IEP progress should be used (e.g., use both running records and DRA2 to measure the same fluency or comprehension goal). Additionally, our intent in presenting the different

Table 8.2 Culturally Responsive Progress-Monitoring Practices and Associated Tools

Monitoring Practice	Associated Tool(s)	Cultural/Linguistic Significance
Curriculum-Based Measurement (CBM)	Running records DRA2/EDL2 (Evaluación del desarrollo de la lectura 2)	Properly designed or modified CBMs allow educators to accommodate language and culture diversity features and values
Cross-Cultural Interview	Interview guide	Direct input provided by classroom teachers, family members, and/or students provides perspective to instruction and associated monitoring results
Language Sample	Classroom-based oral/written samples of language usage	Language samples provide direct evidence of student use of both native and English languages in the learning context
Classroom Observations	Observation guide	Instructional observations provide direct evidence of culturally and linguistically responsive instruction indicating level of sufficient opportunities to learn
Work Sample Analysis	Work completed by student in IEP content areas	Progress is illustrated by examining directly instruction-based student work samples associated with IEP goals and objectives
Performance-Based	Summative product	Product generated and completed by student over a defined period of time or instructional unit provides opportunity to incorporate cultural values within his/her own English language proficiency
Portfolio Assessment	Work artifacts	Portfolios provide evidence of progress over time by drawing on learner's interests and collection of artifacts along with written language skills used to reflect on the learning and growth
Functional Behavioral Assessment (FBA)	FBA process and steps	Use of FBAs provides educators with a more comprehensive view of social and behavioral needs and progress associated with IEP annual goals by allowing accommodated procedures to be incorporated into the FBA process, reflecting culturally/linguistically diverse characteristics and qualities

practices for progress monitoring in Table 8.2 is to demonstrate that a variety of appropriate options exist that may go beyond that which is typically used in today's schools (e.g., all students are administered the same and only test such as DIBELS). For additional information about each progress-monitoring practice or device, the reader is referred to the cited sources used to develop Table 8.2.

Data Collection

"Progress monitoring is an assessment structure for identifying effectiveness of instruction" (Hoover, Barletta, & Klingner, 2016, p. 32) and relies on the proper implementation of data collection procedures. Data collection is the process of systematically gathering quantified information about a learner's performance used to evaluate progress and determine instructional effectiveness. When collecting data, several guidelines are suggested (Hoover, 2016b; Wright, 2013):

- Clearly identify the area to be monitored (e.g., reading fluency, on-task behavior)
- Determine most appropriate methods for collecting data (e.g., running records, multiple observations, diagnostic test)
- Adhere to standard procedures including determining the minimum number of scores required (e.g., eight reading fluency scores, three behavior observation rubric scores)
- Establish baseline and intervals for subsequent progress monitoring (e.g., daily, weekly)
- Collect data scores using established standard procedures
- Collect data using multiple measures for diverse learners
- Illustrate scores on chart or graph
- Interpret scores and make necessary instructional adjustments

Often, school or district special education departments provide guidance on required specific data collection necessary to monitor progress toward mastery of IEP goals and associated objectives. Though data collection procedures vary based on skill and desired outcome (e.g., frequency, duration, intensity), adhering to the same data collection procedure each time the skill is measured when monitoring the same skill over time is important, so scores are best interpreted over time (e.g., same number of word problems in math measurement, read for two-minute time segments, observe same time-on-task behavior). When properly collected, data provide the foundation for making important IEP progress-monitoring decisions.

Though a variety of data collection monitoring procedures are appropriate for use with learners, curriculum-based measurement is highly relevant for English language and other diverse learners due to flexibility in its development, modifications, and usage reflecting cultural and linguistic diversity.

Progress Monitoring Using Curriculum-Based Measurement

Testing Skills That You Teach and Teaching Skills That You Test

Curriculum-based measurement (CBM) is an assessment practice that provides educators with "reliable, valid and efficient indicators of academic competence" (Fuchs & Fuchs, 2007, p. 31). Curriculum-based measurement is a highly useful and often preferred method over norm-referenced national devices due to several key qualities (Hoover, 2013):

a. Directly monitors that which has been taught in the curriculum

b. Facilitates recording quantified progress-monitoring data over time

c. Reduces interference with instructional time since CBMs are implemented over time in quick, easy-to-administer, short segments

d. Adheres to standard procedures through which student performance data are gathered, recorded, charted, and interpreted

e. Allows for instructional variables to be altered to improve learning (teacher controlled)

f. Relies on low- rather than high-inference measures (objective)

In addition to these qualities, CBMs provide opportunities for educators to monitor progress that account for and accommodate several cultural and linguistic learning features (Hoover, Klingner, Baca, & Patton, 2008):

- Experiential background relative to instruction
- English language proficiency
- Cultural relevancy of instruction
- Incorporation of research-based ESL/bilingual instructional practices
- Needed culturally responsive progress-monitoring accommodations
- Proper instructional adjustments reflecting cultural and linguistic strengths
- Reduced cultural bias, thereby increasing validity

Through CBM, educators responsible for progress monitoring of English language and other diverse learners are able to clarify instructional procedures, materials, methods, and structures that frame and put into a cultural and linguistic context the monitoring results. Incorporating into the IEP use of CBMs to monitor progress provides educators a *linking instruction to monitoring* perspective, leading to more accurate (a) teaching and learning, (b) measured performance, (c) interpreted results, and (d) adjusted instruction for all learners.

CBM Strengths and Procedures

Curriculum-based measurement is differentiated from other types of progress monitoring through its unique characteristics, as summarized in Tables 8.3 and 8.4.

CBMs are highly valuable in that they include a standard set of procedures, which is essential for comparing results over time.

Collectively, the CBM characteristics and procedures listed in Tables 8.3 and 8.4 provides educators with IEP progress-monitoring evidence, rich in value for determining (a) response to instruction, (b) rate of progress, (c) need to revise IEP goals or objectives, and (d) required instructional adjustments. In summary, using CBMs to monitor progress of IEP annual goals and objectives has many advantages over extensive use of nationally normed devices including these features: (a) meets MTSS principles and parameters, (b) aligns progress monitoring with actual instruction, (c) uses periodic data collection for making ongoing instructional decisions, (d) illustrates progress over time, and (e) uses selected devices or developed procedures that are easily made culturally and linguistically responsive.

Table 8.3 CBM Progress Monitoring Features

CBM Characteristic	Unique Contribution to Monitoring
Curriculum Alignment	Assesses taught knowledge and skills
Acceptable Reliability/ Validity	Research-based process
Standardized	Uses/follows standard procedures
Objective	Performance is based on observed behaviors linked to instruction
Decision Rules	Specified rules for decision making concerning use of scores are followed
Repeated Measures	Same CBM is used on a repeated basis
Efficient	Easy to administer, score, and interpret
Charted	Visually depicts student progress

Table 8.4 CBM Standardized Procedures

CBM Procedure	Unique Contribution to Monitoring
Directions	Standard directions provided each time
Time	Same time frame (e.g., 2 minutes each)
Materials	Similar skills/different materials
Scoring	Standard scoring each time
Charting	Same procedures for charting
Interpretation Procedures	Defined decision-making procedures

PROGRESS-MONITORING INTERPRETATION FOR DIVERSE LEARNERS: SPECIAL CONSIDERATIONS

Irrespective of the selected progress-monitoring devices and/or practices incorporated into the overall instruction documented on the IEP, several items unique to English language and other diverse learners require consideration as discussed by various researchers (see Basterra et al., 2011; Hoover, 2009; Hoover, Baca, & Klingner, 2016; Hoover et al., 2008; Ortiz et al., 2011):

Consideration 1. Some students in the process of acquiring English as a second language and/or adjusting to a new cultural environment may experience increased anxiety in completing progress monitoring until they develop proficiency in use of more advanced language skills and/or have time to adjust to a new environment.

Consideration 2. Unfamiliarity with behavioral expectations found in test taking may affect some learners' initial understanding of progress-monitoring procedures, requiring additional support to fully demonstrate acquired knowledge and skills.

Consideration 3. The manner in which students prefer to demonstrate learning through progress monitoring is influenced by values/teachings and must be respected so as not to conflict with cultural expectations.

Consideration 4. Progress-monitoring devices and procedures may be unfamiliar to some diverse learners, in which case the results may underestimate actual progress in acquiring knowledge/skills.

Consideration 5. Progress monitoring in English often becomes an English test for students in the process of acquiring English as a second language. This situation affects results by inaccurately reflecting that the learner lacks assessed knowledge and skills, which may actually exist and be accurately demonstrated if a more appropriate monitoring process was used to accommodate English language proficiency and cultural teachings.

These and similar considerations challenge IEP developers to make certain that the selected progress-monitoring devices and procedures do not conflict with cultural teachings and do not require the learner to use English language skills above those consistent with current stage of second language acquisition and associated expected skill sets (e.g., WIDA Can Do Descriptors).

CONCLUSION

The monitoring of progress toward IEP annual goals and short-term objectives is fundamental to linking instruction with assessment and necessary to demonstrate learner progress for subsequent IEP meetings with parents, colleagues, and/or students. Effective implementation of IEP instruction requires classroom teachers to adjust the teaching of content/skills based on student responses obtained during both formal and informal progress-monitoring activities (e.g., listening to student discussions in a small group, observing a student completing work during independent work time, paying specific attention to a student's facial or body language, asking probing questions to check for understanding, weekly reading passage comprehension CBM, periodic writing sample scored using a rubric, completion of daily math reasoning problem, running records).

Specifically, curriculum-based measurement procedures and devices are research-based and found to be highly effective to monitor IEP progress. Educators should use multiple progress-monitoring procedures with English language and other diverse learners to best measure progress and gather results necessary to adjust (a) content instruction, (b) instructional management, (c) English language development supports, and (d) culturally responsive related and supplemental supports. When used in consideration of English language proficiency and culturally diverse qualities, CBMs and other progress-monitoring practices discussed in this chapter provide results appropriate for instructing diverse learners with disabilities within general and specialized instruction.

Culturally and Linguistically Responsive Transition Planning and Services

9

Practitioner's Perspective . . .

What is the *transition* component of an IEP? What are the adult implications of effective transition statements on the IEP? Why is it important to consider transition domains when documenting transition plans for life beyond secondary education? What are important culturally and linguistically diverse features to consider when developing transition plans for English language and other diverse learners?

Transitions (i.e., movement/changes from one activity or situation to another) occur throughout everyone's lives. Some of the transitions encountered go smoothly while others are more challenging. For some individuals, transitions can be abrupt, traumatic, and often unsettling, requiring empathic support, encouragement, and deliberate planning. Formal transition planning and services for people with disabilities are mandated for two types of individuals: (1) young children identified under Part C of the IDEA legislation who are approaching their third birthday, and (2) students with Individualized Education Programs (IEPs) who are aged fourteen or sixteen, depending upon the states in which they reside. At both of these two points in time, early intervention personnel for young children and school educators for the school-aged students in secondary education are mandated by law to provide transition planning. Many of the transitions that children and youth with disabilities encounter are related to school or other services for which they might qualify, which is the topic of this chapter.

Specifically, the transition of secondary level students who are moving from high school to community settings is examined. While other school-related transitions (e.g., elementary to middle school) are important, transition planning for life beyond secondary education is mandated by the IDEA legislation. However, regardless of when transition occurs, it is highly influenced by personal or family choice. For this reason, it is essential for professionals to be particularly aware of and value family and personal perspectives to best facilitate the postsecondary transition decision-making process.

Building on the excellent material documented in other resources on transition planning, this chapter also discusses transition through a cultural and linguistic lens to best meet the hopes and dreams of English language and other diverse learners as they move from secondary education into community settings. To accomplish this, the chapter is organized into three major sections: (1) successful adult functioning; (2) the transition planning process, including a definition of secondary transition, IDEA requirements, transition domains, and a model for transition planning; and (3) special considerations relevant to transition planning for culturally and linguistically diverse students and their families. Additionally, throughout the chapter, readers are provided insight into ways to incorporate diverse values and supports in the transition planning.

SUCCESSFUL ADULT FUNCTIONING

To understand the importance of good transition planning, it is useful to consider the adult outcomes that are major goals of transition planning efforts. Figure 9.1 illustrates the adulthood implications of transition, as first introduced by Patton and Dunn (1998). In this model, the ultimate outcome for which all transition efforts should be directed is to create life situations where the individual feels personally fulfilled, being able to value her/his particular culturally and linguistically diverse heritage and teachings. This perspective clearly relates to the concept of quality of life. Halpern (1993) suggested that quality of life, or personal fulfillment as used in the Patton and Dunn conceptualization,

Figure 9.1   Adulthood Implications of Transition

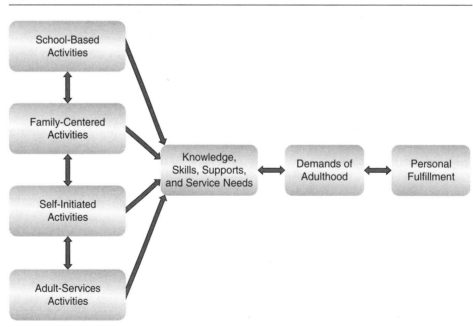

Source: Patton (2016a).

relates to three elements: happiness (transient state of affect), satisfaction (feelings and behavior patterns associated with different adult roles), and sense of general well-being (enduring sense of satisfaction with one's life). All three of these factors are heavily influenced by one's values and culture. Therefore, from the initial stages of transition planning, educators should be familiar with the learner's cultural perspectives, preferences, and values to best assist in the overall process. For example, the *Family-Centered Activities* component of the model illustrated in Figure 9.1 may assume particular relevance for some culturally and linguistically diverse learners by reflecting the potential significance of cooperative and family contributions to one's own success and fulfillment.

To enjoy some sense of personal fulfillment, an individual must be reasonably successful in meeting the challenges of everyday life, whether at work, at home, in school, or in the community. The specific nature of transition varies as a function of (a) cultural values, (b) where one lives, and (c) with whom one has regular contacts (e.g., family, friends, coworkers). Various literature sources (e.g., Cronin, Patton, & Wood, 2007; Wandry, Wehmeyer, & Glor-Scheib, 2013) provide listings of the major demands typically encountered in adulthood. However, as emphasized, the exact interpretation and significance of the demands must be understood within the student's cultural and family contexts (e.g., the need to display competence in using public transportation becomes less of an immediate concern if a student lives in an area where this public service is not provided; assisting with immediate family needs in the home or community may override other opportunities).

Additionally, it is important to note that people who feel personally fulfilled do not always deal successfully with the day-to-day issues that arise in their lives. So how does one become competent to deal with their daily life challenges? Three factors are essential:

1. An individual must possess knowledge of an array of facts, procedures, and events composing his/her post-school environments.

2. The individual needs to acquire specific skills typically demanded in the settings in which the person must function.

3. The learner must identify, access, and use a host of supports and/or services that will be of important assistance in dealing with everyday events. Often, these types of supports are provided by family, friends, community organization members, and others in the person's life.

Therefore, as can be seen in Figure 9.1, four sources of influence share the responsibility for preparing students for adulthood. These four sources—school, family, the student, and adult services—are intricately involved in the transition process. Specifically, the role of parents and perhaps the extended family in the lives of the children may be a very important factor. Concomitantly, the role that school personnel assume in connection to that of the parents' roles should be understood clearly, especially as varying levels of family involvement occur due to factors such as family preference, values about life decision making, interest in the process, and the reality of availability. Though it is essential that family and parental involvement occur, the reality is that this involvement will vary by family, cultural perspective, and other life circumstances that must be incorporated into the transition planning process. And, as discussed, depending on the particular situation, one or more of these four features may assume a greater or lesser role in the transition planning for culturally and linguistically diverse (CLD) learners.

BASIC CONCEPTS ASSOCIATED WITH TRANSITION PLANNING AND SERVICES

Transition services for students with disabilities became a mandate in IDEA in 1990. The 1990 reauthorization of IDEA required transition planning and services for students with special needs when they attained the age of sixteen, with some states requiring efforts beginning at age fourteen. This IDEA mandate, which is addressed on the IEP, assures students that an array of services will be initiated during the last years of high school to assist in their transition into postsecondary education adult life.

Rationale for Implementing Transition Services

A number of reasons explain why transition services became a required component of the special education process in the United States. One of the most compelling reasons was found in the data about adult outcomes of many individuals with disabilities in society. Research conducted as a component of a number of different follow-up studies substantiated less than desirable outcomes beyond secondary education including unemployment or underemployment, few individuals living independently, limited social lives, and little community involvement, to name a few. In addition to the adult outcome data, information related to high school graduation rates indicating high dropout rates of students with disabilities contributed to the IDEA movement to better prepare students with disabilities for life after secondary school.

Definition of Transition Services and Implications for Practice

The current version of IDEA, which was most recently reauthorized in 2004, defines "transition services" as

> *a coordinated set of activities for a child with a disability that is designed within a results-oriented process that is focused on improving the academic and functional achievement of a child with a disability to facilitate movement from school to post-school activities including postsecondary education, vocational training, integrated employment, continuing adult education, adult service, independent living, or community participation. [§300.42(a)(1)]*

This definition clearly conveys the fundamental goal of providing transition-related activities and supports in school prior to students' graduation or completion of school. However, the definition is somewhat broad and does not provide a detailed sense of the level of comprehensiveness about specific transition areas required to ensure that transition services have the most effect on future success. The following discussions provide increased clarity to best understand the comprehensive nature of transition planning and services.

Major Domains of Transition. Although the actual transition domains used across the country vary, a number of key areas for which transition planning should be conducted have been identified. Table 9.1, based on the domains used in the assessment device, *Transition Planning Inventory* (Patton & Clark, 2014), lists eleven transition domains. The scope of these domains shows the type of comprehensiveness that should be addressed when providing transition planning and services. The table also provides a few examples of key features within each domain. It is important to note that most students possess skills in some or all of these domains. However, all areas should be examined for transition strengths, qualities, and areas of need as part of the overall process.

Table 9.1   Transition Domains

Domain	*Featured Content*
Working	
Career Choice and Planning	Knows about jobs Knows how to get a job
Employment Knowledge and Skills	Can acquire and perform general and specific skills related to a job or jobs Knows how to change jobs
Learning	
Further Education/ Training	Knows about options for further development beyond high school Has the skills to be successful Knows how to use support services
Functional Communication	Is able to read, write, listen, and speak in applied settings
Self-Determination	Understands one's strengths and weaknesses Has the ability to plan, set goals, and make decisions Has the ability to be in charge of one's Life
Living	
Independent Living	Has skills related to a variety of everyday demands, such as cooking, cleaning, and making simple repairs Has the ability to solve everyday problems that arise Has the skills to use current technology
Personal Money Management	Has skills associated with buying everyday items Has the ability to pay bills, maintain checking/savings accounts, and budget money

(Continued)

Table 9.1   (Continued)

Community Involvement and Usage	Has skills associated with being a capable citizen Has the ability to use services and resources in the community Has the ability to use local public transportation
Leisure Activities	Has awareness of a range of leisure activities Participates in indoor and outdoor activities Is engaged in various types or entertainment
Health	Has knowledge and skills associated with staying physically healthy Has knowledge and skills associated with staying emotionally/mentally healthy Has knowledge of appropriate sexual behavior
Interpersonal Relationships	Has skills to interact appropriately with a range of other people Has the ability to make and keep friends Has the ability to deal with conflict Has knowledge and skills required to be a good parent

Source: Patton and Clark (2014, p. 7). Reprinted by permission.

Model of Transition Planning Process.   A second area necessary to best understand the comprehensive nature of transition is seen in the actual planning process. Figure 9.2 illustrates a recommended transition model, which was originally developed by Patton and Dunn (1998) and recently enhanced by Patton and Clark (2014). As shown, the model emphasizes the notion that the transition planning process is a multicomponent/multistep process. Additionally, within the broad scope of life development, the transition process begins in the early years of schooling, continuing until such time that the student leaves school through graduation, aging out, or dropping out before completing his/her program. Aspects of this model are addressed in subsequent discussions in this chapter.

Figure 9.2   Transition Planning Process

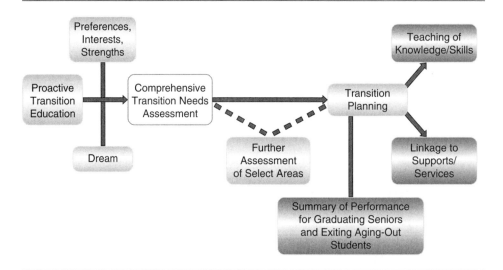

Source: Patton and Clark (2014, p. 4). Reprinted by permission.

TRANSITION PLANNING FOR CULTURALLY AND LINGUISTICALLY DIVERSE STUDENTS

Though all the same transition features illustrated in the above table and figures apply to all learners (e.g., parental involvement, self-determination, community resources, health care, money management), select items warrant particular attention when designing and planning transition for diverse learners. The following discussion is intended to highlight cultural and linguistic qualities and strengths that warrant special consideration by school-based transition personnel in order to deliver the quality transition planning and services to which English language and other diverse learners and their families are entitled under the IDEA legislation. One guiding question is presented after discussion of each transition feature to assist educators to frame the transition aspect of the IEP for diverse learners.

Transition Feature 1: Cultural and Linguistic Responsiveness

Fundamentally, school personnel who are involved in the transition process for diverse learners must maintain cultural integrity, and when English as a second language is present, they must include proper language supports and representation as discussed in several of the previous chapters of this book. As Trainor and Patton (2008) note, "The term *culturally responsive* refers to the ability of teachers to apply a sophisticated understanding of culture and to respond to the needs of families that have as their basis culturally held values and beliefs" (p. 362). Situated within the broader context of language diversity and cultural heritage, the above quotation reminds us of the importance of blending transition planning with diverse values and qualities.

Specifically, IEP documentation of transition planning and services for CLD students relies upon a set of considerations that reflect direct relevance to families who represent culturally and linguistically diverse backgrounds and expectations. Based on material found in Harry, Kalyanpur, and Day (1999), several of the most relevant considerations include these:

- Knowledge of cultural perspectives of teachers and schools that impact preferences, beliefs, and values of school personnel regarding students with disabilities and special education services
- Knowledge and awareness of the values and beliefs held by families and students in transition planning
- Explicit articulation of goals, values, and beliefs of the school and those of the family, attending in particular to the cultural values of the family and how these may differ from those of the school
- Planning in collaboration with the parents so educators ensure that family beliefs and values are integrated into the scope of transition expectations

IEP Transition Planning Question: Are the postsecondary options included on the IEP for an English language or other diverse learner reflective of the student's community values, heritage, and teachings?

Transition Feature 2: Parent/Family Participation

Parental engagement is a fundamental tenet of the IDEA legislation in general and IEP development specifically. However, parents can, and often do, maintain expectations and attitudes that might differ from those of school personnel. One common example of this is seen in the differences between striving for independence, as promoted by many school professionals, and the notion of a more cooperative-oriented interdependence preferred by many diverse families.

The importance of family involvement cannot be overstated. However, the "look" of that involvement may take different shapes. Most school personnel prefer that families be actively involved in IEP meetings and other activities related to the transition process (e.g., assessment). While it is possible that some families will not engage in the transition process in the same way that educators prefer, most parents are very interested in the outcomes of their children. That is, parents want to feel like the process is meaningful to them and their children, and that school personnel truly listen to what they are saying by understanding and incorporating their preferences and interests into the process.

Building on the overall topical emphasis of this book, school professionals involved in the transition planning process must recognize and value the rich funds of knowledge that parents of CLD students bring to the situation. As Trainor and Patton (2008) note, "Families have entire funds of knowledge that can help transition teams incorporate active participation of family members in both planning and instruction" (p. 356). To be successful in engaging parents in this process, adherence to the following suggestions is recommended:

- Involve parents early in the process and provide them ample time to understand the various aspects of the transition planning process.
- Determine parents' preferred language and provide information to them in this language, making sure that communications are truly understood.
- If translators are needed, refer to the guidelines provided in Chapter 7 for the appropriate use of translators with families in which English is not the home or first language.
- Listen attentively and without judgment to what parents of diverse learners wish to share.
- Accept and value differences of perspective (e.g., importance of independence, cultural teachings, home values) in regard to selecting specific transition topics (e.g., preferred employment or school options, living arrangements, role of family and community).

These and similar best practices are built upon in discussions provided in Chapter 10 of this book to ensure meaningful and relevant parental IEP engagement.

IEP Transition Planning Question: Does the process for developing the transition aspect of the IEP for an English language or other diverse learner solicit parental input in the preferred language of communication and subsequently incorporate this input into the final document?

Transition Feature 3: Preferences, Interests, Strengths

An important initial step in the "formal" transition planning process is to develop and use culturally responsive practices (e.g., home visits, cross-cultural interviews, attending community events with family/student) to identify preferences, interests, and strengths in regard to future careers and other life-related areas most valued by both the student and family. Successful transition beyond secondary schooling will best occur if grounded in learner and family preferences, even if these differ from those which school educators prefer. Therefore, a sufficient amount of time is to be expended gathering background material about the student, to be used to ultimately inform the transition aspects of the IEP. For example, in the instrument *Transition Planning Inventory*, Second Edition, (*TPI-2*; Patton & Clark, 2014), forms are provided to obtain interest and preference information from both students and parents. The "home" preference and interest forms provided in the *TPI* are available in a number of different languages. Use of these types of forms to learn about preferences and interests is very helpful. Results should be incorporated with other information gathered through time spent with the student and parents/family to clearly understand their transition values, preferences, strengths, and expectations. Additional considerations to ensure that responsive gathering of diverse learners' transition strengths and preferences are discussed in the next section.

IEP Transition Planning Question: Do the transition aspects of the IEP for an English language or other diverse learner clearly reflect the preferences and strengths expressed by the student and family?

Transition Feature 4: Diversity and Responsive Assessment Qualities

As discussed above, determination of transition preferences, values, and strengths is key to an effective transition planning process. Initiating this information gathering early in the process is recommended to ensure that sufficient time is devoted to developing a working knowledge about the learner's preferences and strengths to best prepare them for life beyond secondary schooling.

The previously referred to *Transition Planning Inventory*, Second Edition, instrument can serve as an example of how to determine transition needs. The *TPI-2* contains three primary rating forms: school, student, and home. Each of these forms contains the same fifty-seven items; however, the student and home forms are written at a lower readability level for ease of use. Once the information is gathered from these three primary sources, it is transferred to a profile for interpretation. In turn, the results obtained provide sufficient information upon which to base transition plan development, though occasionally further assessment information is needed, adding to the *TPI-2* results.

However, whether the *TPI* or some other transition tool is used, an important point to reiterate is that the tool needs to be comprehensive so that all of the areas of transition discussed in the above sections are considered. Also, when used with English language or other diverse learners, the process and use of a transition tool must be culturally and linguistically responsive. To facilitate the use of the *TPI* or other transition planning tool with diverse learners, a checklist such as the one illustrated in Table 9.2 should be used. The guide, developed from material found in Trainor and Patton (2008), provides educators with several important items to consider during the transition planning.

Table 9.2   Guide for Conducing a Culturally and Linguistically Responsive Transition Assessment

---

Instructions: Check each item once the transition development team confirms the item is properly incorporated or considered in the transition planning.

Diverse Learner Considerations

_____ Student has been provided time to express and pursue his/her dreams

_____ Educators ask student about personal preferences, strengths, and interests regarding adult reference topics

_____ Student's preferred response style (e.g., oral interview, written, use of computer) is used to gather information

_____ Student possesses sufficient language skills to express ideas and respond to questions or other items either orally or in writing

---

Family of Diverse Student Considerations

_____ Educators have provided the parents with sufficient information and supports to clarify for them the transition planning purpose and process

_____ Parents are provided relevant and adequate opportunities to meaningfully participate in the transition planning process

_____ Parents are provided a specific opportunity to share their preferences and interests concerning their child's future with adult reference topics

_____ Parents are clearly able to understand transition topics, questions, or other related items, whether provided orally or in writing

_____ If necessary, the translation of print documents and use of translators for interviews occur to interact with or convey critical transition planning information to the parents

_____ Educators solicit and incorporate family values and funds of knowledge in the planning and development process

_____ Parental level of participation to assist the child in achieving transition goals and activities is determined and incorporated into the IEP

Transition Assessment Considerations

_____ Individuals collecting transition information do so in unbiased and culturally responsive ways

_____ Individuals collecting transition planning information possess culturally and linguistically responsive training and maintain use of developed competencies during the transition assessment gathering activities

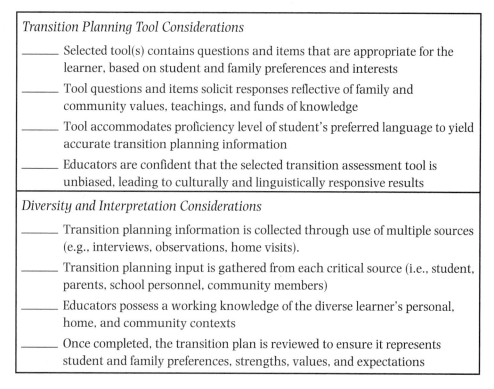

Transition Planning Tool Considerations

_____ Selected tool(s) contains questions and items that are appropriate for the learner, based on student and family preferences and interests

_____ Tool questions and items solicit responses reflective of family and community values, teachings, and funds of knowledge

_____ Tool accommodates proficiency level of student's preferred language to yield accurate transition planning information

_____ Educators are confident that the selected transition assessment tool is unbiased, leading to culturally and linguistically responsive results

Diversity and Interpretation Considerations

_____ Transition planning information is collected through use of multiple sources (e.g., interviews, observations, home visits).

_____ Transition planning input is gathered from each critical source (i.e., student, parents, school personnel, community members)

_____ Educators possess a working knowledge of the diverse learner's personal, home, and community contexts

_____ Once completed, the transition plan is reviewed to ensure it represents student and family preferences, strengths, values, and expectations

As shown, a variety of key items compose a culturally and linguistically responsive transition planning process. However, though the best laid plans may appear sufficient, the reality is that often schools will not be able to obtain some important information, especially if a home form is not completed or returned. Potential reasons for inability to obtain home information may include situations such as parents' inability to complete the form due to (a) work demands or other factors, (b) not understanding some or many of the statements, or (c) the parents feeling disassociated from the process in general. Should this situation arise, school personnel must attempt ways to engage parents in a way that helps them feel comfortable and supported, with their input valued and appreciated. The following suggestions should be helpful when trying to get parents to provide information that will be useful for planning purposes.

- Make sure parents receive the home form in their native language.
- Periodically contact the parents to see if they have any questions or concerns.
- Provide explanatory information (i.e., descriptions of the items or questions) in their native language.

Therefore, as emphasized above, attending to select special considerations will facilitate positive and productive parental engagement in the transition planning process for their children.

IEP Transition Planning Question: How is the assessment for transition planning reflective of the cultural and linguistic items found on the tool illustrated in Table 9.2?

Transition Feature 5: Documentation of Transition Plan

Upon completion of the interest and preference assessment collection phase, specific transition planning documentation should commence. As noted in the model in Figure 9.2, two forms of planning can and should be considered: (1) *instructional goals* associated with the "teaching of knowledge/skills" necessary for successful transition and (2) *linkage goals* associated with "linkage to supports/services" students may access upon leaving postsecondary education. Instructional goals are designed to teach the knowledge and skills associated with transition skill areas that require continued development while the student is still in secondary school. Linkage goals refer to the community connections that need to be made to identify supports and services that will be needed by the student in the future.

As previously expressed, it is essential that parents feel that they are respected members of this process and transition planning team. It is not uncommon for parents, when they feel that their voices have not been heard, to merely go along with what the school has developed when in fact they may not understand, do not necessarily agree with, or may not follow the plans that have been developed. Appropriate sensitivity to family culture and values applied during the transition information gathering phase leads to more culturally and linguistically responsive transition documentation on the IEP.

IEP Transition Planning Question: What evidence exists to confirm that both *instructional* and *linkage* goals are incorporated into the transition component of the IEP and that these are responsive to English language and other diverse learners?

CONCLUSION

As shown in Figure 9.2 and discussed in this chapter, the transition planning process involves several phases and requires various pieces of information. School personnel, families, and students each must contribute to this process to make it successful. Additionally, since this process is highly personal for both the student and family, it is essential that transition planning and the services that accompany the planning process be sensitive and responsive to the cultural and linguistic features of English language and other diverse learners. This includes consideration of several features including preferences, strengths, values, aspirations, and cultural teachings, to name a few. In summary, if culturally and linguistically responsive transition planning is implemented as discussed in this chapter, the likely outcome is an increased probability that the student, and his/her family, will be better prepared for those community settings in which the young adult will live, play, and work beyond secondary education.

Guidelines for Successful IEP Meetings for Diverse Learners

10

By Dr. Leah Teeters

Practitioner's Perspective . . .

What is meant by "funds of knowledge" and how does this inform effective IEP development? What should educators consider prior to the IEP meeting for an English language or other diverse learner? What is important to address during the IEP meeting to value culturally and linguistically diverse qualities and expectations? What is important to consider after the IEP meeting to ensure effective delivery for diverse learners?

IMPORTANCE OF FUNDS OF KNOWLEDGE IN EDUCATION

In today's schools and classrooms nationwide, culturally and linguistically diverse students bring unique and valuable historically developed skills, abilities, practices, and ways of knowing, referred to as *funds of knowledge,* that define the fabric of each family (Moll & Gonzalez, 2004).

Funds of Knowledge Perspective

Students from culturally and linguistically diverse backgrounds may have funds of knowledge that, although integral to their learning experiences, may differ from the dominant culture of the school, curricula, educators, and mainstream students and that are all too often overlooked or viewed as inconsequential in teaching and learning. When schools aim to provide all students with what is perceived as "equal education" reflective of the knowledge, values, and norms of the dominant culture, it may result in diverse learners' cultural backgrounds not being incorporated into teaching and learning. The many references to diverse family and community perspectives, skills, and cultural teachings found in the previous chapters of this book shape learners and represent multiple examples of funds of knowledge that require schools to abandon the equal education perspective to adjust and differentiate instruction for all learners.

Effects on Learners

Incorporating diverse funds of knowledge in classroom instruction supports all learners. Conversely, limited emphasis on diverse funds perpetuates the subtraction of students' cultures, languages, and values (Valenzuela, 2002), which has significant detrimental effects on students' motivation, attention, task completion, family involvement and support, and community engagement, to name a few. Unfortunately, the school that does not maintain and value diverse cultures, languages, and communities through funds of knowledge not only deprives English language and other diverse learners of a rich and well-rounded education, but also expects students and their families to navigate the dominant set of rules and expectations with little or no support. To mitigate the risk that we educate diverse students from a subtractive paradigm, it is important to understand the backgrounds, heritages, values, and beliefs that compose cultural and linguistic diversity. We need to consider how to best incorporate this knowledge into students' learning experiences to develop responsive and relevant Individualized Education Programs (IEPs) for diverse learners.

Learning is supported by social interaction and the social construction of knowledge (Brown, Collins, & Duguid, 1989), occurring within the school, home, and community settings. Learners acquire, develop, and use cognitive tools daily through both planned and unplanned academic or recreational activities. As discussed in each chapter throughout this book, to best facilitate success for students from diverse backgrounds, we need to understand various factors contributing to one's development including (a) home and community contexts, (b) family and cultural views toward education and success, and (c) second language acquisition.

Additionally, when working with English language and other diverse learners with disabilities, we must consider how learning differences and special education identifications are interconnected, misunderstood, or culturally constructed. For example, we previously discussed the notion that different cultures identify, understand, and orient themselves toward learning differences, disabilities, and special education in unique ways, which may vary significantly from how we view these in US schools. Therefore, understanding how the family identifies with the student's strengths and struggles, as well as the associated cultural consequences, informs educators of student learning characteristics and essential funds of knowledge.

Why, then, are funds of knowledge critical to development and implementation of an English language or other diverse learner's IEP? First, the IDEA legislation requires active involvement of families in the IEP development phase. Second, through this active involvement, families share their funds of knowledge, which educators are expected to value and incorporate into an IEP's present levels of performance, annual goals, related services, and accommodations. Third, lack of insight into a family's cultural funds of knowledge limits educators' abilities to develop, implement, and monitor IEPs in culturally and linguistically responsive ways. Therefore, the task of generating IEPs necessitates understanding how families and communities perceive student learning, expectations, and outcomes. Specifically, how might educators bring parents into the IEP process so as to generate more successful academic or functional behavioral plans for learners utilizing their funds of knowledge? Throughout the rest of this chapter, we provide relevant suggestions responding to this question, specific to the three phases of an IEP meeting: pre-meeting activities, during-meeting considerations, and post-meeting follow-ups.

PRE-MEETING SUGGESTIONS

Begin With Self-Reflection

Similar to students and families, educators bring funds of knowledge to the school setting. Selection of instructional practices and materials is influenced by experiences, training, cultural values, teaching preferences, and assumptions about what is considered valuable knowledge. The work of generating IEPs that successfully address the individual student as a unique learner begins by breaking down one's own cultural background and preferences toward teaching and learning. For example: (a) How are student abilities perceived? (b) How are learning characteristics defined? (c) What educational decisions result from responses to a and b? Ultimately, the learning environment created by the teacher is reflective of responses to these and similar questions, leading to selected classroom teaching practices, curricular activities, classroom management, and instructional groupings (Hoover, 2012). Though educators approach teaching with the best of intentions for learners, without self-reflection and critical awareness, the "best" intentions may conflict with diverse learners' cultural values and norms.

To facilitate self-reflection, it is often beneficial to critically examine one's own assumptions about culturally and linguistically diverse education. Specifically: What is culture? What is *my* culture? To respond, consider several factors such as attitudes and perceptions toward authority, role of formal education, learning styles, learning differences, gender, group identification, abstract learning, or discipline perspectives, while honestly acknowledging one's own biases and privileges. Check to determine if the way culture is self-perceived is similar to the culture of the school, classroom, and families or communities. Then, consider how it might feel if the way teaching and learning are shaped varies significantly from one's own cultural background and experiences.

To continue in this process, revisit the stages of cultural proficiency in Table 1.2 to further clarify your own perspective about the value of diverse cultures in teaching and learning. Once this self-reflection process begins, collaborate with colleagues to continue the conversation by identifying the cultural school structures that grade- or school-level teams have constructed. In turn, examine the cultural and linguistic qualities and features diverse learners with disabilities bring to the same grade or school environment.

Subsequently, engage in team self-examination, identifying consistencies and inconsistencies between cultural expectations of educator teams and those of diverse students and their families. Make necessary instructional adjustments to close any cultural gap between how educators and families view education. Consistency between views provides a meaningful foundation for developing a culturally and linguistically responsive IEP and delivering associated instruction to English language and other diverse learners who require special education.

Learn About the Family

Learning about students' families and communities requires educators to engage with the families in their place of comfort, oftentimes the home or a community location. The school is often laden with unspoken cultural codes and formalities that are unknown or misunderstood by many nondominant families, leading to unintended intimidation. Visiting families on "neutral turf" at home or in a community setting (e.g., local community center) allows for parents to be more comfortable and breaks down intimidating factors (e.g., English as dominant language, professional climate, expert views) that are typically experienced in the school setting. For example, a home or community visit demonstrates to the family and child an interest in their lives typically not seen in a school setting. A visit to the home may begin with the teacher sharing about himself/herself in efforts to establish rapport. As conversation continues, the teacher is able to demonstrate to the parents a personal interest in their child by better understanding the home environment necessary to prioritize quality educational experiences, safety, and emotional well-being structures in school. Throughout the visit, as the teacher, you would allow the parents to guide the conversation, providing them opportunity to tell you about what they consider to be important. In these visits once rapport is established, *speak less, listen more* is a good general rule, as you are there to learn about their funds of knowledge and perspectives about school. As the conversation progresses, attempt to gather specific information about the child's way of being at home:

1. What are the child's strengths?

2. What are the child's challenges?

3. What does the child do during free time?

4. What is his/her favorite game?

5. What is his/her favorite TV show or movie (if that is part of the home culture)?

6. With whom does she/he play?

7. For what household responsibilities is the child responsible?

8. How is she/he disciplined?

Also, gather information about the child's family and home culture by asking about family:

1. History

2. Hopes/dreams for the child's experience with school

3. Concerns for the child's experience with school

4. Views of the disability and associated strengths

5. Views of discipline

6. Cultural figure(s) the child most identifies with in her/his life

Not all of the above items may be appropriate to question during one visit, so attention to sensitive or personal topics is necessary to engage parents personally, empathetically, and in nonjudgmental and nonthreatening ways. For example, sharing about home country history and challenges, traumas, and celebrations may be too sensitive for some families, particularly in this era of immigration status. In order for parents to share more sensitive and personal information, a certain level of trust must be established, and waiting to gather some important information may be prudent until such time as trust and security have been maintained.

However, information about these types of topics reveals much about students' backgrounds, learning influences, and preferred ways of learning and should be gathered when possible. Similar suggestions apply when asking about their culture's relationship with disability, learning difference, and academics. Be certain to provide the parents sufficient opportunity to share how they relate to their child's learning and to views about disability and overall education. Also, building on the above qualities of effective meetings with families, it is critical to ask parents what they view as important to address in the IEP and incorporate into the finalized document.

Language Considerations

The fact that parents speak little or no English should not discourage making a home visit or creating situations to facilitate meaningful involvement. Remember, these could be the parents who are reluctant to call the school or attend school-led conferences due to perceived language barriers. In addition to including a team member or translator who is fluent in the family's home language, there are several simple practices to establish rapport and learn about the family. Some family members may understand some English and appreciate efforts made to communicate directly in simple exchanges using English. Additionally, though some English is spoken, family members may prefer to communicate in their native language. Therefore, educators should attempt to communicate in the family's home language and/or English based on family member preference. Modeling a hybrid language or bilingual practice for the family and the student demonstrates that both languages are valued. Also, as discussed in Chapters 2 and 3, the process of second language acquisition initially includes more extensive use of receptive skills before productive skills, meaning that individuals may understand the second language yet not be able to reply in that language. If this is the case, encourage family and team members to respond in the language each prefers, with assistance from a translator if necessary.

Further, if it is the case that some family members or school professionals do not understand any of the other language, engagement with each other is still necessary and required by the IDEA legislation. In this situation, in addition to communicating with a translator, engage with the family directly by facing the parents, rather the translator, when speaking to make eye contact and engage in nonverbal communication. Also, an effective practice is to bring examples of the student's work and ask to see examples of the student's activities in the home. In summary, be creative and recognize that language differences do not need to translate into barriers to basic human interaction. Overall, educators acquire a tremendous amount of knowledge about the learner and family through home/community visits and conversational interactions.

The Student

In addition to meeting with the family as a pre-IEP event, it is extremely important to meet with the student to understand how the learner perceives his/her own learning abilities. Ask students to discuss what they enjoy doing, what they find challenging, and what strategies they use when they find something difficult to complete. Allow them opportunity to discuss most/least favorite activities outside of school, what they are good at, what makes them feel happy, and how they perceive their own learning. Similar to interactions with parents, use open-ended questions with some specific questions, and listen more and speak less. Maintain eye contact, portray interest, and respond in positive ways to what the student is sharing.

Establishing an Interdisciplinary Team

When establishing the IEP team, it is important to consider the diversity of services that the student may receive, ensuring educators are on the team who can best represent the various elements of the learner's educational experience. This includes, but is not limited to, the classroom teacher(s), the parents, the English language development (ELD) teacher, the bilingual educator, the special education teacher, needed special education support or related service providers, and a school administrator. In addition, once all members of the team are identified, one individual is to be identified to oversee, direct, and lead the IEP meeting.

The professional leading the IEP meeting should initially determine the number of meetings needed with other members to gather sufficient material prior to developing the student's IEP at the IEP meeting (i.e., a portfolio of body of evidence that demonstrates a student's learning). This can include, but is not limited to, (a) evidence from home visits, (b) in-class writing samples, (c) authentic assessments, (d) observational data, (e) standardized test results, or (f) benchmark data. The learner's classroom teachers and multi-tiered interventionists should share their experiences with the student relative to the identified areas of need, making certain to emphasize the student's strengths, preferred ways of learning, and other assets as previously presented in this book. Also, as discussed in Chapter 4, when constructing the IEP, it is important that the learning plan be based upon the student's present levels of academic achievement and functional performance.

It is important to note that the official IEP is not constructed until the official IEP meeting occurs that is attended by the parents and other identified educators. However, through pre-meeting discussions with the parents, students, and educators, items to include in the IEP may be listed and documented. Again, this is only a draft and should be used as such, with the official IEP not completed until parental input is shared and included at the IEP meeting. However, given that educators understand the IEP as a legal document, it is important to have a draft structure going into the meeting to make certain all due process items and other essential parental supports are in place in order to meet the IDEA mandates associated with IEP development and implementation.

Upon generating a draft of key IEP items, educators should develop a concise, one-page outline of items, or a draft of the IEP that will be discussed at the IEP meeting, providing this to parents in their preferred language. In this way, parents are able to review ahead of time what will be discussed, allowing them important "think time" to consider (a) how they will contribute to the IEP, (b) questions they wish to have answered, and (c) other related items they wish to discuss. Providing parents with this type of draft information is within the parameters of the IDEA provisions and crucial to empowering parents to fully participate in the official IEP meeting.

Once the IEP team leader has made certain that the draft materials have been developed and provided to the parents/guardians and that they agree to attend the IEP meeting at the specified time and place, the number of educators to attend the meeting is determined. It is important to remember that if the ratio of educators and specialists to parents is considerably disproportionate, authentic parental participation may be compromised. As a general rule, there should be only two to three specialists for each parent attending the IEP meeting, in addition to the special educator and administrator. Also, the linguistic needs of the parents must be considered and addressed during the pre-meeting time. Even if parents are confident communicating in English, they may not have the technical language by which to discuss their child's learning needs and abilities. In the case that a parent is not fully fluent in English, include a translator, versed in the technical language, at the IEP meeting. Once all the above features are considered and addressed, the meeting is conducted highlighting additional suggestions for development of a culturally and linguistically responsive IEP.

DURING–IEP MEETING SUGGESTIONS

The outcomes of the interdisciplinary team meeting are to (a) determine eligibility for special education and (b) develop the official IEP if placed. That is, IEP development begins once official special education placement is made. During the IEP development phase of the meeting, team members discuss the academic and functional recommendations, constructing the learning plan based on the comprehensive evaluation body of evidence used to base the placement decision. All required IDEA-mandated IEP items, due process elements, and related expectations are addressed and documented as previously identified and discussed in this book.

Generating a Learning Profile: PLAAFP

The meeting should begin with the parents. The interdisciplinary team members have already informally met to discuss their perspectives, and now it is time to hear about how the parents view their child's learning. Once again, remember to talk less and listen more. Encourage the parents to speak holistically about their child and present perspectives that may not be captured in the classroom. Ask them to talk about the student's strengths. Lead with the strengths and use those to frame the conversation about the student's academic or behavioral challenges. Together, consider how the strengths can be leveraged to support the student as the present levels of academic achievement and functional performance (PLAAFP) statements are generated.

Creating an Achievable Plan: Annual Goals

After generating a collective learning profile documented in the PLAAFP statement, members transition into program specifics to identify the IEP annual learning goals. The learning goals should be (a) based on areas of desired growth; (b) meaningful so as to address the student's social, linguistic, and academic needs; and (c) generated using the SMART format. Focus on generating strong, specific goals, emphasizing quality over quantity of instruction. Upon generating a few specific annual goals, use the identified strengths and weaknesses documented in the PLAAFP statement to create meaningful and achievable short-term objectives to break down progress into manageable, measurable segments of learning, as discussed in Chapter 5.

At this point in the process, two of the most critical aspects of the IEP have been collectively developed: PLAAFP and annual goals/short-term objectives. These, in turn, facilitate identification of the other IDEA-mandated IEP items: (a) delivery location (i.e., extent of time or work in general-education curriculum and classroom); (b) specialized, related, and supplemental supports; (c) necessary instructional and assessment accommodations; (d) progress-monitoring specifics; (e) transition supports for secondary learners; and (f) other related requests generated by the parents. During the entire process of framing the IEP, all team members advocate for the learner, including attending to cultural and linguistic responsiveness reflected in the developed plan, as explained in Chapters 1 and 2.

Advocating for the Student

Whether or not the student attends the IEP meeting is based on judgment made by team members under guidance from the team leader. Similar to most other aspects of education, the more involved learners are in their IEP development, the more motivated and committed they are to their own learning (Hoover, Baca, & Klingner, 2016). For some aspects of the meeting, it may be inappropriate for the learner to attend (e.g., during presentation and discussion of sensitive information or concerns), but very appropriate for other aspects (e.g., during discussions about interest, preferences toward learning, self-perceived strengths, transition planning). In some cultures, the decision to attend is informed by cultural values that should be discussed with the parents during the pre-meeting time. If appropriate, English learners (ELs) should attend their first IEP meeting at the start of middle school. English language needs should be addressed by providing the student with appropriate translation services similar to those provided to family members. Additionally, the special education teacher, the classroom teacher, and/or the ELD teacher should meet with the students prior to the IEP meeting (as discussed below), providing an overview of the meeting as well as tips on how to self-advocate. The instructor working most directly with the student should have an idea of what the student's questions and desires may be prior to the meeting, in case the meeting structure is intimidating and discourages participation. Therefore, if the grade/age of the student is at the secondary level, it is often highly appropriate to include the student in the meeting, particularly when transition items and supports are discussed. Within these parameters and cultural considerations, learner attendance for all or part of the meeting is strongly encouraged.

Student Attends. Several items should be considered if the student attends all or part of the IEP meeting. It is extremely important that the student feels comfortable, empowered to better understand his/her own learning profile, and encouraged to discuss self-perceived learning strengths and needs. Through this process, the student is supported in positive, advocacy ways that lead to productive discussions and IEP planning. To facilitate learner involvement during the meeting, encourage the student to share information he/she is most comfortable sharing, and at no time coerce the student into discussing a topic or providing consent. Within this framework, ask the student about strengths, likes, challenges, dislikes, and how learning best occurs. Similarly, it is important to help the student reframe previously encountered negative experiences or discourses related to classroom instruction or learning challenges.

However, the student may decline to share negative school experiences for a variety of reasons (e.g., cultural teaching, parents in room, concern for possible repercussions), which must be supported and respected. Instead, provide the student with examples, acquired through the comprehensive evaluation, focusing on strengths, qualities, performance, and expectations. These are shared from a positive rather than deficit perspective to encourage discourse with the student. Input from the learner is documented and incorporated into one or more of the most appropriate mandated components of the IEP.

Student Does Not Attend. If the student is not present at the IEP meeting, two tasks should be completed: (1) one or more team members should meet with the student individually during the pre-meeting time, facilitating similar discourse described above for the student who attends the meeting, gathering the information to share at the meeting; and (2) the team member(s) should have a similar conversation with the parents/guardians during the meeting, supporting them in discussing their child's strengths, concerns, successes, and needs based on their perspectives and interactions with their child. In this way, though not physically present at the IEP meeting, the student's input is gathered, shared, and used in the IEP development and implementation.

POST-MEETING SUGGESTIONS

After the IEP meeting concludes and all have approved the plan, the team leader or another team educator should have a brief follow-up conversation with the student and the family to maintain contact and provide support and encouragement. A translator should be included if one was present at the meeting. During this follow-up, ask the student and attending family members if there was anything that they did not share during the meeting that they would now like the school staff to be aware of and understand. Briefly revisit the main aspects of the IEP, and ask the student and the family if they still agree with the goals and the plan. Also, ask if they thought of any items to add since the meeting, now that they have had time to process the experience and IEP document. Although limiting the number of specialists at the meeting can help minimize the extent to which it is intimidating, the formal meeting can nonetheless be difficult and confusing for some family members who attend. Much of the unintended intimidation can be minimized during productive conversations with the family and student during the pre-meeting time. However, sometimes thoughts and feelings important to consider in the IEP process do not surface until after the meeting, or these may be uncovered during a post-meeting contact. In addition to follow-up contact, important post-meeting tasks include (a) implementation, (b) progress monitoring, and (c) continued family engagement.

Post-Meeting Implementation

Once approved, the IEP is put into action and all services are provided as documented. Teachers and service providers should closely document how they are implementing the instructional plans and supporting the student in achieving the academic and/or functional goals. Progress monitoring is conducted as stipulated in the IEP, and regular benchmark assessments conducted with all learners (i.e., universal screenings) should be completed with the student receiving special education services to determine the extent to which the student is making adequate progress toward grade-level benchmarks. In regard to the cultural and linguistic aspects of the instruction connected to the IEP, (a) all ELs should continue to receive English language instruction, (b) interventions selected should be those validated with English language and other diverse learners, and (c) all academic language needs are to be coordinated among the different service providers to ensure sufficient opportunities to learn.

Progress Monitoring

During IEP implementation, the different service providers should closely monitor student learning in diverse settings, using multiple monitoring practices (see Chapter 8) to ensure the IEP is being used appropriately as an instructional tool. The interdisciplinary team should generate a calendar for meeting regularly to discuss the student's progress. In these meetings, the extent to which the instruction, settings, and materials are culturally and linguistically responsive—sufficient to supporting adequate progress—should be discussed. If the student is making adequate progress, the team should consider how to continue to strengthen the progress, making certain the student is sufficiently challenged. If the student is not making adequate progress, the teachers should review the academic settings, instructional components, accommodations, and related or supplemental supports recorded on the learner's IEP, and consider if revisions are necessary to better address learner needs and progress. Also, if progress is not made for an English learner, the ELD instruction should be reviewed to ensure that the student is continuing to receive sufficient English academic language development.

Continued Family Engagement

Educators should periodically contact the family, providing them with progress updates and checking on their child's out-of-school learning by soliciting feedback about IEP implementation. That is, educators should seek parental input about how they perceive the implementation of the IEP, changes they may have seen in their child, and if they have any feedback, questions, or concerns. This cycle of iteration and parental engagement should be integrated into the learner's plan throughout the year.

This chapter concludes with a summary guide (Table 10.1) that contains several of the key aspects of the IEP process discussed above and that are necessary to complete the pre-meeting, during-meeting, and post-meeting tasks, to ensure effective parental and student involvement is leading to the development of a highly functional IEP that will be used as an instructional tool.

Table 10.1   Guide for Conducting Successful IEP Meeting

Instructions: Check each item once it is implemented during the IEP development process.
Pre-Meeting
_____ Educators reflect on their own perspectives toward the language and culture of the learner
_____ Learn about the family
_____ Consider parental language preference(s) so parents can become valued contributors at IEP meeting
_____ Meet with learner to gather essential IEP information
_____ Establish interdisciplinary IEP team members, including translator if necessary
_____ Meet with parents to gather input on educational expectations
_____ Provide parents a list or rough draft of the IEP components

(Continued)

Table 10.1   (Continued)

During Meeting
_____ Create achievable and relevant educational plan
_____ Present levels of academic achievement and functional performance (PLAAFP) are developed that include strengths in learning, areas of concern, and preferred ways of instruction
_____ Parental input is solicited and incorporated into the IEP development
_____ Student input is incorporated into the IEP
_____ Allow parents to share ideas, ask questions, and participate in meaningful ways
_____ Translator is included and used in development of the IEP
_____ Educator team advocates for the student and family during IEP development
_____ Cultural and linguistic teachings and perspectives are solicited and incorporated into plan
Post-Meeting
_____ IEP implementation progress is monitored, recorded, and charted
_____ Follow-up contact with parents initially occurs soon after completion of the IEP meeting
_____ Educators meet periodically to examine IEP progress toward goals and objectives
_____ Collaboration with family continues with periodic contacts, updates, and opportunities for ongoing dialogue
_____ Progress monitoring is conducted as documented on IEP in culturally and linguistically responsive ways

CONCLUSION

Students and their families bring rich life experiences and funds of knowledge to the teaching and learning environment. Learners have notions about how the world works and how they relate to their role within its complicated elements. Students possess skills, literacies, and background knowledge often neglected in today's curriculum and instruction. As educators, it is our responsibility to learn about the vast cultural and linguistic repertoires of practice that diverse students bring into the classroom. Recognizing that students and their families represent broad, dynamic communities creates the foundation for delivery of culturally and linguistically responsive instruction through IEP development and implementation. Additionally, when considering the influences of students' cultures on teaching and learning, it is important to remember that while cultures contain basic underpinnings consistent over time, they are also dynamic and ever changing, highlighting the notion that the process of understanding one's own culture and those of others is a lifelong skill that continues to evolve. Adhering to the chapter's pre-meeting, during-meeting, and post-meeting suggestions for English language and other diverse learners shapes a collaborative environment among family, students, and educators, necessary for development and delivery of culturally and linguistically responsive IEPs.

Putting the IEP Pieces Together 11

This practical book provides educators with research findings, professional guidance, and best practices for developing Individualized Education Programs (IEPs) for English language and other diverse learners. The intent of this final chapter is to summarize key ideas and practices discussed in the earlier chapters that frame the development and implementation of an IEP as both a compliance and instructional tool. Though key components of an IEP are mandated by the IDEA legislation, the content documented for each component for English language and other diverse learners must go beyond that which is typically included to account for unique qualities and strengths of culturally and linguistically diverse learners.

SUMMARY OF IEP SKILL SETS FOR ENGLISH LANGUAGE AND OTHER DIVERSE LEARNERS

Figure 11.1, developed from material previously discussed in this book, illustrates ten key knowledge and skill sets necessary to develop effective IEPs for diverse learners as addressed in this book. Collectively, proficiency with each of the ten skill sets provides educators a solid foundation for developing culturally and linguistically responsive IEPs for English language and other diverse learners. We begin by summarizing the IEP skill areas discussed throughout this book along with application examples.

Academic Language Proficiency

Skill Set: Proficient use of academic language is foundational to unlocking success in school for students who bring cultural and linguistic diversity to the teaching and learning environment (Gottlieb & Ernst-Slavit, 2014). Academic language, at minimum, includes the three interrelated areas of vocabulary, grammar, and discourse (Frantz, Bailey, Starr, & Perea, 2014). Four interrelated processes frame academic language in teaching and learning: sociocultural, developmental, academic, and cognitive, each of which is essential to incorporate into classroom instruction for diverse learners.

Application to IEPs: English language academic proficiency levels inform and shape the content documented in at least three key IEP components:

Figure 11.1   Skill Sets Essential for Developing Culturally and Linguistically Responsive IEPs

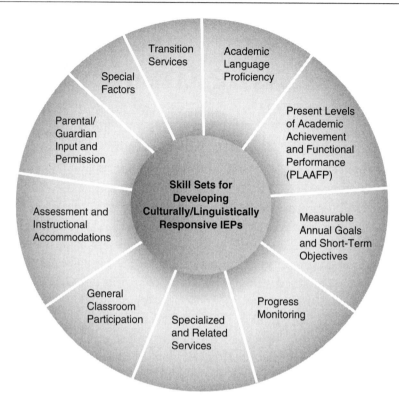

(a) present levels of academic achievement and functional performance (PLAAFP) by describing learner strengths relative to language, (b) measurable annual goals and associated short-term objectives addressing needed academic language proficiency supports required to improve learning, and (c) accommodations and/or supplemental supports that must include consideration of the learner's academic language proficiency and amount of English language development (ELD) instruction.

Present Levels of Academic Achievement and Functional Performance

Skill Set: Academic performance includes core academic skills and abilities relevant to the disability, especially reflective of reading, writing, and/or mathematics. Functional skills are those abilities that reflect necessary daily living and classroom performance expectations essential to success regardless of academic area.

Application to IEPs: Academic achievement performance should be summarized in both quantitative (e.g., assessment test or rubric scores) and qualitative terms (i.e., statements about conditions under which student best learns). Functional skills documented on the IEP include abilities necessary for effective functional performance in school and society that require support or teaching. When developing the PLAAFP statements on the IEP, since culturally and linguistically diverse values, teachings, and norms affect both academic achievement and functional performance, these should be identified as student strengths clarifying ways of learning.

Measurable Annual Goals and Short-Term Objectives

Skill Set: Once PLAAFP statements are developed, annual goals stated in measurable terms within a defined time frame are discussed and documented. Adhering to SMART goal procedures provides a structured approach to annual goal, and associated short-term objective, development and is the preferred method in many of today's schools. Through development of meaningful, specific, and attainable IEP goals, English language and other diverse learners are provided IEPs that reflect culturally and linguistically diverse values and qualities consistent with the students' second language acquisition stage of development, cultural heritage and teachings, as well as family expectations.

Application to IEPs: Building on the above ideas, the IEP team develops SMART goals to guide IEP delivery for English language and other diverse learners. SMART goals improve outcomes for students by offering specific applications to the skill being taught, mastered, and progress monitored. Interconnected to the PLAAFP, IEP team members create annual goals unique to the student's identified disability and English language proficiency levels by documenting *specific, measurable, attainable, relevant,* and *time-bound* material to guide implementation of special services. Once developed, necessary progress monitoring, accommodations, and related services are best identified.

Progress Monitoring

Skill Set: Fundamental to all IEPs is documentation of how progress toward annual goals and short-term objectives will be measured, charted, and results interpreted. Progress monitoring refers to the task of systematically gathering assessment data to determine the extent to which a student responds to evidence-based instruction on a regular, frequent basis (e.g., monthly, weekly, daily; Hoover, 2009). It is essential to consider that English learners (ELs) at developing or emerging levels of English proficiency are especially vulnerable to misinterpretation of progress-monitoring results, due to second language development behaviors. Also, progress-monitoring tools (e.g., AIMSweb, DIBELS) used with ELs often have lower validity than when used with fluent English learners, especially for those at the lower end of the English language proficiency continuum (Abedi, 2004).

Application to IEPs: Progress monitoring of diverse learners is influenced by several instructional features including English language proficiency level, test validity, need for multiple means of assessment, and selection of best devices and practices to ensure cultural and linguistic responsiveness. Though several monitoring practices and associated devices exist, curriculum-based measurement (CBM) is one of the most relevant for monitoring IEP progress. CBMs are especially appropriate for English language and other diverse learners, due to flexibility in development and use to account for diverse learning qualities, such as experiential background, English proficiency, and cultural relevance to instruction.

Specialized and Related Services

Skill Set: Specialized and related services include a variety of supports such as counseling, medical, occupational therapy, transportation, speech therapy, or social work delivered by various professionals including those trained as a guidance counselor, school psychologist, social worker, school nurse, or speech and language specialist. In addition, many students require supplemental services or aids necessarily provided for education with nondisabled peers to the maximum extent possible (Gibb & Dyches, 2016). Specialized and related services along with supplemental supports are documented on the IEP, monitored for appropriate delivery, and effects assessed on a periodic basis.

Application to IEPs: When used with English language and other diverse learners, the selection and implementation of these services and supports should be made within a cultural and linguistic context to be meaningful and relevant. Parental input should be sought and valued when one or more specialized or related services are provided. In addition, supplements to the curriculum should include use of various ESL instructional practices (e.g., CEIP tool; Hoover, Hopewell, & Sarris, 2014) and daily ELD to ensure delivery of culturally and linguistically responsive teaching and learning in both general and special education settings.

General Classroom Participation

Skill Set: The extent to which English language and other diverse learners with IEPs continue to receive instruction with general education peers is also documented. This includes attention to English language development as well as access to core curriculum in the general classroom. As emphasized, lack of emphasis on ELD once delivery of an IEP begins facilitates potential lack of progress, since English development directly influences academic progress. English language and other diverse learners who receive special education should continue to receive as much instruction as possible in the general setting, which includes ELD instruction with peers.

Application to IEPs: Continued English language development—for example, daily ELD for forty-five minutes—in addition to incorporating research-based ESL instructional practices in general class core instruction, which should be documented on the IEP, are both essential and necessary for successful IEP progress. It is important to note that ELD instruction provided to all ELs in the school or district must continue for ELs with IEPs. Education with peers provides diverse students sufficient opportunities to learn. Therefore, IEPs for English language and other diverse learners should contain specific information about (a) ELD supports in general education, (b) ELD general education pull-out instruction, and (c) strategies to ensure that culturally and linguistically responsive instruction is delivered in daily core general education instruction.

Assessment and Instructional Accommodations

Skill Set: Instructional and assessment accommodations to best improve learning are documented on the IEP. Specifically, five accommodations are typically considered in the delivery of assessment and instruction for learners with an IEP: (a) setting, (b) presentation, (c) response, (d) scheduling/assignments, and (e) time. Though these accommodations are essential to the delivery of appropriate instruction and assessment for all learners with IEPs, they also represent structures specific to providing culturally and linguistically responsive teaching and learning for diverse students.

Application to IEPs: IEPs for English language and other diverse learners should document instructional and assessment accommodations that reflect cultural and linguistic qualities the students bring to the teaching and learning environment. For example, one responsive accommodation allows for the use of reading material that reflects the student's cultural teachings. Or providing a culturally and linguistically diverse (CLD) learner additional time to respond to questions or other items to reflect the level of English language proficiency is an accommodation that is of great benefit. Much latitude exists in the accommodations component of an IEP, and educators should take advantage of the opportunity to document ways to structure learning, providing all service providers with valuable instructional suggestions.

Parental/Guardian Input and Permission

Skill Set: The IDEA legislation provides parents/guardians with necessary safeguards, requiring their input and written permission regarding IEP development and implementation. For English language and other diverse learners, these legal mandates address several items including providing an interpreter in the most proficient language, responding to issues or questions raised about the IEP process and its implementation, obtaining written consent for IEP approval, and informing parents of procedures to follow should they disagree with or otherwise wish to challenge aspects of the IEP. Parental input and approval issues often arise in select areas such as specialized and related services, delivery settings, and culturally and linguistically responsive supports.

Application to IEPs: To best avoid disagreement issues associated with IEP services and supports to be provided or not provided to English language and other diverse learners, instructional plans should incorporate parental input and clearly (a) demonstrate how English language development is continued for ELs with IEPs, (b) incorporate both language development and content objectives into IEPs, and (c) document relevant supplemental supports, aids, and accommodations (e.g., culturally responsive materials, research-based ESL instructional practices, instructional settings with true peers). Overall, IEPs and their delivery must be responsive to (a) culturally and linguistically diverse needs, (b) second language acquisition proficiency levels, and (c) use of instructional methods and assessments validated to the learners' cultural and linguistic present levels of performance.

Special Factors

Skill Set: This area includes use of behavioral intervention plans and assistive technology in the teaching and learning environment.

Application to IEPs: If the learner exhibits specific behavior that interferes with his/her own learning or the learning of others, a behavioral intervention plan is required, which in turn is incorporated into the IEP. Assistive technology devices and services required to access instruction and classroom tasks are evaluated with appropriate technologies identified and incorporated into the IEP.

Transition Services

Skill Set: All secondary-aged learners with IEPs are required by the IDEA legislation to have a documented plan for transitioning beyond secondary education. The transition component requires input and efforts from educators, families, community organization members, as well as the student, through a process that includes planning, implementation, and coordination (Trainor & Patton, 2008). Cultural influences on family and student expectations beyond secondary education are critical to consider (Hoover, Klingner, Baca, & Patton, 2008), and are best determined through meaningful parent engagement in IEP development, which is mandated by IDEA.

Application to IEPs: Transition aspects of an IEP include potential (a) employment or postsecondary school options, (b) settings or types of locations for the postsecondary options, and (c) life skills required for success beyond secondary education. Each of these items requires careful consideration and documentation to ensure that the learner is provided meaningful preparation for life beyond secondary schooling. In regard to English language and other diverse learners, unique cultural and linguistic supports, aspirations, family expectations, and related heritage teachings shape transition plans and outcomes.

These skill sets represent the most important features necessary to develop, implement, and evaluate progress associated with IEPs for English language and other diverse learners. As educators move forward in efforts to make the IEP a useful instructional tool, the many practical suggestions discussed in previous chapters will help provide an integrated education to best deliver culturally and linguistically responsive instruction through implementation of the IEP.

THE INTEGRATED IEP FOR DIVERSE LEARNERS

We conclude this chapter and book with Table 11.1, which provides a checklist to use to ensure that IEPs developed for English language and other diverse learners are culturally and linguistically responsive. The checklist reflects key items discussed throughout this book.

CONCLUSION

The development of an IEP for English language and other diverse learners requires educators to consider factors that go beyond those addressed for English speakers. Culturally and linguistically diverse qualities remain central to

Table 11.1 Culturally and Linguistically Responsive IEP Guide

Instructions: Based on consensus, circle Yes/No to indicate whether the team confirms that the item is incorporated into the diverse learner's IEP. Leave item blank if not relevant to learner (e.g., student is not an EL, yet item refers to an EL).		
IEP Item/Team Consensus		
1. Academic Language		
Academic language strengths/needs are incorporated into PLAAFP	**Y**	**N**
Academic language supports are incorporated into the annual goals/objectives	**Y**	**N**
2. Present Levels of Academic Achievement and Functional Performance (PLAAFP)		
PLAAFP include statements describing instructional conditions through which student best learns, reflecting cultural/linguistic strengths	**Y**	**N**
PLAAFP address both academic and functional learning abilities, if both are indicated as areas of disability concern	**Y**	**N**
PLAAFP include both qualitative and quantitative evidence	**Y**	**N**
PLAAFP include statements about English language proficiency level	**Y**	**N**
PLAAFP highlight diverse learner's strengths as well as areas of need	**Y**	**N**
3. Annual Goals		
Annual goals and/or short-term objectives include use of ESL/bilingual research-based instructional practices	**Y**	**N**
English language development is incorporated into IEP goals	**Y**	**N**
Content objectives use SMART principles connected to diverse needs	**Y**	**N**
4. Progress Monitoring		
Monitoring practices/devices are aligned directly to what will be taught	**Y**	**N**
Monitoring practices/devices are unbiased for ELs or other diverse learners	**Y**	**N**
Monitoring includes use of curriculum-based measurements	**Y**	**N**
Monitoring results inform both language development and content progress	**Y**	**N**
5. Specialized/Related Services and Supplemental Supports/Aids		
Specialized and related services are documented on IEP	**Y**	**N**
Specialized and related services were discussed with parents/guardians prior to incorporation into IEP in most proficient language	**Y**	**N**
Supplemental supports/aids include use of ESL instructional practices in both general and special education settings	**Y**	**N**
Specialized and related services include input from a bilingual educator if student is a second language learner	**Y**	**N**
Specialized and related services, and supplemental supports/aids receive parental approval for incorporation into IEP in most proficient language	**Y**	**N**
6. General-Education Instruction With Peers		
General-education curriculum access with true peers is clearly articulated on IEP	**Y**	**N**
General-education participation for English learners includes services in ELD	**Y**	**N**
If appropriate, special education service delivery includes push-in supports in general-education classroom	**Y**	**N**
Pull-out special education services are based on disability need and not English language proficiency level	**Y**	**N**

ESL/bilingual instructional modifications to meet disability needs in general classroom are identified on IEP	*Y*	*N*
7. Accommodations		
Necessary instructional accommodations are appropriate for diverse learners	*Y*	*N*
Necessary assessment accommodations are appropriate for diverse learners	*Y*	*N*
Accommodations support culturally/linguistically responsive instruction	*Y*	*N*
Accommodations reflect English language proficiency levels of English learners	*Y*	*N*
8. Parental Input/Permission		
Parents/guardians are informed of rights and supports in IEP development in most proficient language	*Y*	*N*
Parents/guardians are consulted in IEP development prior to formal meeting	*Y*	*N*
Parents/guardians provide written consent for IEP	*Y*	*N*
Parents/guardians are provided interpreter if necessary during IEP meeting	*Y*	*N*
Parents/guardians are provided translated material if necessary during IEP meeting	*Y*	*N*
Follow-up to IEP meeting with parents is scheduled	*Y*	*N*
9. Special Factors		
Behavioral intervention plan, if needed, is developed and incorporated into IEP	*Y*	*N*
Required assistive technology devices are used as necessary in culturally and linguistically responsive ways	*Y*	*N*
Needed assistive technology services are provided in culturally and linguistically responsive ways	*Y*	*N*
10. Transition Supports (Learners 14 and older)		
Transition plans are developed with learner input in most proficient language	*Y*	*N*
Parents are consulted about transition needs of learner in most proficient language	*Y*	*N*
Cultural values/teachings are considered when developing transition plan	*Y*	*N*
Life skills to be developed for effective transition are incorporated into goals and objectives (i.e., Instructional Goals)	*Y*	*N*
Appropriate community organizations are identified on IEP to best reflect transition expectations of family and student (i.e., Linkage Goals)	*Y*	*N*

Source: Adapted from Hoover (2016a), *Culturally and linguistically responsive IEP guide.* Boulder, CO: Hamilton.

the education of CLD learners in both special and general education once the IEP is developed and implementation begins. It is essential to maintain English language development for ELs with IEPs and avoid reducing English language development services at the expense of special education services. Parental engagement, input, and approval are central to effective IEP development, as is the need to document necessary accommodations, specialized and related services, and supplemental supports/aids consistent with cultural values and second language acquisition. For secondary learners, emphasizing life skills required for success beyond secondary schooling is essential to ensure effective transition. Access to general education curricula and general classroom participation, including ELD, should continue for all diverse learners with IEPs, with the present levels of academic achievement and functional performance serving as the foundation for developing effective IEPs for all students.

Appendix

The appendix includes a table describing various devices to measure learner progress and determining present levels of performance along with samples of IEPs for two English learners.

The table "Commercially Available Instruments for Determining Present Levels of Performance," though not all-inclusive, is presented to further explain many devices that are appropriate for developing and implementing an IEP. The devices may be used with English language and other diverse learners provided their use aligns with necessary English proficiency levels required by the test and possessed by the learner, and when incorporated into a comprehensive assessment set of procedures. *None of the devices presented is sufficient for use as a single measure with an English learner; multiple measures are required to best determine present levels.*

IEP examples are provided for an elementary 2nd grade student and a secondary 11th grade student, highlighting some of the many suggestions about how to create culturally and linguistically responsive IEPs for English language and other diverse learners discussed in this book. Though the template used for these two sample IEPs is authentic and based on a tool currently used in a midwestern US school system, these IEPs are presented with the recognition that different districts generate their own IEP templates and formats; therefore, our sample IEPs may vary from others used in readers' schools. However, each IEP contains mandated IDEA (2004) components.

***Note:* For illustrative purposes, written statements and responses to the IEP items specific to culturally and linguistically responsive instruction are presented in bold text.**

Also, other diverse examples in these IEPs are appropriate; our intent is to provide a few relevant examples of ways to easily incorporate culturally and linguistically responsive material into the IEP.

Note: The template used for the sample IEPs was adapted from the Lawrence, Kansas, Public Schools Elementary and Secondary IEPs (2016) and used with permission.

COMMERCIALLY AVAILABLE INSTRUMENTS FOR DETERMINING PRESENT LEVELS OF PERFORMANCE

Instrument/Publisher	Brief Description	Results/Products
Adaptive Behavior Planning and Instruction Guide	Informal instrument with 1000+ items that can be used to pinpoint current levels of function across multiple adaptive behavior skill areas	• indication of mastery levels for individual items
Basic Assessment System for Children—3rd ed. (BASC-3)	Standardized instrument that comprises a set of rating scales for measuring behavior	• standard score (T-score) • percentiles
Behavioral Intervention Planning—3rd ed. (BIP-3)	Informal instrument for conducting functional behavioral assessments and developing behavioral intervention plans	• system for organizing observational and other behavioral data
Bilingual Verbal Ability Tests (BVAT)	Standardized instrument for use in bilingual education entry, program planning, and determination of academic readiness	• standard scores • relative proficiency index • "instructional zones" index
Brigance Comprehensive Inventory of Basic Skills II	Criterion-referenced instrument that provides comprehensive assessment of reading/English language arts and mathematics	• criterion measures • NOTE: a standardized component is also available
Developmental Reading Assessment-2	Criterion-referenced instrument that provides indications of reading proficiency (reading engagement, oral reading fluency, and comprehension)	• criterion measures • benchmarks
Dynamic Indicators of Basic Early Literacy Skills (DIBELS)	Informal procedures/ measures for assessment of early literacy skills	• benchmarks
English Language Proficiency Assessment for the 21st Century (ELPA21)	System that measures development of English language proficiency— identifies initial placement, need for reassessment, instructional guidance	• screener • summative assessment information
Informal Assessments for Transition Planning: Employment and Career Planning	Set of informal measures that generate information about careers and other areas related to future employment	• depends on the measure • checklists • rating scales
Informal Assessments for Transition Planning: Independent Living and Community Participation	Set of informal measures that generate information about how an individual is able to deal with the demands of everyday life	• depends on the measure • checklists • rating scales
Measures of Academic Progress (MAP)	Standardized measures of mathematics and reading	• RIT (Rasch Unit) • lexiles

Instrument/Publisher	*Brief Description*	*Results/Products*
Pragmatic Language Observation Scale (PLOS)	Standardized rating scale that assesses student daily classroom spoken language behaviors	• Pragmatic Language Observation Index • percentiles
Reading A-Z	Collection of researched- based leveled reading resources with phonics assessments (29 levels of reading difficulty)	• downloadable resources
Reading Observational Scale (ROS)	Standardized rating scale that assesses student reading behaviors	• Reading Observation Index • percentiles
Scholastic Reading Inventory (SRI)	Reading comprehension assessment (literature and expository text) that uses the Lexile Framework	• lexiles
Study Skills Inventory	Informal rating scale of study skills organized across 12 key areas	• rating scale that includes four levels of proficiency (highly proficient; proficient; partially proficient; not proficient)
WIDA ACCESS Language Proficiency	Large-scale English language proficiency assessment focusing on listening, speaking, reading, and writing	• proficiency levels for each language domain (1 to 6) • scale scores for each language domain (100 to 600)
Written Language Observations Scale (WLOS)	Standardized rating scale that assesses student written language behaviors	• Written Language Observation Index percentiles
6+1® Trait Writing Model of Instruction and Assessment	Model used to evaluate written language across text types and are based on specific traits: ideas, organization, voice, word choice, sentence fluency, conventions, presentation	• rubrics: K–2 or 3–12

IEP: ELEMENTARY INDIVIDUALIZED EDUCATION PROGRAM

Student Information

Name: *Antonio Tomas*   **Age:** *7*   **Grade:** *2*
Parent/Guardian: *Mr. Robert Tomas*
Parent/Guardian: *Mrs. Silvia Tomas*
Language of Parent/Guardian: *Spanish* *and English*

IEP Type/Dates

Type of IEP: *Initial*   **IEP Date: Initial:** *10/05/16*
Annual Review: *10/05/17*   **3-Year Review:** *10/05/19*

IEP Meeting Participants

Title	Name
Special Educator	Mrs. Smith
General Educator	Mr. Jones
Administrator/Designee	Principal Gonzalez
Parent/Guardian	Mr. Tomas
Parent/Guardian	Mrs. Tomas
Student	Not in Attendance
School Psychologist	Ms. Hamilton
Bilingual Educator	Ms. Martinez
ELD Instructor	Mr. Gomez

✓ A person to interpret the instructional implications of evaluation results attended this meeting.

Other Agency Involvement

☑ No Agency Involvement needed at this time.

☐ A representative of another agency was invited to this meeting with parent consent.

☐ An agency representative was invited to the meeting with parent consent, but did not attend.

Notifications

Federal law requires school districts to notify students and parents at least one year prior to the student's 18th birthday that at age 18 all rights afforded parents under special education law will transfer to the student unless he/she has been legally adjudicated to be an incapacitated person or a child in need of care. This means that in the absence of court directive, the student will become the educational decision maker.

Notice provided: ☑ Education/Decision Maker ☐ Student

Notice to Parent (student 18 or older): You have been provided a copy of your parental rights annually prior to this IEP meeting or at this IEP meeting. You may also request a copy of these rights at any time.

Notification of Destruction of Records: Special education records for each child with an exceptionality are maintained by the school district until no longer needed to provide educational services to the child. This notice is to inform you that the special education records for this student will be destroyed after (5) years following the end of your child's educational services unless the student or the student's guardian has taken possession of the records prior to that time.

IEP CONSIDERATIONS

Strengths of the Student

Antonio is an active second grader who enjoys climbing on the jungle gym with his friends at recess, and PE is his favorite subject in school. **Antonio is an English learner who functions at the expanding stage, based on a current English proficiency test.** *Antonio reads near or at grade level, his favorite color is black, and he enjoys circle time because he likes to sing and dance. During whole-class time, he performs best when he receives questions about reading and mathematics tasks ahead of time,* **where he is given ample time to process questions and then respond in English.** *Antonio does not do well when put in the spotlight with an expectation to respond immediately; he requires some extra time to process information given in English.* **His learning disability in mathematics is observed at school, home, and in the community and when both Spanish and English languages are used.** *His behavioral outbursts occur most frequently during reading instruction yet are also seen during math although less frequently. Also, Antonio performs well when teachers use visuals and manipulatives to help him* **understand new content in English and build connections with prior knowledge. Additionally, during mathematics and reading instruction, Antonio should be paired with a Spanish-speaking peer to assist with clarifying English vocabulary and concepts, and increase appropriate behavior. Antonio is more successful in the classroom when provided these types of English language development supports.**

Concerns of the Parents/Educational Decision Maker

☑ The IEP Team has requested and considered the concerns of Parent(s)/ Educational Decision Maker.

Educationally Relevant Medical Issues

Does the student have a health condition that impacts the student's involvement and progress in the general curriculum and general education classroom and other education-related settings?

☐ No relevant medical issues noted.

☐ Student has Individual Health Care Plan.

☑ No Individual Health Care Plan; however, relevant information is noted below:

> *Diagnosis of ADHD—hyperactivity/ impulsivity. Antonio does not take medication per family decision. They would like to wait and try other methods to help Antonio before they talk about the use of medication with the pediatrician.* Teachers will provide feedback to family and pediatrician will monitor. *Antonio exhibits these behaviors during instruction provided in both English and Spanish and both in and out of school settings.* Progress in mathematics is most impacted by these behaviors.

Blind/Visually Impaired

☐ Yes ☑ No **Is the student Blind or Visually Impaired?**

If yes, the use of Braille should be provided unless the IEP team determines otherwise. If after consideration the IEP team deems Braille not an appropriate method, provide reason for not using Braille.

Deaf/Hard of Hearing

☐ Yes ☑ No **Is the student Deaf or Hard of Hearing?**

If yes, describe unique communication needs relating to opportunities for direct communications with peers and professional personnel in the student's language/communications mode:

Evaluation Results

In developing this IEP, the team has considered the results of the initial or most recent evaluation of the student including, as appropriate, the results of district or state assessments.

Limited English Proficiency

☑ Yes ☐ No **Is the student an English Language Learner?**

> *Student tested at level 4 (Expanding) for English proficiency on the WIDA ACCESS test.*

Special Communication Needs

☑ The unique communication needs of the student have been considered. If unique communication needs are present, IEP team must con- sider how these needs affect the student's achievement toward educational goals.

Assistive Technology

☑ **The Assistive Technology needs of the student have been considered.** If needed, Assistive Technology is addressed in the following place(s) within the IEP:

☐ Program Modifications/Accommodations

☐ Assistive Technology Plan

☐ Service Plan

Social/Behavioral/Emotional Needs

☑ Yes ☐ No **Does the student have behaviors which impede his/her learning or the learning of others?**

If yes, team must consider positive behavioral interventions, strategies, and supports to address behavior. Behavior is addressed in the following place(s) within the IEP:

☑ Goal(s)

☐ Behavioral Intervention Plan (attached)

☑ Accommodations

> *Antonio gets very excited and wants to share his thoughts with the class at most times, but particularly during reading instruction time, and sometimes during mathematics time. He struggles with raising his hand and waiting to be called on. He yells out whatever comes to his mind before he thinks through whether the time or content of his response is appropriate for the class discussion or topic. Antonio is motivated by use of a simple token system to earn a reward (e.g., Iron Man stickers) when he demonstrates appropriate group behavior, by refraining from calling out his answers prior to raising his hand and waiting to be recognized. Teachers should model the appropriate behavior by giving him visual cues to remind him to wait or raise his hand prior to speaking. He will also be provided a self-monitoring chart to be kept at his desk and used during reading instruction, which is when he has the most issues with inappropriate group behaviors.*

Physical Education

☐ Yes ☑ No **Does the student need Adaptive PE in order to participate in physical education?**

If yes, describe services in service plan.

PRESENT LEVELS OF ACADEMIC ACHIEVEMENT AND FUNCTIONAL PERFORMANCE, GOAL AND OBJECTIVES

Standard Associated with this Annual goal: *Mathematics*

PLAAFP: Present levels of academic achievement and/or functional performance related to particular area of need.

Current Academic Achievement and/or Functional Performance: *As of November 2016, Antonio is able to count to 100 in English, with 90% accuracy,* **and in Spanish to 20, with 100% accuracy.** *In random order, he is able to identify numbers to 20 in English with 85% accuracy* **and in Spanish with 60% accuracy.** *Antonio performs best in small group settings rather than large group.* **Antonio counts objects in Spanish then translates to English for quantities under 20. Antonio performs best when provided extra time to process information in English given his proficiency level in using English academic language. Also, he is most successful when mathematics problems are related to prior experiences in his home language of Spanish and when provided opportunity to examine the similarities and differences in the use of mathematics between his home culture and that of the classroom.**

Impact of Exceptionality upon ability to access and progress in the general curriculum (or appropriate activities for preschool children): NA

Baseline Data for Goal:	**How will progress toward goal be measured?**
Antonio is *able to count to 100 in English, with 90% accuracy,* **and to 20 in Spanish**, *with 100% accuracy. Is able to identify numbers to 20 in English with 85% accuracy* **and in Spanish with 60% accuracy.**	*Mathematics fluency test along with performance-based projects.*

Annual Goal:
By November 2017, when provided a mathematics task being able to ask clarifying questions with **a Spanish-speaking peer,** *Antonio will independently solve double-digit addition and subtraction without regrouping with 80% accuracy, and addition and subtraction with regrouping with 70% accuracy each within a 20-minute session.*

Parents will receive written reports of the student progress toward meeting annual IEP goals in accordance with the district's established grade reporting schedule.

PRESENT LEVELS OF ACADEMIC ACHIEVEMENT AND FUNCTIONAL PERFORMANCE, GOAL AND OBJECTIVES

Standard Associated with this Annual goal: *Behavior*

PLAAFP: Present levels of academic achievement and/or functional performance related to particular area of need.

Current Academic Achievement and/or Functional Performance: *As of November 2016, Antonio verbally expresses his thoughts aloud to the class and teachers at inappropriate times during group classroom instruction particularly during reading instruction. He blurts out on average 10 times and raises his hand on average 2 times per 30-minute activity (frequency count across 4 different group activities). Behavior concern is highest during reading instruction. Based on Reading A-Z assessment he performs at an instructional level with comprehension at a 70% success rate. Antonio performs best behaviorally when* **academic tasks include sufficient time for him to build background knowledge about the topic with a Spanish-speaking peer and when approximations to the correct response are initially accepted to encourage his success. His inappropriate behavior decreases when a concept is delivered in concrete ways using visuals, diagrams, or concept mapping to assist with English academic language development.**

Impact of Exceptionality upon ability to access and progress in the general curriculum (or appropriate activities for preschool children): NA

Baseline Data for Goal:	How will progress toward goal be measured?
Outbursts occur on average 10 times per 30-minute activity (frequency count across 4 different reading group activities and independent work). He raises his hand to be recognized on average two times in the 30-minute reading period.	*Behavior rating scale, self-monitoring checklist*

Annual Goal:
By November 2017, after using a self-monitoring chart, visual cues, concrete examples, **and approximations in reading responses,** *Antonio will increase appropriate expressive behavior 80% by reducing his inappropriate outbursts to no more than 2 per 30-minute reading group session.*

Parents will receive written reports of the student progress toward meeting annual IEP goals in accordance with the district's established grade reporting schedule.

PROGRAM ACCOMMODATIONS AND MODIFICATIONS

The following unique accommodations and modifications are needed to enable the child to advance appropriately in attaining the annual goals, be involved and make progress in the general curriculum and participate in extracurricular and nonacademic actives, and be educated and participate with other children with and without disabilities in these activities as appropriate.

☐ No accommodations or modifications are necessary OR

In the boxes below indicate whether an accommodation or modification is stated along with location, duration, frequency.

Accommodation and Modifications	Location	Duration	Frequency
☑ **Accommodation:** *Oral responses to math problems* ☐ **Modification:**	*Inclusive and special education classrooms*	*Each math session during 2016–17 year*	*During all math instruction*
☐ **Accommodation:** ☑ **Modification:** *Chunk assignments into smaller sections*	*Inclusive and special education classrooms*	*Each math session during 2016–17 year*	*During all math instruction*
☑ **Accommodation:** *Frequent breaks especially when he is feeling overwhelmed and having trouble staying focused* ☐ **Modification:**	*Inclusive and special education classrooms*	*Each instruction and work session during 2016–17 year*	*During all content sessions*
☑ **Accommodation:** *Response approximations are accepted when reading concepts and material are new to learner to reduce behavior outbursts* ☐ **Modification:**	*Inclusive and special education classrooms*	*Each reading session during 2016–17 year*	*During all reading sessions*
☑ **Accommodation:** ***Spanish speaking peer provided during math and reading to assist with English academic vocabulary and reduce outbursts*** ☐ **Modification:**	*Inclusive and special education classroom*	*Each reading and math session during 2016–17 year*	*During all reading and math sessions*
☑ **Accommodation:** *Self-monitoring system to manage own behavior during reading whole group instruction* ☐ **Modification:**	*Inclusive and special education classrooms*	*Each reading session during 2016–17 year*	*During all reading sessions*

*Only state-approved accommodations will be used for State Assessments.

*Only those accommodations/modifications routinely provided the student in daily classroom instruction should be listed.

PARTICIPATION IN RELEVANT DISTRICT AND STATE ASSESSMENTS

State Assessments

	General Assessment	General Assessment With Accommodation
Math Grades 3–8 & 10		✓
English / Language Arts Grades 3–8 & 10		✓
History / Government Grades 6, 8, & 11		✓
Science Grades 5, 8, & 11		✓

*Accommodations found on program Modifications and Accommodations.

*Content/grade levels are state determined. Tests made available by the state will be administered.

District K–12 Assessments

*All school-aged students have the opportunity to participate in District Assessments.

☐ Student will participate in available District Assessment without accommodations.

☑ Student will participate in available District Assessment with accommodations.

☐ The IEP team determined the following District Assessments are not appropriate:

SERVICE PLAN

Special Education and Related Services and Supplementary Aids and Services

The school is unable to provide regularly scheduled special education and/or related services when the following occurs: inclement weather closures, scheduled school closures, unforeseen emergencies, student absences, school field trips, assemblies, non-late arrival weeks, emergency drills, and summer break.

☑ Yes ☐ No The student will have the same opportunities to participate with children without disabilities in extracurricular and other non-academic activities.

If no, explain:

```
```

Describe the special education services to be provided, and describe the related services (if any) that the student needs in order to benefit from his/her special education services. Also describe the supplementary aids and services necessary to enable the student to be educated with children without disabilities to the maximum extent appropriate.

Service Delivery Statement (include service frequency, location, and duration):

> *Antonio will receive special education mathematics instruction daily for 30 minutes. In addition, Antonio will receive direct social work support for 30 minutes, 1 day per week at a time that does not interfere with direct instruction in content areas.* **Classroom instruction should include some extended wait time to provide Antonio increased opportunities to process information, questions, and tasks in English.** *General classroom teacher will use a self-monitoring system with Antonio to help reduce behavior outbursts during reading instruction, to be supported through contact with the social worker.* **Antonio will continue to receive English language development instruction in the general education classroom and in a pull- out setting for 30 minutes per day, 5 days per week, that does not interfere with direct instruction in content areas or special education services.**

☐ Yes ☑ No **Is Special Transportation needed?**

If yes, provide description if necessary (e.g., lift).

```
```

Supports for School Staff

Describe the supports for school personnel that need to be provided for the student to enable him/her to advance appropriately toward attaining his/her measurable annual goals and to be involved and progress in the general education curriculum.

☐ No supports for school staff are necessary.

Teachers and staff will be trained on the use of Antonio's token system to earn rewards and nonverbal cues

---

☐ Yes ☑ No **Is Extended School Year (ESY) necessary based on current and available data?**

Description of ESY Services to be provided (include service frequency, location, and duration):

Other Considerations not noted elsewhere in IEP:

None

IEP: SECONDARY INDIVIDUALIZED EDUCATION PROGRAM

Student Information

Name: *Luna Garcia*   **Age:** *17*   **Grade:** *11*
Parent/Guardian: *Ms. Ella Ocampo*
Parent/Guardian:
Language of Parent/Guardian: ***Filipino*** *and English*

IEP Type/Dates

Type of IEP: *Annual*   **IEP Date:** *04/19/12*
Annual Review: *04/19/17*   **3-Year Review:** *04/19/18*

IEP Meeting Participants

Title	*Name*
Special Educator	*Mrs. Prentice*
Math Educator	*Mr. Garcia*
English Lang Arts Educator	*Ms. Sheppard*
Science Educator	*Ms. Kim*
Social Worker	*Ms. Crickard*
Administrator/Designee	*Principal Hernandez*
Parent/Guardian	*Ms. Ocampo*
Student	*Luna Garcia*
Bilingual Educator	*Ms. Martinez*
ELD Instructor	*Mr. Gomez*

☑ A person to interpret the instructional implications of evaluation results attended this meeting.

Other Agency Involvement

☑ No Agency Involvement needed at this time.

☐ A representative of another agency was invited to this meeting with parent consent.

☐ An agency representative was invited to the meeting with parent consent, but did not attend.

Notifications

Federal law requires school districts to notify students and parents at least one year prior to the student's 18th birthday that at age 18 all rights afforded parents under special education law will transfer to the student unless he/she has been legally adjudicated to be an incapacitated person or a child in need of care.

This means that in the absence of court directive, the student will become the educational decision maker.

Notice provided: ☑ Education/Decision Maker   ☐ Student

Notice to Parent (student 18 or older): You have been provided a copy of your parental rights annually prior to this IEP meeting or at this IEP meeting. You may also request a copy of these rights at any time.

Notification of Destruction of Records: Special education records for each child with an exceptionality are maintained by the school district until no longer needed to provide educational services to the child. This notice is to inform you that the special education records for this student will be destroyed after (5) years following the end of your child's educational services unless the student or the student's guardian has taken possession of the records prior to that time.

IEP CONSIDERATIONS

Strengths of the Student

> *Luna is an 11th-grade student who is involved with the fine arts department.* **Luna is an English learner who functions at the higher end of the intermediate stage of language acquisition, based on a current English proficiency test. Though possessing near fluency with English proficiency, Luna still requires language supports to access and use grade-level academic English vocabulary (e.g., word walls, sentence stems) and extra time to process higher-level comprehension tasks.** *Though her disability is in writing, her favorite medium to work with is clay and mixed textures. Her favorite classes are ceramics and sculpture. She is currently working with the art teacher to create a sculpture for the school garden. Luna prefers activities that allow her to express her creativity at her own pace. When completing her work, Luna works best when given a task and ample processing time. She needs time to construct her thoughts before beginning a task.* **At home, she is very active in her community, assisting elders with translating.** *She tutors and babysits kids from the community on the weekends.* **Filipino is her primary language, which she speaks at home with her family. Luna does well in school when her teachers establish goals with her that include daily check-ins, additional wait time prior to responding to questions to process the English academic vocabulary, and building background knowledge about the topic or concept being studied.**

Concerns of the Parents/Educational Decision Maker

   ☑ The IEP Team has requested and considered the concerns of Parent(s)/ Educational Decision Maker.

Educationally Relevant Medical Issues

Does the student have a health condition that impacts the student's involvement and progress in the general curriculum and general education classroom and other education-related settings?

☐ No relevant medical issues noted.

☐ Student has Individual Health Care Plan.

☑ No Individual Health Care Plan; however, relevant information is noted below:

> *Diagnosis of anxiety, medication listed in health history. Luna takes her medication at home on a daily basis. School will not administer. If Luna forgets to take medicine, a family member will bring it to school. Her psychologist monitors her medication. She sees her psychologist every other week, which requires her to miss parts of the school day and select academic activities. She makes up all missed work within 3 school days. **Anxiety appears most frequently during writing activities and assignments in English.***

Blind/Visually Impaired

☐ Yes   ☑ No   **Is the student Blind or Visually Impaired?**

If yes, the use of Braille should be provided unless the IEP team determines otherwise. If after consideration the IEP team deems Braille not an appropriate method, provide reason for not using Braille.

Deaf/Hard of Hearing

☐ Yes   ☑ No   **Is the student Deaf or Hard of Hearing?**

If yes, describe unique communication needs relating to opportunities for direct communications with peers and professional personnel in the student's language/communications mode:

Evaluation Results

In developing this IEP, the team has considered the results of the initial or most recent evaluation of the student including, as appropriate, the results of district or state assessments.

Limited English Proficiency

☑ Yes   ☐ No   **Is the student an English Language Learner?**

> *Student tested at level 5 (Bridging) for English proficiency on the WIDA ACCESS test.*

Special Communication Needs

☑ The unique communication needs of the student have been considered. If unique communication needs are present, IEP team must consider how these needs affect the student's achievement toward his/her educational goals.

Assistive Technology

☑ **The Assistive Technology needs of the student have been considered.** If needed, Assistive Technology is addressed in the following place(s) within the IEP:

☐ Program Modifications/Accommodations

☐ Assistive Technology Plan

☐ Service Plan

Social/Behavioral/Emotional Needs

☑ Yes   ☐ No   **Does the student have behaviors which impede his/her learning or the learning of others?**

If yes, team must consider positive behavioral interventions, strategies, and supports to address behavior. Behavior is addressed in the following place(s) within the IEP:

☑ Goal(s)

☐ Behavioral Intervention Plan (attached)

☑ Accommodations

> *Luna taps her fingers and feet loudly when she experiences anxiety particularly during written language tasks. Often she is not able to monitor her behavior, which affects her ability to complete writing tasks successfully. Occasionally, she becomes very anxious, and when this occurs, she asks to be allowed to leave the room and meet with the special education teacher. Another result of Luna's anxiety is that she periodically picks at her fingers, injuring herself and requiring a bandage or other minor first aid. Luna struggles with, yet will benefit from, self-monitoring to reduce the tapping and finger picking as a way to reduce anxiety associated with written tasks.*

Physical Education

☐ Yes   ☑ No   **Does the student need Adaptive PE in order to participate in physical education?**

If yes, describe services in service plan.

PRESENT LEVELS OF ACADEMIC ACHIEVEMENT AND FUNCTIONAL PERFORMANCE, GOAL AND OBJECTIVES

Standard Associated with this Annual goal: *Writing*

PLAAFP: Present levels of academic achievement and/or functional performance related to particular area of need.

Current Academic Achievement and/or Functional Performance: *As of April 2016, Luna is able to write a 5-paragraph narrative essay with a topic of her choice with the following scores based on a 6 +1 trait writing rubric: Ideas: 2, Organization: 2, Voice: 2, Word choice: 3, Sentence fluency: 2, Conventions: 3, Presentation: 3, yielding a total of 17/35. When Luna dictates her writing to a teacher/paraeducator to get her ideas on a word processor, she can more easily make her edits than editing a hard copy.* ***The teacher/ paraeducator helps Luna with spelling during the dictation, which allows her to focus on formulating her thoughts in English, prior to taking on the task of writing down her ideas. Scaffolding the generation of thoughts and ideas followed by the actual writing helps Luna deal with English academic vocabulary in more productive ways, leading to improved writing. However, Luna becomes anxious when she struggles with selecting correct English vocabulary in her writing, which in addition to scaffolding the task is frequently best addressed by pairing her with a peer fluent in her home language.*** *Also, when the teacher takes some **extra time to help Luna build relevant background knowledge and use word walls and sentence stems**, she demonstrates less anxiety and more productive written assignments.*

Impact of Exceptionality upon ability to access and progress in the general curriculum (or appropriate activities for preschool children): NA

Baseline Data for Goal:	How will progress toward goal be measured?
6+1 trait writing rubric yields a total score of 17/35.	*6+1 trait writing rubric; performance-based writing projects*

Annual Goal:
*By April 2017, with the **aid of word walls, sentence stems, and scaffolding in writing instruction**, Luna will write a 5-paragraph narrative essay based on a research topic of her choice, obtaining a score of 4 or higher for each of the 6+1 writing traits in an untimed writing session (28/35 total score).*

Parents will receive written reports of the student progress toward meeting annual IEP goals in accordance with the district's established grade reporting schedule.

PRESENT LEVELS OF ACADEMIC ACHIEVEMENT AND FUNCTIONAL PERFORMANCE, GOAL AND OBJECTIVES

Standard Associated with this Annual goal: *Study Skills*

PLAAFP: Present levels of academic achievement and/or functional performance related to particular area of need.

Current Academic Achievement and/or Functional Performance: *As of April 2016, based on YES/NO ratings on a study skills inventory completed independently by two teachers, Luna struggles with self-management and organizational study skills particularly when managing and completing both in-school and homework writing assignments. She does not use a daily planner and frequently loses her draft papers, does not meet stated deadlines for submission of assignments, and requires extra time to organize her thoughts in writing. Her backpack, desk, and folders are often highly disorganized. Also, Luna completes tasks more frequently when she asks for help, though she infrequently requests assistance leading to 50% of both in-school and homework writing assignments either late or not submitted.* **When completing writing assignments, her struggles with English academic language cause embarrassment, often resulting in anxiety, late submissions, and periodic finger picking.** *However, when* **provided sufficient wait time**, *a self-management tool to monitor her own time and organization,* **along with extensions to the due dates to best build the English academic background** *necessary to complete tasks, Luna is more successful with both organization and task completion in writing.*

Impact of Exceptionality upon ability to access and progress in the general curriculum (or appropriate activities for preschool children): NA

Baseline Data for Goal:	**How will progress toward goal be measured?**
Scores of Yes/No for different study skills using a study skills inventory shows struggle with self-management and organizational skills.	*Scores from teacher ratings using a study skills inventory; performance-based observations using a student self-management tool to monitor her own organization and time.*

Annual Goal:
By April 2017, after using a self-management study skills tool and a daily planner, Luna will demonstrate an organized backpack and desk when asked 90% of the time, and complete 90% of writing in-school assignments and 80% of writing homework assignments by stated due dates.

Parents will receive written reports of the student progress toward meeting annual IEP goals in accordance with the district's established grade reporting schedule.

PROGRAM ACCOMMODATIONS AND MODIFICATIONS

The following unique accommodations and modifications are needed to enable the child to advance appropriately in attaining the annual goals, be involved and make progress in the general curriculum and participate in extracurricular and nonacademic actives, and be educated and participate with other children with and without disabilities in these activities as appropriate.

☐ No accommodations or modifications are necessary OR

In the boxes below indicate whether an accommodation or modification is stated along with location, duration, frequency.

Accommodation and Modifications	*Location*	*Duration*	*Frequency*
☑ **Accommodation:** *Frequent breaks* ☐ **Modification:**	*All classes*	*2016–17 school year*	*Daily*
☑ **Accommodation:** *Notes provided* ☐ **Modification:**	*All classes*	*2016–17 school year*	*Daily*
☑ **Accommodation:** ☑ **Modification:** **Dictation in English when completing writing assignments of more than two paragraphs**	*All classes*	*2016–17 school year*	*As needed*
☑ **Accommodation**: *Chunk writing assignment* ☐ **Modification:**	*All classes*	*2016–17 school year*	*Daily*
☑ **Accommodation:** *Extended time for writing tasks and assessments, 3 extra days, if more time is needed, student will request with teacher* ☐ **Modification:**	*All classes*	*2016–17 school year*	*As needed*
☑ **Accommodation:** *Self-management and organization tool completed daily* ☐ **Modification:**	*All classes*	*2016–17 school year*	*Daily*
☑ **Accommodation:** *Separate and/or quiet setting to limit distractions and reduce anxiety* ☐ **Modification:**	*All classes*	*2016–17 school year*	*As needed*

*Only state-approved accommodations will be used for State Assessments.

*Only those accommodations/modifications routinely provided the student in daily classroom instruction should be listed.

PARTICIPATION IN RELEVANT DISTRICT AND STATE ASSESSMENTS

State Assessments

	General Assessment	*General Assessment With Accommodation*
Math Grades 3–8 & 10		✓
English / Language Arts Grades 3–8 & 10		✓
History / Government Grades 6, 8, & 11		✓
Science Grades 5, 8, & 11		✓

*Accommodations found on program Modifications and Accommodations.

*Content/grade levels are state determined. Tests made available by the state will be administered.

District K–12 Assessments

*All school-aged students have the opportunity to participate in District Assessments.

☐ Student will participate in available District Assessment without accommodations

☑ Student will participate in available District Assessment with accommodations.

☐ The IEP team determined the following District Assessments are not appropriate:

SERVICE PLAN

Special Education and Related Services and Supplementary Aids and Services

The school is unable to provide regularly scheduled special education and/or related services when the following occurs: inclement weather closures, scheduled school closures, unforeseen emergencies, student absences, school field trips, assemblies, non-late arrival weeks, emergency drills, and summer break.

☑ Yes   ☐ No   The student will have the same opportunities to participate with children without disabilities in extracurricular and other non-academic activities.

If no, explain:

Describe the special education services to be provided, and describe the related services (if any) that the student needs in order to benefit from his/her special education services. Also describe the supplementary aids and services necessary to enable the student to be educated with children without disabilities to the maximum extent appropriate.

Service Delivery Statement (include service frequency, location, and duration):

Luna will receive special education in written language and study skills instruction one period every other day for 90 minutes, per block schedule. In addition, Luna will receive direct social work support 30 minutes, 1 day per week at times that do not conflict with direct content instruction. Also, the first and last 15 minutes per day, 5 days per week, Luna will check in with her special education teacher or social worker to discuss study skills development in self-management and organization. **Luna will continue to receive English language development supports in all classes through use of word walls, sentence stems, additional wait time prior to responding, and being encouraged to connect new material to events/people in home community with a peer.**

☐ Yes   ☑ No   **Is Special Transportation needed?**

If yes, provide description if necessary (e.g., lift).

Supports for School Staff

Describe the supports for school personnel that need to be provided for the student to enable him/her to advance appropriately toward attaining his/her measurable annual goals and to be involved and progress in the general education curriculum.

☐ No Supports for School Staff are necessary.

> *Teachers and staff will be trained to identify when Luna is experiencing an anxiety attack or feeling anxious and encourage her to see the social worker or special education teacher nonverbal cues.*

☐ Yes ☑ No **Is Extended School Year (ESY) necessary based on current and available data?**

Description of ESY Services to be provided (include service frequency, location, and duration):

Other Considerations not noted elsewhere in IEP:

None

TRANSITION PLAN: AGE 14 AND UP
(Required for all students turning 14 or older during the duration of this IEP)

Transition Goals

Student's post-secondary Education/Training goal:
After graduation, Luna will attend either a community college or 4-year college and study art or art education.

Student's post-secondary Employment goal:
Luna will seek a job working as a retailer at a local boutique while attending college and pursue a career as an artist or art teacher after college.

Student's post-secondary Independent Living goal (if needed):
    ☑ Not applicable

The following transition assessment was used: *Student Questionnaire*
Date: *04/01/16*

Preferences, Strengths and Interests Based on Present Levels of Performance, Age-Appropriate Transition Assessments and Needs:

At school: Luna enjoys her art classes especially sculpture and ceramics. Her favorite medium to work with is clay and mixed textures. She is an active member of the school Art Club and hopes to be an officer next year. She is currently working with the art teacher to create a sculpture for the school garden. She would love to own an art studio one day and teach art to elementary-aged students. Her plans are to attend college and double major in art and art education.

*At home: She helps the young kids in her community with their homework and attends school meetings with the parents. **She primarily speaks Filipino with her family and community**. She helps elders in the community with translating when she can.*

*Overall: Luna prefers to try and resolve issues independently that frequently leads to incomplete in-school and homework assignments, particularly in writing. She struggles with asking for help and informing her teachers when she is confused or does not understand an assignment, academic language, or behavior expectation. **However, when interacting with a peer who is fluent in her home language, her academic performance and behavior improve.***

STATEMENT OF NEEDED TRANSITION SERVICES

The following is not required until the IEP year in which the student turns 16.

Skills	Activities Timeline (Duration/Frequency)	Responsible Parties
Needed Instructional Activities: *Organization of papers and time management;* **interact with peer to clarify writing tasks in native language**	*Daily during 2016–17 school year*	*Student Special Education Teacher Social Worker General Educators*
Needed Community Experiences: *(1) College tours—Local 4-year Universities or Community College* **(2) Strategies to locate cultural diversity centers / supports and resources on college campuses**	*(1) 2–4 days during 2016–17 school year depending on number of tours scheduled* *(2) Monthly during 2016–2017 school year*	*Student Family Transition Coordinator Special Education Teacher Social worker*
Needed Post-Secondary Training and Adult Living Activities: *Self-monitoring, organization, and anxiety management skills*	*Daily during 2016–17 school year*	*Student Social Worker Special Education Teacher General Educators*
Functional Vocational Evaluation (if appropriate):	*Not applicable*	
Referral notification of post-secondary related service needs and activities:	*Not applicable*	

References

Abedi, J. (2004, November). *Psychometric issues in ELL assessment and special education eligibility.* Paper presented at the English Language Learners Struggling to Learn: Emergent Research on Linguistic Differences and Learning Disabilities Conference, Tempe, AZ.

Abedi, J. (2006). Psychometric issues in the ELL assessment and special education eligibility. *Teachers College Record, 108*(11), 2282–2303.

Aceves, T. C., & Orosco, M. J. (2014). *Culturally responsive teaching* (Document No. IC-2). Retrieved from http://ceedar.education.ufl.edu/wp-content/uploads/2014/08/culturally-responsive.pdf

Alt, M., Arizemendi, G. D., Beal, C. R., & Hurtado, J. S. (2013). The effect of test translation on the performance of second grade English learners on the KeyMath-3. *Psychology in the Schools, 50,* 27–36.

August, D., & Shanahan, T. (2010). Effective English literacy instruction for English learners. In F. Ong (Ed.), *Improving education for English learners: Research-based approaches* (pp. 209–249). Sacramento: California Department of Education.

August, D., Shanahan, L., & Shanahan, T. (2006). *Developing literacy in second-language learners: Report of the National Literacy Panel on language-minority children and youth.* Mahwah, NJ: Lawrence Erlbaum.

Baca, L., & Cervantes, H. (2004). *The bilingual special education interface.* Upper Saddle River, NJ: Pearson, Merrill, Prentice Hall.

Barrera, I. (1996). Thoughts on the assessment of young children whose sociocultural background is unfamiliar to the assessor. In *New visions for the developmental assessment of infants and young children* (pp. 69–84). Washington, DC: Zero to Three.

Basterra, M. D. R., Trumbull, E., & Solano-Flores, G. (2011). *Cultural validity in assessment: Addressing linguistic and cultural diversity.* New York, NY: Routledge.

Bateman, B. D. (2007). *From gobbledygook to clearly written annual IEP goals.* Verona, WI: Attainment.

Bateman, B. D., & Herr, C. M. (2006). *Writing measurable IEP goals and objectives.* Verona, WI: Attainment.

Baxter, C., & Mahoney, W. (2016). *Developmental disability across cultures.* Retrieved from http://www.kidsnewtocanada.ca/mental-health/developmental-disability

Beck, I., McKeown, M. G., & Kucan, L. (2002). *Bringing words to life: Robust vocabulary instruction.* New York, NY: Guilford Press.

Blanton, L. P., Pugach, M. C., & Florian, L. (2011, May). *Preparing general education teachers to improve outcomes for students with disabilities* (Policy Brief). Retrieved from http://www.aacte.org/pdf/Publications/Reports_Studies/AACTE%20NCLD%20Policy%20Brief%20May%202011.pdf

Boele, A. L. (2016). Select reading methods for teaching English learners. In J. J. Hoover, L. M. Baca, & J. K. Klingner, *Why do English learners struggle with reading?*

Distinguishing language acquisition from learning disabilities (2nd ed., pp. 101–116). Thousand Oaks, CA: Corwin.

Brown, J. S., Collins, A., & Duguid, P. (1989). Situated cognition and the culture of learning. *Educational Researcher, 18*, 32–42.

Can Do Descriptors. (2014). Retrieved from https://www.wida.us/standards/CAN_DOs/

Center for Parent Information and Resources. (2013). *Supplementary aids and services.* Retrieved from http://www.parentcenterhub.org/repository/iep-supplementary/

Center for Parent Information and Resources. (2016). *Special factors in IEP development.* Retrieved from http://www.parentcenterhub.org/repository/special-factors/#idea

Center on Response to Intervention. (n.d.). Home page. Retrieved from http://www.rti4success.org/

Chamot, A. U., & O'Malley, J. M. (1994). *The CALLA handbook: Implementing the cognitive academic language learning approach.* Reading, MA: Addison-Wesley.

Cipani, E., & Schock, K. M. (2010). *Functional behavioral assessment, diagnosis, and treatment: A complete system for education and mental health settings.* New York, NY: Springer.

Common Core State Standards Initiative. (2015a). Grade four: Numbers and operations in base ten. *Mathematics Standards.* Retrieved from http://www.corestandards.org

Common Core State Standards Initiative. (2015b). Grade three: Numbers and operations in base ten. *Mathematics Standards.* Retrieved from http://www.corestandards.org

Cronin, M. E., Patton, J. R., & Wood, S. J. (2007). *Life skills instruction: A practical guide for integrating real-life content into the curriculum at the elementary and secondary levels for students with special needs or who are placed at risk.* Austin, TX: PRO-ED.

Cross, T., Bazron, B., Dennis, K., & Isaacs, M. (1989). *Towards a culturally competent system of care, volume I.* Washington, DC: Georgetown University Child Development Center, CASSP Technical Assistance Center.

Cummins, J. (1979). Cognitive/academic language proficiency, linguistic interdependence, the optimum age question, and some other matters. *Working Papers on Bilingualism, 19*, 121–129.

Cummins, J. (1999). BICS and CALP: Clarifying the distinction. Retrieved from http://files.eric.ed.gov/fulltext/ED438551.pdf

Darling-Hammond, L. (2002). What's at stake with high-stakes testing. *The Brown University Child and Adolescent Behavior Letter, 18*, 1–3.

Doran, G. T. (1981). There's a S.M.A.R.T. way to write management's goals and objectives. *Management Review, 70*(11), 35–36.

Duran, R. P. (2011). Ensuring valid educational assessments for ELL students: Scores, score interpretation and assessment uses. In M. Basterra, E. Trumbull, & G. Solano-Flores (Eds.), *Cultural validity in assessment: Addressing linguistic and cultural diversity* (pp. 115–142). New York, NY: Routledge.

Echevarria, J., Vogt, M. E., & Short, D. J. (2008). *Making content comprehensible for English learners: The SIOP model.* Boston, MA: Pearson.

Frantz, R. S., Bailey, A. L., Starr, L., & Perea, L. (2014). Measuring academic language proficiency in school-age English language proficiency assessments under new college and career readiness standards in the United States. *Language Assessment Quarterly, 11*(4), 432–457.

Fuchs, D., & Fuchs, L. S. (2007). The role of assessment in the three-tier approach to reading instruction. In D. Haager, J. Klingner, & S. Vaughn (Eds.), *Evidence-based reading practices for response to intervention* (pp. 29–42). Baltimore, MD: Paul H. Brookes.

Garcia, S. B. (2014, March). *Developing culturally and linguistically responsive services for English learners with special needs.* Paper presented at MABE Annual Conference for Dual Language Programs: Cross-Cultural Connections, New Haven, CT.

Gay, G. (2000). *Culturally responsive teaching: Theory, research, and practice.* New York, NY: Teachers College Press.

Gay, G. (2002). Preparing for culturally responsive teaching. *Journal of Teacher Education, 53,* 106–116.

Gay, G. (2010). *Culturally responsive teaching: Theory, research, and practice.* New York, NY: Teachers College Press.

Gibb, G. S., & Dyches, T. T. (2007). *Guide to writing quality individualized education programs.* Boston, MA: Pearson Education/Allyn & Bacon.

Gibb, G. S., & Dyches, T. T. (2016). *IEPs: Writing quality individualized education programs.* Boston, MA: Pearson Education/Allyn & Bacon.

Goh, D. S. (2004). *Assessment accommodations for diverse learners.* Boston, MA: Pearson.

Goldenberg, C. (2008). Teaching English language learners: What the research does—and does not—say. *American Educator, 32*(2), 8–23, 42–44.

Goldenberg, C. (2013). Unlocking the research on English Learners: What we know—and don't yet know—about effective instruction. *American Educator, 37*(2), 4–11, 38.

Gottlieb, M. (2006). *Assessing English language learners: Bridges from language proficiency to academic achievement.* Thousand Oaks, CA: Corwin.

Gottlieb, M., & Ernst-Slavit, G. (2014). *Academic language in diverse classrooms: Definitions and contexts.* Thousand Oaks, CA: Corwin.

Grossman, H. (1995). *Special education in a diverse society.* Boston, MA: Allyn & Bacon.

Halpern, A. S. (1993). Quality of life as a conceptual framework for evaluating transition outcomes. *Exceptional Children, 59,* 486–498.

Harry, B., Kalyanpur, M., & Day, M. (1999). *Building cultural reciprocity with families: Case studies in special education.* Baltimore, MD: Paul H. Brookes.

Harry, B., & Klingner, J. K. (2014). *Why are so many minority students in special education? Understanding race and disability in schools* (2nd ed.). New York, NY: Teachers College Press.

Haynes, J., & Zacarian, D. (2010). *Teaching English learners across the content areas.* Alexandria, VA: Association for Supervision and Curriculum Development.

Hoover, J. J. (2009). *Differentiating learning differences from disabilities: Meeting diverse needs through multi-tiered response to intervention.* Boston, MA: Pearson, Allyn & Bacon.

Hoover, J. J. (2011). Making informed instructional adjustments in RTI models: Essentials for practitioners. *Intervention in School and Clinic, 47*(2), 82–90.

Hoover, J. J. (2012). Reducing unnecessary special education referrals of diverse learners: Guidelines for practitioners. *Teaching Exceptional Children, 44*(4), 38–47.

Hoover, J. J. (2013). *Linking assessment to instruction in multi-tiered models: A teacher's guide to selecting reading, writing, and mathematics interventions.* Boston, MA: Pearson.

Hoover, J. J. (2016a). *Culturally and linguistically responsive IEP guide.* Boulder, CO: Hamilton.

Hoover, J. J. (2016b). Data-driven decision making: Distinguishing language acquisition and cultural behaviors from a disability. In J. J. Hoover, L. M. Baca, & J. K. Klingner, *Why do English learners struggle with reading? Distinguishing language acquisition from learning disabilities* (2nd ed., pp. 141–162). Thousand Oaks, CA: Corwin.

Hoover, J. J. (2017). *How to select reinforcers* (2nd ed.). Austin, TX: PRO-ED.

Hoover, J. J., Baca, L. M., & Klingner, J. K. (2016). *Why do English learners struggle with reading? Distinguishing language acquisition from learning disabilities* (2nd ed.). Thousand Oaks, CA: Corwin.

Hoover, J. J., & Barletta, L. M. (2016). Special education assessment of ELs. In J. J. Hoover, L. M. Baca, & J. K. Klingner, *Why do English learners struggle with reading? Distinguishing language acquisition from learning disabilities* (2nd ed., pp. 117–139). Thousand Oaks, CA: Corwin.

Hoover, J. J., Barletta, L. M., & Klingner, J. K. (2016). Multi-tiered system of supports (MTSS) and English learners. In J. J. Hoover, L. M. Baca, & J. K. Klingner, *Why do English learners struggle with reading? Distinguishing language acquisition from learning disabilities* (2nd ed., pp. 25–55). Thousand Oaks, CA: Corwin.

Hoover, J. J., & deBettencourt, L. U. (in press). Educating culturally and linguistically diverse exceptional learners: The need for continued advocacy. *Exceptionality.*

Hoover, J. J., Hopewell, S., & Sarris, J. (2014). *Core ESL instructional practices (CEIP).* Boulder: University of Colorado, BUENO Center.

Hoover, J. J., & Klingner, J. (2011). Promoting cultural validity in the assessment of bilingual special education students. In M. Basterra, E. Trumbull, & G. Solano-Flores (Eds.), *Cultural validity in assessment: Addressing linguistic and cultural diversity* (pp. 143–167). New York, NY: Routledge.

Hoover, J. J., Klingner, J. K., Baca, L. M., & Patton, J. M. (2008). *Methods for teaching culturally and linguistically diverse exceptional learners.* Upper Saddle River, NJ: Pearson, Merrill, Prentice Hall.

Hoover, J. J., Sarris, J. S., & Hill, R. (2015). Increasing usage of ESL instructional practices in a rural county. *Rural Educator, 36*(3). Retrieved from http://epubs.library .msstate.edu/index.php/ruraleducator/index

IDEA. (2004). Individuals with Disabilities Education Improvement Act of 2004, 20 U.S.C. § 1400 *et seq.* (2012).

IRIS Center for Training Enhancements. (2011). *Teaching English language learners: Effective instructional practices.* Retrieved from http://iris.peabody.vanderbilt.edu/ module/ell/

IRIS Center for Training Enhancements. (2015). *Dual language learners with disabilities: Supporting young children in the classroom.* Retrieved from http://iris.peabody .vanderbilt.edu/module/dll/

IRIS Center for Training Enhancements. (2016). *Accountability: High stakes testing for students with disabilities.* Retrieved from http://iris.peabody.vanderbilt.edu/ module/hst/

Kieffer, M. J., Lesaux, N. K., Rivera, M., & Francis, D. J. (2009). Accommodations for English language learners taking large-scale assessments: A meta-analysis on effectiveness and validity. *Review of Educational Research, 79*(3), 1168–1201.

Klingner, J. K., Artiles, A. J., & Barletta, L. M. (2006). English language learners who struggle with reading: Language acquisition or LD? *Journal of Learning Disabilities, 39*(2), 108–128.

Klingner, J., Vaughn, S., Boardman, A., & Swanson, E. (2012). *Now we get it! Boosting comprehension with collaborative strategic reading.* San Francisco, CA: Jossey-Bass.

Ladson-Billings, G. (1995). Toward a theory of culturally relevant pedagogy. *American Educational Research Journal, 32*(3), 465–491.

Lloyd, J. W., Kameenui, E. J., & Chard, D. J. (Eds.). (2014). *Issues in educating students with disabilities.* Mahwah, NJ: Lawrence Erlbaum.

Martin, C. C., & Hauth, C. (2015). *The survival guide for new special education teachers.* Arlington, VA: Council for Exceptional Children.

Mason, J. L. (1993). *Cultural competence self-assessment questionnaire.* Portland, OR: Portland State University, Multicultural Initiative Project.

McConnell, K., Patton, R., & Polloway, E. A. (2006). *Behavioral intervention planning: A comprehensive guide for completing a functional behavioral assessment and developing a behavior intervention plan (BIP 3).* Austin, TX: PRO-ED.

McLaughlin, M. J., & Nolet, V. (2004). *What every principal needs to know about special education.* Thousand Oaks, CA: Corwin.

McWilliam, R. A. (2009). Goal functionality scale III. *TEIDS-Plus study, Siskin Children's Institute.* Retrieved from http://www.ectacenter.org/~pdfs/topics/families/GoalFunctionalityScaleIII2.pdf

Moll, L., & Gonzalez, N. (2004). Engaging life: A funds-of-knowledge approach to multicultural education. In J. Banks & C. Banks (Eds.), *Handbook of research on multicultural education* (2nd ed., pp. 699–715). San Francisco, CA: Jossey-Bass.

Moreno, G., Wong-Lo, M., & Bullock, L. M. (2014). Assisting students from diverse backgrounds with challenging behaviors: Incorporating a culturally attuned functional behavioral assessment in prereferral services, preventing school failure. *Alternative Education for Children and Youth, 58*(1), 58–68. doi: 10.1080/1045988X.2012.763156

National Association of Special Education Teachers. (2006/2007). *IEP components—Supplementary aids and services.* Retrieved from http://www.naset.org/3429.0.html

National Center on Response to Intervention. (2011, August). *RTI considerations for English language learners (ELLs).* Washington, DC: U.S. Department of Education, Office of Special Education Programs.

Navarrete, L., & Watson, S. M. R. (2013). *English language learners: The impact of language and socio cultural factors on learning.* Retrieved from http://www.council-for-learning-disabilities.org/english-language-learners-impact-of-language-and-socio-cultural-factors-on-learning

Norlin, J. W. (2009). *What do I do when—: The answer book on individualized education programs* (3rd ed.). Horsham, PA: LRP.

O'Malley, J. M., & Pierce, L. V. (1996). *Authentic assessment for English language learners: Practical approaches for teachers.* London, England: Longman.

Orosco, M. J. (2005). Accommodations in assessment and instruction to meet special needs. In J. J. Hoover (Ed.), *Current issues in special education: Meeting diverse needs in the twenty-first century* (pp. 87–94). Boulder: University of Colorado, BUENO Center.

Orosco, M. J., de Schonewise, E. A., de Onis, C., Klingner, J. K., & Hoover, J. J. (2016). Distinguishing between language acquisition and learning disabilities among English learners: Background information. In J. J. Hoover, L. M. Baca, & J. K. Klingner, *Why do English learners struggle with reading? Distinguishing language acquisition from learning disabilities* (2nd ed., pp. 1–14). Thousand Oaks, CA: Corwin.

Orosco, M. J., & Klingner, J. (2010). One school's implementation of RTI with English language learners: "Referring into RTI." *Journal of Learning Disabilities, 43,* 269–288.

Ortiz, A. A., Robertson, P. M., Wilkinson, C., Y., Liu, Y., McGhee, B. D., & Kushner, M. I. (2011). The role of bilingual education teachers in preventing inappropriate referrals of ELLs to special education: Implications for response to intervention. *Bilingual Research Journal, 34*(3), 316–333. doi:10.1080/15235882.2011.628608

Patton, J. R. (2016a). *Adulthood implications of transition.* Austin, TX: jplearning4living.com

Patton, J. R. (2016b). *Transition resources.* Austin, TX: jplearning41iving.com

Patton, J. R., & Clark, G. M. (2014). *Transition planning inventory* (2nd ed.). Austin, TX: PRO-ED.

Patton, J. R., & Dunn, C. (1998). *Transition from school to young adulthood: Basic concepts and recommended practices.* Austin, TX: PRO-ED.

Pennell, D. (2011). Fulfilling the purpose of IDEA through academic and functional skill development. Retrieved from http://education.wm.edu/centers/ttac/resources/articles/iep/fulfillingthepurposeofidea/

Pennock-Roman, M., & Rivera, C. (2011). Mean effects of test accommodations for ELLs and non-ELLs: A meta-analysis of experimental studies. *Educational Measurement: Issues and Practice, 30*(3), 10–28.

Regan, L. M. (2013). *Supporting English learners with disabilities.* Los Angeles, CA: LAUSD Division of Special Education.

Richards, H., Brown, A., & Forde, T. (2007). Addressing diversity in schools: Culturally responsive pedagogy. *Teaching Exceptional Children, 23*(3), 64–68.

Rowland, C. M., Quinn, E. D., & Steiner, S. A. (2015). Beyond legal: Crafting high-quality IEPs for children with complex communication needs. *Communication Disorders Quarterly, 37*(1), 53–62.

Rowland, C. M., Quinn, E. D., Steiner, S. A., & Bowser, G. (2013). Design to Learn IEP development guide. Retrieved from http://communicationmatrix.org/uploads/pdfs/Design_to_LearnIEPDevelopmentGuide.pdf

Saunders, W., Goldenberg, C., & Marcelletti, D. (2013). Guidelines for English language development instruction. *American Educator, 37*(2), 13–25, 38–39.

Shinn, M. R., & Shinn, M. M. (2000). Writing and evaluating IEP Goals and making appropriate revisions to ensure participation and progress in general curriculum. In C. F. Telzrow & M. Tankersley (Eds.), *IDEA amendments of 1997: Practice guidelines for school-based teams* (pp. 351–381). Bethesda, MD: National Association of School Psychologists.

Siegel, L. M. (2014). *The complete IEP guide* (8th ed.). Berkeley, CA: NOLO.

Skinner, C. H., Pappas, D. N., & Davis, K. A. (2005). Enhancing academic engagement: Providing opportunities for responding and influencing students to choose to respond. *Psychology in the Schools, 42,* 389–403.

Steege, M. W., & Watson, T. S. (2009). *Conducting school-based functional behavioral assessments: A practitioner's guide* (2nd ed.). New York, NY: Guildford Press.

Tharp, R. G. (1997). *From at-risk to excellence: Research, theory, and principles for practice* (Research Report 1). Santa Cruz, CA: Center for Research on Education, Diversity and Excellence.

Tharp, R. G., Doherty, R. W., Echevarria, J., Estrada, P., Goldenberg, C., & Hilberg, R. S. (2004, March). *Five standards for effective pedagogy and student outcomes* (No. G1). Berkeley: University of California, Berkeley. Retrieved from http://crede.berkeley.edu/research/crede/products/print/occreports/g1.html

Thomas, W. P., & Collier, V. P. (1997). Two languages are better than one. *Educational Leadership, 55,* 23–26.

Trainor, A. A., & Patton, J. R. (2008). Culturally responsive transition planning and instruction form early childhood to postsecondary life. In J. J. Hoover, J. K. Klingner, L. M. Baca, & J. M. Patton (Eds.), *Methods for teaching culturally and linguistically diverse exceptional learners* (pp. 342–367). Boston, MA: Pearson Merrill.

Twachtman-Cullen, D., & Twachtman-Bassett, J. (2011). *The IEP from A to Z: How to create meaningful and measurable goals and objectives.* San Francisco, CA: Jossey-Bass.

Valenzuela, A. (2002). Reflections on the subtractive underpinnings of education research and policy. *Journal of Teacher Education, 53*(3), 235–241.

Valle, M. S., Waxman, H. C., Diaz, Z., & Padrón, Y. N. (2013). Classroom instruction and the mathematics achievement of non-English learners and English learners. *Journal of Educational Research, 106*(3), 173–182.

Vanderwood, M. L., & Nam, J. (2007). Response to intervention for English language learners: Current developments and future directions. In S. R. Jimmerson, M. K. Burns, & A. M. VanDerHeyden (Eds.), *The handbook of response to intervention: The science and practice of assessment and intervention* (pp. 408–417). New York, NY: Springer.

Vaughn, S., & Bos, C. S. (2012). *Strategies for teaching students with learning and behavior problems* (8th ed.). Boston, MA: Pearson, Allyn & Bacon.

Villegas, A. M., & Lucas, T. (2007, March). The culturally responsive teacher. *Educational Leadership*, pp. 28–33.

Vygotsky, L. S. (1986). *Thought and language.* Cambridge, MA: MIT.

Wandry, D., Wehmeyer, M. L., & Glor-Scheib, S. J. (2013). *Life centered education: The teacher's guide.* Arlington, VA: Council for Exceptional Children.

Wright, J. (2011). How RTI works' series. Retrieved from http://www.jimwrightonline.com/mixed_files/sage/RTI_defs_core_instruction_intv_accomm_mod.pdf

Wright, J. (2013). *How to: Structure classroom data collection for individual students.* Retrieved from http://www.interventioncentral.org/blog/assessment-progress-monitoring/how-structure-classroom-data-collection-individual-students

Wright, P. W., & Wright, P. D. (2006). *SMART IEPs: An introduction.* Retrieved from http://www.ldonline.org/article/24690?theme=print

Wright, P. W., & Wright, P. D. (2016). *High stakes testing.* Retrieved from http://www.wrightslaw.com/info/highstak.index.htm

Wright, P. W., Wright, P. D., & O'Connor, S. W. (2010). *All about IEPs: Answers to frequently asked questions about IEPs.* Hartfield, VA: Harbor House Law Press.

Wlodkowski, R. J., & Ginsburg, M. B. (1995). A framework for culturally responsive teaching. *Educational Leadership, 53*(1), 17–21.

Yell, M. L., Katsiyannis, A., Collins, J. C., & Losinski, M. (2012). Exit exams, high-stakes testing, and students with disabilities: A persistent challenge. *Intervention in School and Clinic, 48*(1), 60–64.

Yell, M. L., & Stecker, P. M. (2003). Developing legally correct and educationally meaningful IEPs using curriculum-based measurement. *Assessment for Effective Intervention, 28*, 73–88.

Zacarian, D. (2011). *Transforming schools for English learners: A comprehensive guide for school leaders.* Thousand Oaks, CA: Corwin.

Zacarian, D. (2013). *Mastering academic language: A framework for supporting student achievement.* Thousand Oaks, CA: Corwin.

Zacarian, D., & Haynes, J. (2012). *The essential guide to educating English learners.* Thousand Oaks, CA: Corwin.

Zainuddin, H., Yahya, N., Morales-Jones, C. A., & Ariza, E. N. (2011). *Fundamentals of teaching English to speakers of other languages in K–12 mainstream classrooms.* (3rd ed.). Dubuque, IA: Kendall Hunt.

Zhang, C., & Bennett, T. (2003). Facilitating the meaningful participation of culturally and linguistically diverse families in the IFSP and IEP process. *Focus on Autism and Other Developmental Disabilities, 18*(1), 51–59.

Zweirs, J., & Crawford, M. (2011). *Academic conversations: Classroom talk that fosters critical thinking and content understandings.* Portland, ME: Stenhouse.

Index

A SAGE Publishing Company

Helping educators make the greatest impact

CORWIN HAS ONE MISSION: to enhance education through intentional professional learning.

We build long-term relationships with our authors, educators, clients, and associations who partner with us to develop and continuously improve the best evidence-based practices that establish and support lifelong learning.

Solutions you want. Experts you trust. Results you need.

Author Consulting

On-site professional learning with sustainable results! Let us help you design a professional learning plan to meet the unique needs of your school or district. www.corwin.com/pd

Institutes

Corwin Institutes provide collaborative learning experiences that equip your team with tools and action plans ready for immediate implementation. www.corwin.com/institutes

eCourses

Practical, flexible online professional learning designed to let you go at your own pace. www.corwin.com/ecourses

Read2Earn

Did you know you can earn graduate credit for reading this book? Find out how: www.corwin.com/read2earn

Contact an account manager at (800) 831-6640 or visit **www.corwin.com** for more information.